TM

References for the Rest of Us!®

BESTSELLING BOOK SERIES

Are you intimidated and confused by computers? Do you find that traditional manuals are overloaded with technical details you'll never use? Do your friends and family always call you to fix simple problems on their PCs? Then the *...For Dummies*® computer book series from IDG Books Worldwide is for you.

...For Dummies books are written for those frustrated computer users who know they aren't really dumb but find that PC hardware, software, and indeed the unique vocabulary of computing make them feel helpless. *...For Dummies* books use a lighthearted approach, a down-to-earth style, and even cartoons and humorous icons to dispel computer novices' fears and build their confidence. Lighthearted but not lightweight, these books are a perfect survival guide for anyone forced to use a computer.

"I like my copy so much I told friends; now they bought copies."

— Irene C., Orwell, Ohio

"Quick, concise, nontechnical, and humorous."

— Jay A., Elburn, Illinois

"Thanks, I needed this book. Now I can sleep at night."

— Robin F., British Columbia, Canada

Already, millions of satisfied readers agree. They have made *...For Dummies* books the #1 introductory level computer book series and have written asking for more. So, if you're looking for the most fun and easy way to learn about computers, look to *...For Dummies* books to give you a helping hand.

1/99

by Paul Hoffman

IDG Books Worldwide, Inc.
An International Data Group Company

Foster City, CA ♦ Chicago, IL ♦ Indianapolis, IN ♦ New York, NY

Perl For Dummies®, 2nd Edition

Published by
IDG Books Worldwide, Inc.
An International Data Group Company
919 E. Hillsdale Blvd.
Suite 400
Foster City, CA 94404
www.idgbooks.com (IDG Books Worldwide Web site)
www.dummies.com (Dummies Press Web site)

Library of Congress Catalog Card No.: 98-88389

ISBN: 0-7645-0460-6

Printed in the United States of America

10 9 8 7 6 5 4 3

2B/SW/QT/ZZ/IN

Distributed in the United States by IDG Books Worldwide, Inc.

Distributed by CDG Books Canada Inc. for Canada; by Transworld Publishers Limited in the United Kingdom; by IDG Norge Books for Norway; by IDG Sweden Books for Sweden; by Woodslane Pty. Ltd. for Australia; by Woodslane (NZ) Ltd. for New Zealand; by TransQuest Publishers Pte Ltd. for Singapore, Malaysia, Thailand, Indonesia, and Hong Kong; by ICG Muse, Inc. for Japan; by Norma Comunicaciones S.A. for Colombia; by Intersoft for South Africa; by Le Monde en Tique for France; by International Thomson Publishing for Germany, Austria and Switzerland; by Distribuidora Cuspide for Argentina; by Livraria Cultura for Brazil; by Ediciones ZETA S.C.R. Ltda. for Peru; by WS Computer Publishing Corporation, Inc., for the Philippines; by Contemporanea de Ediciones for Venezuela; by Express Computer Distributors for the Caribbean and West Indies; by Micronesia Media Distributor, Inc. for Micronesia; by Grupo Editorial Norma S.A. for Guatemala; by Chips Computadoras S.A. de C.V. for Mexico; by Editorial Norma de Panama S.A. for Panama; by American Bookshops for Finland. Authorized Sales Agent: Anthony Rudkin Associates for the Middle East and North Africa.

For general information on IDG Books Worldwide's books in the U.S., please call our Consumer Customer Service department at 800-762-2974. For reseller information, including discounts and premium sales, please call our Reseller Customer Service department at 800-434-3422.

For information on where to purchase IDG Books Worldwide's books outside the U.S., please contact our International Sales department at 317-596-5530 or fax 317-596-5692.

For consumer information on foreign language translations, please contact our Customer Service department at 1-800-434-3422, fax 317-596-5692, or e-mail rights@idgbooks.com.

For information on licensing foreign or domestic rights, please phone +1-650-655-3109.

For sales inquiries and special prices for bulk quantities, please contact our Sales department at 650-655-3200 or write to the address above.

For information on using IDG Books Worldwide's books in the classroom or for ordering examination copies, please contact our Educational Sales department at 800-434-2086 or fax 317-596-5499.

For press review copies, author interviews, or other publicity information, please contact our Public Relations department at 650-655-3000 or fax 650-655-3299.

For authorization to photocopy items for corporate, personal, or educational use, please contact Copyright Clearance Center, 222 Rosewood Drive, Danvers, MA 01923, or fax 978-750-4470.

About the Author

Paul E. Hoffman has written more than a dozen computer books, many of them about the Internet (including *Netscape Communicator 4.5 For Dummies* and *The Internet,* the official book of the PBS presentation "The Internet Show," both from IDG Books Worldwide, Inc.); in fact, he's been active on the Internet for more than 15 years. As a founder of the Internet Mail Consortium, he is responsible for the popular Web service there as well as the mail response system.

ABOUT IDG BOOKS WORLDWIDE

Welcome to the world of IDG Books Worldwide.

IDG Books Worldwide, Inc., is a subsidiary of International Data Group, the world's largest publisher of computer-related information and the leading global provider of information services on information technology. IDG was founded more than 30 years ago by Patrick J. McGovern and now employs more than 9,000 people worldwide. IDG publishes more than 290 computer publications in over 75 countries. More than 90 million people read one or more IDG publications each month.

Launched in 1990, IDG Books Worldwide is today the #1 publisher of best-selling computer books in the United States. We are proud to have received eight awards from the Computer Press Association in recognition of editorial excellence and three from Computer Currents' First Annual Readers' Choice Awards. Our best-selling *...For Dummies®* series has more than 50 million copies in print with translations in 31 languages. IDG Books Worldwide, through a joint venture with IDG's Hi-Tech Beijing, became the first U.S. publisher to publish a computer book in the People's Republic of China. In record time, IDG Books Worldwide has become the first choice for millions of readers around the world who want to learn how to better manage their businesses.

Our mission is simple: Every one of our books is designed to bring extra value and skill-building instructions to the reader. Our books are written by experts who understand and care about our readers. The knowledge base of our editorial staff comes from years of experience in publishing, education, and journalism — experience we use to produce books to carry us into the new millennium. In short, we care about books, so we attract the best people. We devote special attention to details such as audience, interior design, use of icons, and illustrations. And because we use an efficient process of authoring, editing, and desktop publishing our books electronically, we can spend more time ensuring superior content and less time on the technicalities of making books.

You can count on our commitment to deliver high-quality books at competitive prices on topics you want to read about. At IDG Books Worldwide, we continue in the IDG tradition of delivering quality for more than 30 years. You'll find no better book on a subject than one from IDG Books Worldwide.

John Kilcullen
Chairman and CEO
IDG Books Worldwide, Inc.

Steven Berkowitz
President and Publisher
IDG Books Worldwide, Inc.

Eighth Annual Computer Press Awards ≥1992

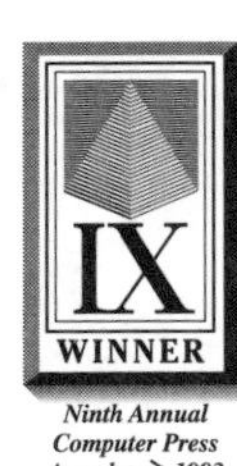

Ninth Annual Computer Press Awards ≥1993

Tenth Annual Computer Press Awards ≥1994

Eleventh Annual Computer Press Awards ≥1995

IDG is the world's leading IT media, research and exposition company. Founded in 1964, IDG had 1997 revenues of $2.05 billion and has more than 9,000 employees worldwide. IDG offers the widest range of media options that reach IT buyers in 75 countries representing 95% of worldwide IT spending. IDG's diverse product and services portfolio spans six key areas including print publishing, online publishing, expositions and conferences, market research, education and training, and global marketing services. More than 90 million people read one or more of IDG's 290 magazines and newspapers, including IDG's leading global brands — Computerworld, PC World, Network World, Macworld and the Channel World family of publications. IDG Books Worldwide is one of the fastest-growing computer book publishers in the world, with more than 700 titles in 36 languages. The "...For Dummies®" series alone has more than 50 million copies in print. IDG offers online users the largest network of technology-specific Web sites around the world through IDG.net (http://www.idg.net), which comprises more than 225 targeted Web sites in 55 countries worldwide. International Data Corporation (IDC) is the world's largest provider of information technology data, analysis and consulting, with research centers in over 41 countries and more than 400 research analysts worldwide. IDG World Expo is a leading producer of more than 168 globally branded conferences and expositions in 35 countries including E3 (Electronic Entertainment Expo), Macworld Expo, ComNet, Windows World Expo, ICE (Internet Commerce Expo), Agenda, DEMO, and Spotlight. IDG's training subsidiary, ExecuTrain, is the world's largest computer training company, with more than 230 locations worldwide and 785 training courses. IDG Marketing Services helps industry-leading IT companies build international brand recognition by developing global integrated marketing programs via IDG's print, online and exposition products worldwide. Further information about the company can be found at www.idg.com. 1/24/99

Author's Acknowledgments

The Perl world is full of very helpful people who will answer questions for just about anyone. Perl's main developer, Larry Wall, started this trend when he released Perl, and there are now hundreds of people on various Usenet news groups and mailing lists who are keeping alive the spirit of cooperation. Many of my ideas in this book have come from things these people have said in different forums over the past few years. Tens of thousands of hours have been spent on making Perl free and useful, and I'm grateful for all this effort by Perl enthusiasts all over the world (and you should be too!).

This is my second book in the ...*For Dummies* series, and I'd like to repeat what I said in my first book. Writing for computer novices is always easier if you have a few of them around asking you questions. My close circle of novices and ex-novices keeps me on my toes and reminds me what is not obvious, how frustrating it can be when the system is designed by know-it-all dweebs, and what parts are fun. I am indebted to my friends, my family, and my family-by-choice.

Special thanks to Nancy DelFavero, the project editor, who spent long hours improving this edition of the book, and for this I am very grateful (and you should be too!). Many other folks at IDG Books Worldwide, Inc. (and you can find out who they are on the next page) also helped to bring this book to your hands, and I am thankful for their effort and patience.

Publisher's Acknowledgments

We're proud of this book; please register your comments through our IDG Books Worldwide Online Registration Form located at `http://my2cents.dummies.com`.

Some of the people who helped bring this book to market include the following:

Acquisitions, Editorial, and Media Development

Project Editor: Nancy DelFavero

Acquisitions Editor: Joyce Pepple

Copy Editors: Constance Carlisle, Paula Lowell, Phil Worthington

Technical Editors: Allen Wyatt

Associate Media Development Technical Editor: Joell Smith

Associate Permissions Editor: Carmen Krikorian

Editorial Manager: Mary C. Corder

Media Development Manager: Heather Heath Dismore

Media Development Coordinator: Megan Roney

Editorial Assistants: Donna Love, Paul E. Kuzmic, Alison Walthall

Production

Project Coordinators: E. Shawn Aylsworth, Karen York

Layout and Graphics: Lou Boudreau, Valery Bourke, Linda M. Boyer, J. Tyler Connor, Maridee V. Ennis, Angela F. Hunckler, Brent Savage, Rashell Smith, Kate Snell

Proofreaders: Michelle Croninger, Rachel Garvey, Nancy Price, Rebecca Senninger, Christine Snyder, Janet M. Withers

Indexer: Sherry Massey

General and Administrative

IDG Books Worldwide, Inc.: John Kilcullen, CEO; Steven Berkowitz, President and Publisher

IDG Books Technology Publishing: Brenda McLaughlin, Senior Vice President and Group Publisher

Dummies Technology Press and Dummies Editorial: Diane Graves Steele, Vice President and Associate Publisher; Mary Bednarek, Director of Acquisitions and Product Development; Kristin A. Cocks, Editorial Director

Dummies Trade Press: Kathleen A. Welton, Vice President and Publisher; Kevin Thornton, Acquisitions Manager

IDG Books Production for Dummies Press: Michael R. Britton, Vice President of Production and Creative Services; Cindy L. Phipps, Manager of Project Coordination, Production Proofreading, and Indexing; Kathie S. Schutte, Supervisor of Page Layout; Shelley Lea, Supervisor of Graphics and Design; Debbie J. Gates, Production Systems Specialist; Robert Springer, Supervisor of Proofreading; Debbie Stailey, Special Projects Coordinator; Tony Augsburger, Supervisor of Reprints and Bluelines

Dummies Packaging and Book Design: Patty Page, Manager, Promotions Marketing

♦

The publisher would like to give special thanks to Patrick J. McGovern, without whom this book would not have been possible.

♦

Contents at a Glance

Cartoons at a Glance

By Rich Tennant

The 5th Wave
By Rich Tennant
Re·al Pro·gram·mers
Real Programmers drive Volkswagen vans or cars made before 1968.

page 5

The 5th Wave
By Rich Tennant

"This part of the interview tells us whether or not you're personally suited to the job of systems administrator."

page 69

The 5th Wave
By Rich Tennant

"Sure, at first it sounded great—an intuitive network adapter that helps people write memos by finishing their thoughts for them."

page 147

The 5th Wave
By Rich Tennant
The Perils of Pauline
Help! I'm losing depth recursion! My subroutines are confusing!! My hash tables are degrading—heeeeellp!!

page 239

The 5th Wave
By Rich Tennant
...AND THESE ARE OUR OBJECT-ORIENTED PROGRAMMING SPECIALISTS.

page 295

Fax: 978-546-7747 • E-mail: the5wave@tiac.net

Table of Contents

Part II: The Basic Perl Programming Ingredients 69

Part IV: Advanced Perl Demystified 239

Introduction

Assuming that you want to venture into programming, your first step is to pick a specific programming language to start out with. Because you're reading this book, I'm guessing you're seriously thinking about programming with Perl. I applaud your choice. Like human languages, some programming languages are easier to learn than others. Perl is one of the easiest programming languages to work with, yet it's as powerful as many languages that are much more difficult to master.

The Perl programming language allows you to create fully working computer programs with just a few steps. It is particularly good at common programming tasks such as reading and writing text files, but it also excels at reducing the work that programmers have to do, more so than other popular languages such as C and Java.

Who You Are

Your reasons for wanting to learn a programming language probably boil down to the following:

- A fascination with how computers work
- A desire to create your own programs to control your computer
- For professional development (that is, you want to advance to programmer status)

You may also want to get acquainted with a programming language because you work with programmers and you wonder what it is that they do all day. Understanding programming definitely helps you appreciate what it takes to be a good programmer, even if you don't become one yourself.

If you're interested in discovering how to program (or how others program), *Perl For Dummies, 2nd Edition* is for you. If you already know something about programming (but not about Perl), this book is also for you. If you are already an expert programmer, you're still welcome to read this book; you can just skip the basic stuff (you never know what kind of new tips and tricks you'll pick up).

After finding out how to program with Perl, you may decide to go on and become someone who makes his or her living as a Perl programmer. Or, you may decide that, although programming is interesting, it isn't something that you want to do full time. And, a chance exists (although a slight one) that after you learn how to program in Perl, you may discover that you like programming but you don't like Perl.

Fortunately, most of the Perl programming skills that you can pick up from this book can also be applied to another programming language later on. Perl is simpler to work with than most other programming languages — and Perl uses many of the same concepts as other languages do, making it an excellent introductory language.

What You Need to Know First

This book covers how to use Perl under four different operating systems: UNIX, Windows 95/98, Windows NT, and Macintosh. To use this book to learn Perl programming, you need to know at least one of these operating systems. You don't need to know more than one operating system, and very few folks out there know how to use all four. If you are one of those people who's familiar with all four operating systems, you can enjoy the title of Total Computer Dweeb and be comfortable in the fact that few others in the world share your unique skills.

In short, you don't need to know anything about programming up front, or even what Perl is, to get lots of value from this book. However, you do need to know the basics of using your computer system so that you can load Perl and create text files that Perl can use as programs.

What You'll Find in This Book

Because *Perl For Dummies, 2nd Edition* is meant for both programming novices and folks who already know something about programming, I've arranged the book so that both groups of people can find what they want quickly. You may want to read this book straight through from beginning to end, or you may be one of those folks who enjoys skipping to just what you need. In either case, you'll need to know how the book is arranged.

Part I: Getting Started with Perl

Part I tells you what programming is all about, what Perl is, what makes it different from other programming languages, and what it means "to program." This part contains some example programs so that you can see what they look like and how they are put together. You also get some help in installing Perl and running Perl on various operating systems.

Part II: The Basic Perl Programming Ingredients

Here, I cover the basic elements of programming with Perl — including techniques for working with text and numbers, plus in-the-trenches programming stuff like lists, strings, operators, loops, and conditional statements. When you're done perusing this part, you can probably write a few short programs of your own.

Part III: More on the Nuts and Bolts of Perl

This part of the book shows you how to structure a complete Perl program, put together larger and more complex programs, tell Perl to read and write files on your computer, and write programs that know how to talk to a Web server.

Part IV: Advanced Perl Demystified

After you're comfortable with Perl and feeling adventurous, you can dip into this part of the book, which covers a number of advanced Perl topics. Novice programmers aren't expected to use these features immediately, but if you zoom ahead to these chapters (maybe you're saying, "Nah, that's not me," but you may surprise yourself later), you'll find lots of useful information to rev up your Perl programs.

Part V: The Part of Tens

This part of the book contains some nice, quick lists of interesting information about Perl. If you like round numbers, you'll be happy to know that they're all organized in groups of ten.

A Word about Program Examples

Throughout the book, you can find examples of Perl code that look like the following line:

```
print "Hello, world!\n";
```

You will also see examples of this same kind of typestyle in the body text `like this` to indicate that `this text` is a part of a Perl program. You can also find multiple lines of code neatly enclosed in gray boxes. The single lines of code are usually Perl statements (or portions of a statement) and the multiple lines are generally Perl programs. (Yes, you can write an entire program in Perl with just three or four lines.) Not to worry, though. This books tells you all about the difference between statements and programs (and functions and strings and other programming conventions) that are displayed in code font.

Icons Used in This Book

One of the fun things about writing a *...For Dummies* book is that you get to use these clever icons to point out items of special interest.

Hopefully, you'll find everything in the book really useful, but these items are especially noteworthy.

This alerts you to something that you should definitely watch out for. A couple of important "gotchas" are buried in Perl, and these warnings can help steer you clear of them.

This icon appears next to anything you need to remember later on when you're doing other kinds of stuff with Perl.

Stop here for a side note about something especially high-end. This icon points out technical information that isn't critical to know, but handy nonetheless.

Because most readers of this book are Windows users (either Windows 95, Windows 98, or Windows NT), this icon helps point them to information that's specific to Windows.

Part I
Getting Started with Perl

The 5th Wave
By Rich Tennant
Re·al Pro·gram·mers
©RICHTENNANT
Real Programmers drive Volkswagen vans or cars made before 1968.

In this part . . .

You've got to start somewhere, and the beginning is the best place, is it not? In these first few chapters, you find out what a programming language is, what Perl is, how to get Perl up and running on your particular operating system, and what a couple of substantial Perl programs look like.

Chapter 1

How Perl Fits into the Big Programming Picture

In This Chapter

- Understanding the hows and whys of programming languages
- Comparing Perl with other languages

Some people want to know exactly what it is that makes their computer programs tick. They have a nagging itch to find out what's "under the hood" of their computers, beyond the chips and wires. They want to find out how they can create new and better programs and how it is that programmers can make so much money yet look like they dress in the dark.

On a personal note: Don't assume that everyone who programs or writes books about programming is a young whippersnapper. Without getting too specific, let's just say that my college days are way, way behind me. When I worked with computers back then, I often used punched cards and paper tape — ah, those wonderful pre-PCs days.

In those olden days, BASIC was the easy language to learn, and serious programmers learned FORTRAN or COBOL to do "real work." But many people discovered that you could accomplish a lot with plain old BASIC. Today, many people have discovered that Perl is a great beginning programming language because it's simple to use and yet you can create powerful programs with little effort. Sure, you can immerse yourself in more difficult languages, such as C++ or Java, but you can probably learn Perl faster and find yourself doing what you want to do just as well, if not better.

The Purpose of Programming

If you're new to the concept of programming you may be asking yourself, "Why am I learning to program at all?" Sure, programs control computers, but that doesn't mean that everyone should learn to be a programmer.

When personal computers appeared on the scene about 25 years ago, almost no commercial software existed, and the software that did exist was pretty primitive. If you wanted to do anything special you had to learn to program so that you could create programs to meet your specific needs. By 1981, when the IBM PC came out, plenty of commercial programs were available and users no longer needed to program their computers — the software did it for them.

Today, very few computer users have any real need to write programs. Tens of thousands of programs are available, many for free, and you can find one for just about anything that you want to do with your computer.

Some people think that once they learn to program they can write any kind of program for their computers. "I have this great idea for a word processor that's different than the ones I've seen." "I'll create an Internet program that makes Netscape look like a kid's toy!" "There are no good programs that convert English into ancient Greek. I'll create one and make a fortune." And on and on.

Although such programs are possible, each one would take months or years to create. When you learn to program, you begin by creating simple applications. To create complex programs, you have to practice, practice, and practice, usually full time. In this book, I show you how to cook up lots of simple programs using Perl (but nothing on the order of a word processor, Internet browser, or English-to-ancient-Greek translator, although the latter is certainly possible with Perl).

You may not have to program, but there are plenty of reasons why you may simply want to learn the art of programming:

- Learning programming is a good way to understand how computer programs work. Because everything that happens on your computer is controlled by one program or another, learning what it takes to create programs is a good way to find out what makes your computer tick.
- Programming is fun, at least to people like us. If you enjoy computers and being creative, writing programs can provide great amusement. Programming also appeals to tinkerers, because after you create a program, you can change it a bit here, add a few features there, and just keep on going with it.
- Professional programmers can get paid big bucks, and jobs exist for them all over the world. Note, however, that most of the programmer jobs you see advertised in the Sunday want ads are for experienced programmers, and the number of entry-level jobs in the field is almost zilch. Still, with a shred of patience and a bit of luck, you can teach yourself programming and turn it into a profession within a few years.

Programming Languages: Making Computers Compute

For starters, take a step back to examine what it is that a computer does and what it takes to control a computer. Don't worry, you can expect only a tiny amount of talk about chips and wires and circuit boards here. But you do need a bit of that sort of information because even though programming is about software, software controls hardware.

A computer is a hardware system that can, well, compute. The main chip in each computer, often called the central processing unit (CPU), takes instructions and data and acts on them, usually to create more data. That's really the basis for all computers. Things get fancy when you start talking about the kinds of instructions and data the CPU can handle.

For example, a CPU can take the data "3" and the data "5" and the instruction "add" and respond with "8." If, instead, you give it data like "4" and "6" but still give it the instruction "add," you'd sure hope that it responded "10." Or, if you still used "3" and "5," but said "multiply" rather than "add," you'd like to see it come back with "15."

All data given to a computer's CPU is in number form. You may find that fact hard to believe because you've seen your computer produce letters, pictures, and maybe even sounds and movies, but everything you see on screen is composed in the computer's mind as numbers. When you use a programming language such as Perl, the language lets you think in terms of letters, but the program actually converts letters to numbers for the CPU.

CPUs can do much more than add and multiply. One common CPU operation is the comparison of two numbers. For example, a CPU instruction may say, "If this number is bigger than 0, do this; otherwise, do that instead." By comparing two numbers and choosing what to do next based on the comparison, the CPU can make decisions about how to work when the numbers aren't known ahead of time.

That's the short-and-sweet introduction to the brain of any computer, including a bit about how it "thinks." Of course, a computer doesn't really think: It reacts. And the way that it reacts is based on the instructions and data given to it. The list of instructions that you give to a CPU is a *program,* and you put together a program with a *programming language.* A programming language like Perl is the means by which you, the programmer, can create a set of CPU instructions.

Making Your Language Your Computer's Language

In order to make CPUs run quickly, the instructions and data that you feed them must be compact and concise. These instructions and data are called *machine language,* and even though machine language is a kind of programming language, very few people know how to use it. Instead, they use more human-friendly languages like Perl (or C, or COBOL, or JAVA, and so on). These languages are called *high-level languages,* and when they run they are converted into machine language to let the CPU know what's going on.

When most folks learn how to program, they use a high-level language because that's what humans can handle best. As long as your computer has a way of translating the high-level language into machine language, you're fine. Note that that's not always an easy (or inexpensive) proposition.

In the Good Old Days of the early 1980s, most computers came equipped with programming languages that you could use to write your own programs. MS-DOS, for example, included a simple programming language called BASIC and a primitive batch-processing language (Windows 95 and Windows 98, in fact, still come with the batch language). Lots of us old fogies learned BASIC mostly because it was included as part of a computer's operating system.

BASIC was certainly not the first programming language. FORTRAN and COBOL, for example, had been around for many years. But both of those languages took up lots of memory and were difficult to run on small computers. Many other smaller languages were around, but they weren't any easier to learn than FORTRAN or BASIC, and in some cases were even more difficult. Two features of BASIC made it popular: It was free and small. Perl's popularity derives from its having similar features: It is free and it is relatively small.

An important feature of a programming language is how quickly people can learn to create useful programs with it. There are other considerations, such as how fast programs run after you write them and how much energy you have to expend to get particular tasks done, but first and foremost is a language's ease of use. A difficult language may be okay for the top 10 or 20 percent of the programming population, but for the rest of us, a difficult language simply means too much struggle in the learning department and, therefore, isn't likely to be very popular.

The Thinking behind Computer Language Design

We sometimes think of human languages as appearing out of nowhere and never changing, but that is clearly not the case. Human languages evolve in a number of ways, and so do computer languages. Computer languages are quite different from human languages, although they do compare in a few respects:

- The main purpose of human language is person-to-person communication; the main purpose of computer languages is human-to-computer communication.
- All computer languages have been created within the past 50 years. Because they haven't developed over a long period of time like most human languages, they don't present some of the challenges that many human languages do, such as having too many exceptions to the rules.
- Computer languages are usually invented by a single person or a small group of people (although larger groups of people may get together later to decide how to modify a language). Because human languages are developed by whole cultures, they are apt to have more quirks and oddities in them than computer languages.

When people create a new computer language, they have to think long and hard about what they want to do with it and why their language will be better than the ones that are already out there. It can be difficult to convince people to stop using their favorite computer language and switch to a new one, so a designer must craft a language to make it as attractive as possible (that is, powerful or easy to use, or both).

Sometimes, a language is created to do just one little thing better than any other language does it, and that one thing is really important to a select group of people. For example, engineers who design robots may want their own computer language to be able to describe how to move an arm or a leg and what direction to move it in, but they don't need the ability to perform calculus. Other languages are designed to do all things fairly well and that makes program writing simpler because the programmer can do everything with just a single tool.

You may think that every language should be simple to learn so that more people can use it. However, that's not really necessary because a fair number of simple languages already exist (Perl being one of them). Instead of creating new, easily mastered languages, language designers are targeting specific groups of programmers who are willing to spend the time to work with special features or interesting language forms.

When creating a new computer language, designers must keep a number of considerations in mind:

- How fast will the language run?
- How easy is it to extend the language to handle tasks unanticipated by the language's authors?
- What sort of background do programmers of that language need?
- What sort of computers will run the language?

Because of these design challenges, relatively few computer languages are widely used. Although at least 100 languages have been disseminated over the past 30 years, a dozen or less are used by more than a few thousand people.

Picky languages versus those that give you lots of leeway

When you first learn a programming language, you're allowed to make minor mistakes along the way. When it comes to actually creating a workable program, however, some languages are very particular about how you write it and will block your progress unless the program is perfect.

Some programming languages, such as C, demand that you're extremely careful about the types of data you are using; if you make a mistake, the program can cause errors without your noticing them. Other languages, such as Perl, are much more lenient, letting you be less specific about the kind of data you're using.

Professional programmers can argue on and on about whether a language should be picky or not. Some say being picky is good because it forces the programmer to dictate exactly what he or she wants, leaving no guesswork for the language. Others say languages should be lenient so that a programmer can write code quickly without having to dot all the is and cross all the ts.

There are other ways in which a programming language can be stringent or lenient. Some languages require that every line of a program line up with each other in a certain way, and others are much more free-form. By the way, you'll discover that Perl is overall a pretty lenient language. However, if you want Perl to get picky, you can tell it to check your programs for probable errors in order to find the things that you may have done wrong.

So, Why Perl?

Computer users can argue ad nauseam about which programming language is "best" or "easiest to use." The fact is, no single language is perfect for every task, and the top three or four languages for most tasks get the job done equally well. For the novice or intermediate programmer, then, the question is not really what is the best program to use, but which is the easiest one to master.

Perl scores high on both the learning-curve and ease-of-use scales. You can write a small Perl program designed to do a simple task after reading just the first few chapters of this book. In fact, if you read through the first part of this book, you'll understand enough about Perl that you can begin to modify programs to your heart's content.

Certainly, other languages are easy to learn and use, but they do not have the features that make Perl a great all-around language, such as flexibility with the kinds of data it can handle or its ability to deal with objects. Good old BASIC has features similar to the "easy" parts of Perl, but it's not very good for modern programming because of its lack of flexibility. Microsoft Visual Basic is not nearly as easy to learn as BASIC; although it's very powerful, many novices find Visual Basic pretty confusing. Some people think C is easy to learn, but difficult to use unless you are very careful because you can create C programs that look great on the surface but do harmful things to your computer. C also loses points in the text-handling area, one of the places in which Perl shines.

Perl surpasses other programming languages on some common tasks. With Perl, it's quite easy to open a file on your computer, read it, and make some changes based on what you find in the file. Perl can handle text files with aplomb, and has no problems with binary files. Perl is also good at handling text in ways that humans do, such as looking at a sentence and breaking it into words, or sorting lines in alphabetical order.

The ten-second summary of Perl's strongest points is this: It works great for reading through text files, summarizing processed files or converting files to a different format, and managing UNIX systems. Other languages strive to be elegant or very small; Perl strives to be complete and easy to use.

Another great reason for using Perl is that it's free. Versions of Perl for use with Windows, Macs, and UNIX systems are included on the CD-ROM in the back of this book, and they are all freeware. This no-cost policy has prompted many people to help out with the Perl development effort and has resulted in widespread usage of Perl over a relatively short period of time.

A Bit of Perl History

Programming languages have been around for several decades. Perl is probably the youngest of the popular programming languages, debuting in the mid-1980s. The idea for Perl pretty much sprang from the head of one person, Larry Wall, who had a bunch of system-administration tasks to do and no one good language to get them all done. (The name Perl stands for *Practical Extraction And Report Language.* Rumor has it that Larry was going to name it "pearl," but another language already had that name so he opted for the phonetic spelling.)

Most system administrators love challenges, and networked computers are always a challenge. The more important a certain computer on a network is, the more important its system administrator becomes. Lots of geek macho surfaces during the process of chasing down system-level bugs and making systems run faster and more smoothly. System administrators love their software tools even more so than auto mechanics love their wrenches, and Perl has become one of the premier system administration tools.

In short, Perl was born out of necessity. Larry Wall needed a language that had the power to open a bunch of text files in different formats, read these different files in one way, and create new files that reported on the original files. He could have used C, a popular language at the time, but C is ornery when dealing with text and is prone to making difficult-to-locate errors if you're not careful.

Interpreters and compilers

Two main types of programming languages exist, *compiled* and *interpreted,* each of which has its advantages and disadvantages. Probably the best-known compiled language is C. Perl, on the other hand, is an interpreted language.

The main difference between the two is that compiled languages generally run faster. Interpreted languages read a program and turn it into machine instructions before executing it; compiled languages already have the machine instructions so they can start executing from the get-go. Many people, particularly C programmers, contend that compiled programs are better because they run faster. In our faster-is-better society, this may be a compelling argument.

The speed difference between a compiler and an interpreter is sometimes infinitesimal, and unnoticeable by mere mortals. For instance, even for large and complex Perl programs, an equivalent C program may take one-half of a second less to run. Another difference is that interpreted languages are a bit easier to debug, because they are executed step-by-step so you can find exactly where a problem occurred and stop right there to fix it.

For a long time, Perl was mostly a UNIX-only language. Perl has been extended to do much more than extract text and then generate a report on it. Thousands of useful system-administration and Internet tools now rely on Perl in order to perform tasks like summarizing log files, taking input from Web users, and displaying parts of databases on the Web. In fact, a few Web server programs are written completely in Perl.

Perl now comes bundled with almost every copy of every flavor of UNIX. Until a few years ago, virtually all work on Perl was done on UNIX systems (and other workstation operating systems). The language hasn't become as popular on PCs and Macintoshes yet, but the interest in Perl by users of small computers is growing by leaps and bounds. Perl is the only popular free programming language available for Windows 95, Windows 98, and Macs, and as these computers need more and more system administration, Perl's acceptance and use is likely to grow even more.

Perl for Windows, Mac, and UNIX is also on the CD-ROM that comes with this book. For the latest versions of Perl, you can go to a number of places on the Internet to access Perl installations. (See Chapters 2 and 23 for more information on Perl resources.)

Many Versions, One Perl

Throughout this book, I talk about Perl as if it were just one programming language. But, like all software, Perl has gone through many changes since the time Larry Wall conceived it. Fortunately, there are only two major versions of Perl that you need to think about: Perl 4 and Perl 5.

Each major version has many minor versions; for instance, as I write this, the current version of Perl is 5.005. All minor versions of a major version act pretty much the same, but higher numbered minor versions usually have a few additions and bug fixes. In fact, each minor version has minor-minor versions, such as 5.005_02.

Perl Version 4 was the stable version of Perl for many years. In fact, many people still use Perl 4 instead of Perl 5 because they just got so used to it, even though Perl 5 added many advanced features. The final subversion of Perl 4 is "patchlevel 36," but most people just refer to it as Version 4.036. Whenever I talk about Perl 4 in this book, I'm referring to Perl Version 4.036.

In early 1996, people started making the switch to Perl 5. The reasons for this trend are all good ones. Perl 5 is not a huge change from Perl 4, but the differences are such that there will probably never be a Perl 6. Perl 5 is pretty stable (although not completely bug-free, of course) and can certainly be used for almost any application.

This book is almost exclusively about Perl 5, which is not to say that a Perl 4 user can't use the programs you find here. In fact, about 95 percent of what's in this book works exactly the same under Perl 4 as it does with Perl 5: a testament to how carefully the folks working on the Perl project engineered a smooth transition from Perl 4 to Perl 5.

There are, however, a few things in Perl 5 that just plain didn't exist in Perl 4, and they, of course, are covered in this book. For example, Chapter 19 covers object-oriented Perl, a feature that doesn't exist in Perl 4. Descriptions of a few smaller, but nevertheless handy, new features in Version 5 are sprinkled throughout the book.

Having said that, however, I urge everyone using Perl 4 to upgrade to Perl 5. It's much easier for people to write programs for each other using Perl 5. In fact, most programs that you find on the CD-ROM that comes with this book are for Perl 5.

Perl in the Future

Before embarking on your Perl expedition, you may be wondering whether Perl is the best language to learn now, given that the computer world and particularly the Internet are changing so quickly. Rest assured, Perl (and particularly Perl Version 5) is as ready for the future as any other programming language.

Mind you, plenty of new technologies get lots of hype but never amount to much. I've been writing for computer publications for almost 20 years and I've seen plenty of new ideas that were supposed to be amazing, revolutionary, and the next big thing that disappeared within a year or two. However, Perl's flexibility lets programmers develop for almost any new application, whether or not that application becomes popular.

A good example of Perl's "future-ready" features is its support for XML (eXtensible Markup Language). XML is a new document format for exchanging data via the Internet that I believe will sweep Webmeisters off their feet in the next five years, and Perl is one of the best languages for reading XML files. XML is still so new that it's difficult to find many XML documents on the Internet. Nevertheless, I introduce you to using Perl for XML programming in Chapter 15.

Perl modules already exist for a few other exciting emerging technologies, including:

- *CORBA,* the *Common Object Request Broker Architecture.* Many people expect that CORBA will be the primary method by which programs pass objects to each other (see Chapter 19 for information on objects).

- *DNS,* the Internet's *Domain Name System.* The DNS is undergoing changes due to political pressure from various nations worldwide that want more control over the registration of domain names within their borders. Because these pressures are likely to bring changes to the DNS in the near future, system administrators need tools to help them understand the current state of the system. Perl already has the building blocks in place to help administrators manage their domain names.
- Y2K (Year 2000) compliance. We can only hope that computer programs around the world won't be making too many dumb assumptions when January 1, 2000, rolls around. Perl itself has no Y2K problems, but as with any programming language, some folks have created programs that may develop problems. Nevertheless, Perl is one of the best languages to write programs designed to ferret out Y2K problems in other programs. (How Perl deals with the Y2K "bug" is covered in Chapter 9.)

Most programming languages can be forced to work with new technologies, but only a few languages give you the tools to do so without your having to write huge amounts of code from scratch. Perl's structure makes it a forward-thinking language, which means that as you decide to use some of these technologies that are still in the development stage, you'll have less work to do in the long run.

Chapter 2

Running Perl on Your Computer

In This Chapter

- Installing Perl on UNIX, Windows 95/98, Windows NT, and Macintosh
- Running Perl programs
- Getting the latest version of Perl
- Finding out about Perl on other systems

Any programming language that runs on a certain type of computer has to be in sync with that computer in order to run any programs. For instance, in order to read and write files, a language must know precisely how the computer on which it is running reads and writes files.

Technically speaking, a programming language such as Perl runs on an operating system, not on a computer. Practically every computer built today comes with its own operating system, and some computers can run many optional operating systems. For instance, IBM-compatible PCs can run MS-DOS, Windows 95 or 98, Windows NT, LINUX and other flavors of UNIX, QNX, and on and on. Perl isn't particular about the computer it's running on, just the computer's operating system.

Perl Isn't Just for UNIX Anymore

Perl was written first and foremost for UNIX and similar operating systems. One of the wonderful things about Perl (or, should I say, "yet another of the wonderful things about Perl") is that it tries valiantly to hide any differences among operating systems. Perl for Windows 95/98 and Perl for the Macintosh have a few features not found on Perl for UNIX, but the vast majority of the interesting stuff in Perl works the same on every operating system. You open files the same way, you do math the same way, and so on.

You do need to be aware of a few important differences between Perl running on UNIX and Perl running on other operating systems. These differences are pointed out in this book with warnings such as this one. Ignoring these words of advice can result in programs that don't work the way you expect.

Most of this book is about the parts of Perl that work the same way on all kinds of computers. Before you can start running Perl programs, however, you need to install Perl on your computer, which requires different steps for each kind of computer. I describe those steps in later sections of this chapter.

The name game

This book describes how to run Perl on four different operating systems: UNIX, Windows 95/98, Windows NT, and Macintosh (MacOS). (***Note:*** No supported Perl exists for Windows 3.1.)

Perl for Windows 95, Windows 98, and Windows NT are actually the same program. In this book, I call the program Perl-Win32 because that's what its authors call it.

Perl on the Macintosh is called MacPerl, and Perl on UNIX is called, well, just plain Perl.

Getting the latest from the Internet

If for some reason you don't want to use the version of Perl supplied on this book's companion CD-ROM, you can get the latest version of Perl from many sites on the Internet. The files on the CD-ROM were the latest available as of this writing. The Perl installations are all stable and run great, so don't feel as if you have to go off and get the latest version in order to get going with Perl.

However, there are those people who do need the up-to-the-minute newest programs. The UNIX and Macintosh Perl installations on the CD-ROM are available from dozens of Internet sites in the Comprehensive Perl Archive Network (CPAN) library. (See Chapter 23 for more information on where to look on the Internet for the latest CPAN library and other Perl resources.)

The Perl-Win32 installation is used with permission from its developer, ActiveState. You can get the most recent version from them at `www.activestate.com`.

UNIX: Perl's First Home

Because Perl started out as a UNIX application, Perl's integration with UNIX is much tighter than its integration with Windows or the Mac. However, this does not mean that installing and using Perl on UNIX is always a minor task.

The following two sections of this chapter should help any UNIX users avoid problems with intalling Perl on their systems.

Determining if you need to install Perl on UNIX

If you've used UNIX for any length of time, you know that a zillion variants of UNIX are available. For some folks, the differences don't amount to much. If you're trying to install a complex program such as Perl, however, those differences can make the installation process utter agony. In my experience, installing Perl can be a cinch or it can be a real mind-bender.

Fortunately, Perl is so popular among UNIX folks that almost every implementation of UNIX now comes with Perl fully installed. A good way to find out whether or not you already have Perl on your system is to enter the following simple UNIX command:

```
perl -v
```

If Perl is installed and in your UNIX search path, you get something on screen that looks like this:

```
This is perl, version 5.005_02 built for i386-bsdos

Copyright 1987-1998, Larry Wall

Perl may be copied only under the terms of either the
Artistic License or the GNU General Public License, which
may be found in the Perl 5.0 source kit.

Complete documentation for Perl, including FAQ lists,
should be found on this system using 'man perl' or
'perldoc perl'.  If you have access to the Internet, point
your browser at http://www.perl.com/, the Perl Home Page.
```

Make note of the version number in the first line of the previous message. It should say `This is perl, version 5.004` or `This is perl, version 5.005`. That means you're running Perl 5, the latest major version of Perl. If the first line says something like `This is perl, version 4.0`, you're running Perl 4, which is okay but not great. As I explain in Chapter 1 and Chapter 24, some of the features described in this book are available only in Perl 5.

Many UNIX systems have both Perl 4 and Perl 5 running simultaneously. Usually, one is invoked as `perl` and the other as `perl4` or `perl5`. In the example screen text shown earlier, `perl` is Perl 5, and there may be a program called `perl4` on your UNIX system which will run Perl 4. If running `perl` gives you Perl 4, you should definitely check whether the command `perl5 -v` results in the version message for Perl 5.

If you don't have Perl in your UNIX search path, when you issue the `perl -v` command you'll see the message

```
perl: command not found
```

Not to worry: You may still have Perl on your system, but you should have UNIX do a bit of searching for you using the `whereis` command:

```
whereis perl
```

If Perl is in any of the standard places where one may expect to find it, you'll probably get something like this:

```
/usr/bin/perl
/usr/contrib/bin/perl
```

(***Note:*** The `whereis` command sometimes puts the response on a single line.)

If you get a blank response from the `whereis` program, most likely you don't have Perl on your system. You must then resort to the one thing that many of us hate to do: Ask someone else. Your best bet is to ask a system administrator where Perl may be hiding. The administrator may have installed a copy but not made it publicly available or you may need just one more person (you!) to pester the administrator about installing Perl.

Installing Perl on UNIX (when you have to)

If you are a UNIX system administrator (welcome, oh wizard!), you can probably install Perl with a minimum of muss or fuss if your flavor of UNIX is supported in the Perl build. Unfortunately, it usually isn't. In the past, I've been able to install Perl using just two commands, and at times I've had to get on the phone with the tech support people at my UNIX vendor to figure out what went wrong.

You can install Perl for other people to use only if you are a system administrator. You can, however, install it for yourself without having system administrator privileges. Perl requires access to some privileged files in order to install it correctly for general use; therefore, you must be the root user when doing the installation. If you aren't a system administrator with root privileges, you need to ask the person who does have those privileges to do the Perl installation for you.

The first thing you need to do is to get the latest version of the Perl program. The easiest way to get it is from the CD-ROM that comes with this book. The Perl distribution files for UNIX on the CD-ROM are located in the directory called UNIX. The Perl 5 distribution file is called perl5.tar.gz, and uses about 3.5 megabytes of memory.

You can install Perl 5 with the following seven basic steps:

1. **Use `gunzip` and `tar` to uncompress and unpack the .tar.gz file.**

   It's a good idea to put the sources in the same place you put your other program sources (typically in /usr/src).

2. **Read the file called INSTALL.**

   This file gives you more information about what you need to install Perl than this numbered list does. The file isn't lengthy, and it lists some of the picky details you need to know for the different flavors of UNIX.

3. **Remove the config.sh file, if you have one in the installation directory.**

   It may be there if, for instance, you previously tried to install Perl.

4. **Issue the command**

   ```
   sh Configure
   ```

   This command is a shell script that can figure out lots of information about your system. The script creates the config.sh file, which contains dozens of variable definitions for your system.

5. **Issue the command**

   ```
   make
   ```

   This command compiles and links all the needed files using the parameters determined in Step 4.

6. **Issue the command**

   ```
   make test
   ```

   This command performs many tests on the copy of Perl that was made in Step 5. The `make test` command should result in the reply `All tests successful`; if it doesn't, the other messages you get should (hopefully) help you figure out which part of the compilation or linking failed.

7. **Last, but certainly not least, issue the command**

   ```
   make install
   ```

   This command installs all the parts of Perl into the various system directories on your computer.

Many parts of Perl exist, and the installer program puts the various Perl files in different places, possibly wiping out previous versions of some system files. Just to be sure, look through the *Makefile* (the file that tells the `make` program what to do) *before* running the `makeinstall` command to be sure everything's going to go where you want it to be.

Running Perl programs under UNIX

Assuming that you have Perl on your system, you can run Perl programs quite easily using the `perl` command. Perl programs are simply text files, and you can create Perl programs with any text editor such as vi or emacs.

For example, if you have a Perl program in a file called proc-invoices, you can run that program with the command

```
perl proc-invoices
```

Perl has myriad command-line options. For example, one of the most useful command line options is `-c`, which tells Perl to *not* run the program but to just check it for any syntax errors. Therefore, to check your proc-invoices program, you can give the command

```
perl -c proc-invoices
```

Under UNIX, Perl acts like a shell interpreter, a subject familiar to UNIX-savvy users. The fact that Perl acts as a shell interpreter means that you can write Perl programs invoked from the UNIX command line without starting the command with `perl`. For instance, you can run the proc-invoices program with the command

```
proc-invoices
```

However, in order to make the previous command work, the very first line of your Perl program must look something like

```
#!/usr/bin/perl
```

The text to the right of the `#!` characters must be the location of Perl on your system. Most UNIX systems stash Perl in /usr/bin/perl. If your system keeps Perl in a location such as /usr/contrib/lang/perl, the first line of your Perl programs is

```
#!/usr/contrib/lang/perl
```

If you use both UNIX and MS-DOS, you may fall into a common trap. Under MS-DOS (or the DOS window in Windows 95/98), don't type the program's extension when you run a program. For example, if you have a program called PROCINV.EXE, you would give the command

```
procinv
```

No actual "extensions" exist under UNIX. Therefore, if you have a program called proc-invoices.pl (.pl being the common way of indicating that a file is a Perl program), you have to give the command

```
proc-invoices.pl
```

and not just `proc-invoices`.

Perl-Win32 on Windows 95/98 and Windows NT

Okay, enough of that UNIX stuff. Installing Perl 5 on Windows 95, Windows 98, or Windows NT by comparison is much easier. Perl-Win32 comes as a *self-installing* program, which means that it comes as a single executable file. When you run that file, it installs all the necessary files in the right places on your hard drive.

Installing Perl-Win32 under Windows

If you are running under Windows 95, Windows 98, or Windows NT, you can find the Perl-Win32 files on the *Perl For Dummies* CD-ROM in the directory called Windows. In that directory, you will find a file called APi502e.exe, which is the installer program for Perl-Win32.

Before you run the installer, you may need to take an extra step if you're a Windows 95 user. (Windows 98 and Windows NT users can skip this step.) You have to install DCOM into Windows 95 before you install Perl-Win32. DCOM, which stands for Distributed Component Object Model, is an extension for Windows 95 from Microsoft. If you don't already have DCOM on your Windows 95 system (and there isn't any easy way to tell whether you do or not), you have to get it from the Microsoft Web site at www.microsoft.com/com/dcom.asp and load it onto your PC. After you do that, you can then install Perl-Win32.

To install Perl, double-click on the icon for the APi502e.exe file. As the installation program runs, it acts like the installation programs for most other Windows software you're probably familiar with. Various dialog boxes prompt you for feedback, such as whether you've read the license agreement.

One of the important questions the Perl-Win32 installer will ask you is where you want to put Perl-Win32; it suggests the directory C:\perl. Unless you have some strong preference against this location, you should accept this suggestion and install Perl-Win32 in that spot. Another reason to accept this location: Every Windows example in this book was written with the assumption that Perl is installed in C:\perl.

After you wade through a few more prompts from the installation program, the program installs all the needed files on your hard drive. After it has copied all the files, the last prompt asks you if you want to read the release notes for Perl-Win32. If you say yes, the installer program launches your Web browser (such as Netscape Communicator or Internet Explorer) to display the release notes. Feel free to say no to the prompt, because you can read the release notes later, and you're probably more interested in starting to use Perl than in reading more about it.

Running Perl-Win32 in a (yuck!) DOS window

I have some sad news: Perl-Win32 *isn't* a Windows program. You run it from the command line in a DOS window. Yes, you read this correctly. That means no menus, no dialog boxes, and lots of typing. At first I was flabbergasted at this discovery, but I've learned to live with it.

First, you need to open a DOS window manually.

1. **Go to the Start menu, and choose MS-DOS Prompt from the Programs item.**

   An MS-DOS window that is probably not in the directory in which you put Perl-Win32 appears.

2. **Use the (ouch!) `MS-DOS CD` command to get to your Perl directory.**

   If you followed the installation instructions, that directory is C:\perl.

After reading this section of the chapter, you can see why I use C:\Perl as my Perl directory: I can get there with very little typing. But, you can go one step better than that. You can create a shortcut so you don't have to give the CD command every time you start an MS-DOS window.

1. **Right-click on the system's desktop.**

   A context-sensitive menu appears.

2. **Select New⇨Shortcut.**

   A dialog box appears asking for the command line of the shortcut you are creating.

3. **Type** C:\Command.com **in the text area for the command line and click Next.**

4. **For the shortcut name, enter** Perl5.

5. **Click Finish.**

   You now have a new icon on your desktop.

6. **Right-click on the new icon for a context-sensitive menu.**

7. **Select Properties.**

8. **In the Properties dialog box, click the Program tab.**

9. **In the Working option, enter the name of the directory where you keep Perl-Win32: for example** C:\Perl.

   You can specify any other options you desire under the other tabs in the Properties window.

10. **Click OK in the Properties window to make sure that the new settings stick.**

Now when you double-click the icon that was created using the previous steps, the MS-DOS prompt window will start in your Perl directory.

Because Perl programs are text files, you can create programs with a text editor such as the Windows Notepad program or the MS-DOS edit command. You can also run Perl programs easily using the `perl` command. For example, if you have a Perl program in the procinv.pl file, you can run that program with the command

```
perl procinv.pl
```

Perl features a number of command line options, and one of the most useful of those options is `-c`, which tells Perl to check a program for syntax errors without running the program. So, to check the proc-invoices program, you can issue the following command:

```
perl -c procinv.pl
```

It does get a bit tiresome typing `perl` for each command and having to remember the file extension every time. Perl-Win32 has a program called pl2bat that turns a Perl program into a batch file that can be run by name.

For example, to change the procinv.pl program into a batch file, you can use this command:

```
pl2bat procinv.pl
```

This `pl2bat` command creates the procinv.bat file, and you can run this program as

```
procinv
```

You can check the version of Perl-Win32 you are running by giving the command

```
perl -v
```

The output of this command is shown in Figure 2-1.

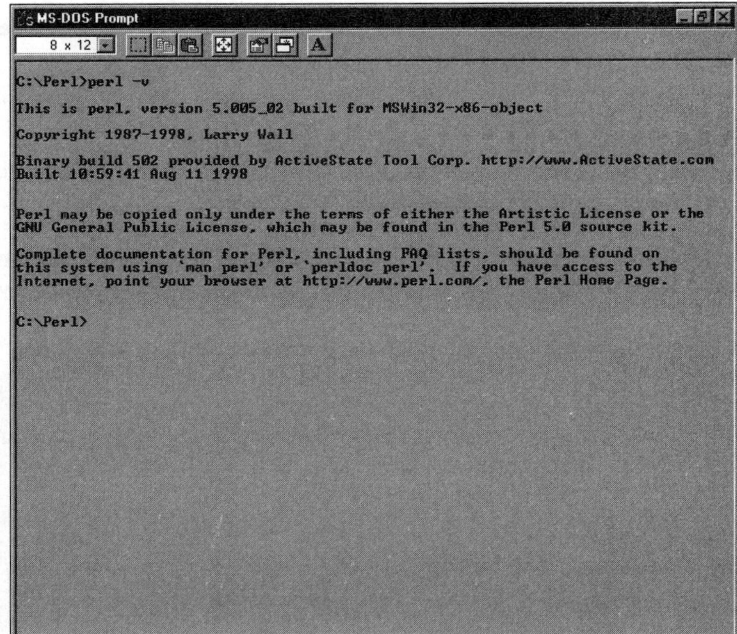

Figure 2-1: Here you can check the version of Perl-Win32 being run.

MacPerl: The User-Friendly Mac Interface You'd Expect

The Macintosh fans in the audience who read the previous sections of this chapter are probably bored silly by now with all the UNIX and Windows command lines. Fear not, it's your turn. Compared with UNIX, installing Perl for the Mac is a breeze.

Installing MacPerl

In the Macintosh folder on the CD-ROM, you can find the MacPerl Installer, which does all the work of installing MacPerl on your hard drive. When you run the MacPerl Installer by double-clicking on it, it asks you where you want the MacPerl folder and then installs 800 or so files that are associated with Perl, including all the online documentation. The result of the installation is a folder like the one shown in Figure 2-2.

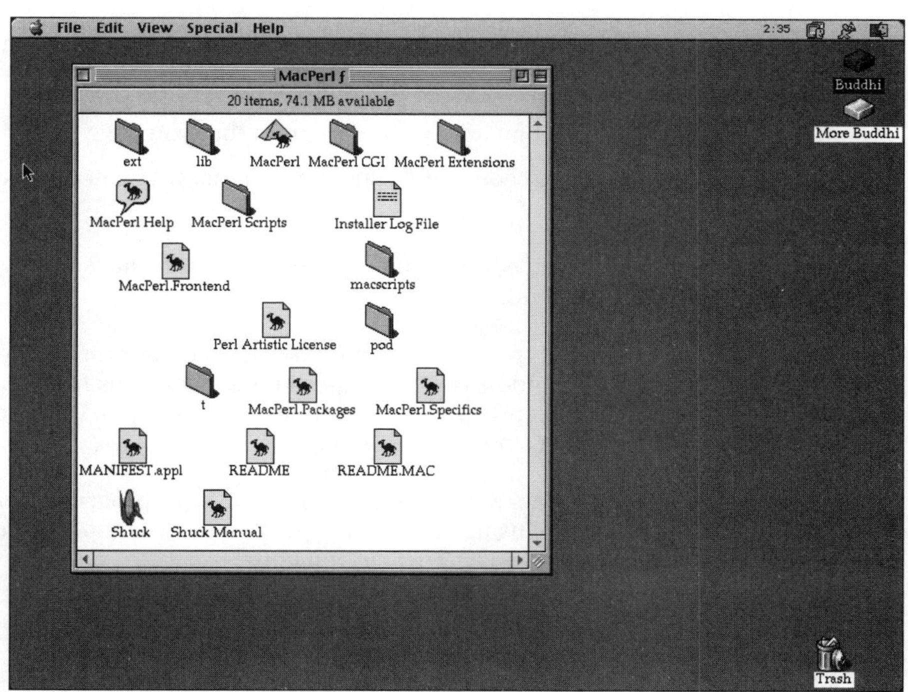

Figure 2-2: The MacPerl folder.

Running MacPerl programs

MacPerl is a program that runs Perl programs. This means that when you run MacPerl, you tell it which Perl programs you want to run. The MacPerl program itself has a nominal user interface. In fact, when you start MacPerl, it doesn't even open up any windows.

MacPerl programs are plain text files, so you can create them with any text editor such as SimpleText or BBEdit. MacPerl also has a very basic text editor built into it.

To create a new text file in MacPerl:

1. **Select File⇨New.**
2. **Enter and edit your program.**
3. **Select File⇨Save.**

   You can also use the Open, Close, Print, Cut, Copy, and Paste commands in the MacPerl editor just like you would in any other Mac program.

To run a Perl program in MacPerl, choose one of the two Run commands from the Script menu.

- The first Run command runs a program that you have on disk.
- The second Run command runs the program that you are editing in MacPerl.

If you want to use an editor other than MacPerl's internal editor, you should use the first command.

When you run a Perl program, MacPerl opens an empty window for input and output. This window is where you can read messages from MacPerl, and also where you can enter your text responses to prompts. (Chapter 3 covers reading and entering in Perl programs.)

You can also use MacPerl to check for errors in your programs before you run them. Instead of using one of the Run commands, simply use one of the Syntax Check commands in the Script menu.

Perl on the Command Line

When you run Perl from the UNIX or MS-DOS command line, you can include command line options that change the way Perl behaves; these options are also available for MacPerl, but not from the command line, because MacOS has no command line. More than a dozen command line options are available for Perl (UNIX dweebs love their command line options!), but only a few are really interesting to most programmers. A few of those options are covered in this section of the chapter.

Methods for entering command line options

You can give command line options in either one of two ways. The first, of course, is on the command line. As an alternative, you can include a line at the beginning of your program that looks like the command line but starts with `#!`. For example, you can indicate that you always want to use the `-w` command line option by inserting `#!perl -w` as the first line of your program. Mac users, who don't have a command line, will be especially thankful for this option.

UNIX users, as described earlier in this chapter in "Running Perl programs under UNIX," must enter the full path to a Perl program in the command line of their programs. Therefore, instead of entering `#!perl -w`, for example, a UNIX user enters

```
#!/usr/bin/perl -w
```

as the first line of the program.

The `-c` option

The most common Perl option you can expect to use is `-c`, which causes Perl to check the syntax of a program without running it. For you Mac users, the Syntax Check command in MacPerl does the same thing as the `-c` command line option.

The `-w` option

Similar to the `-c` option is the `-w` option that causes Perl to carefully examine your program for a number of programming errors. If it finds any of these errors, it prints them so that you can then edit your program in order to fix it. Using the `-w` option before you start to use a Perl program helps you to avoid embarrassing problems later on.

The -v option

The -v option tells you which version of Perl you're running. The -v option also works on Perl-Win32 and MacPerl. For instance, if you include the line

```
#!perl -v
```

at the beginning of a Perl-Win32 file, Perl will print

```
This is perl, version 5.005_02 built for MSWin32-x86-object

Copyright 1987-1998, Larry Wall

Binary build 502 provided by ActiveState Tool Corp.
http://www.ActiveState.com
Built 10:59:41 Aug 11 1998

Perl may be copied only under the terms of either the
Artistic License or the GNU General Public License, which
may be found in the Perl 5.0 source kit.

Complete documentation for Perl, including FAQ lists,
should be found on this system using 'man perl' or
'perldoc perl'.  If you have access to the
Internet, point your browser at http://www.perl.com/, the
Perl Home Page.
```

The -e option

Perl has a mode in which you can run one-line programs without having to enter them into a text file. If you use the -e option, Perl assumes that the rest of the command line is a one-line Perl program, not the name of a text file that has a program in it. For instance, to find the product of two numbers, you can use

```
perl -e "print 27.35 * .0825;"
```

The -i option

The -i option allows you to use Perl programs to edit files. Chapter 13 covers this option in more depth.

The `-d` option

After you get more experience in working with Perl, you may want to use Perl's internal debugging system. The debugger is a program that allows you to find errors in your Perl programs by moving through them step by step. The topic of debugging is beyond the scope of this book, but in case you want to experiment with it, you can turn on the debugger with the `-d` command line option. For example, to debug the proc-invoices simply enter

```
perl -d proc-invoices
```

Other Perls

The Comprehensive Perl Archive Network (CPAN) contains the Perl language for many operating systems other than UNIX, Windows NT, Windows 95/98, and MacOS. Perl has been made to run on a wide variety of systems, and implementations of Perl for all the following operating systems are available:

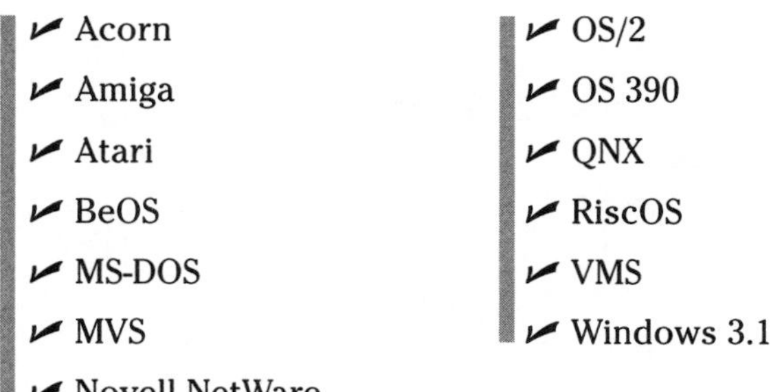

- Acorn
- Amiga
- Atari
- BeOS
- MS-DOS
- MVS
- Novell NetWare
- OS/2
- OS 390
- QNX
- RiscOS
- VMS
- Windows 3.1

Note: Some of the versions of Perl I just listed are old and unsupported. Most notably, the Windows 3.1 version is for Perl 4 only and hasn't been updated in more than four years.

Some of the other versions of Perl are up-to-date and well-supported and you can use them with abandon. If you want to run Perl on one of the other operating systems listed in this section, take a look at the program files on CPAN to see if any documentation exists, and if so, look for e-mail contact information for the program.

This book covers Perl running on UNIX, Windows NT, Windows 95/98, and MacOS only. If you're using Perl on any other operating system, at least 95 percent of the programs presented in this book should work just fine for you, but I make no guarantees.

Chapter 3

Diving into the Guts of Perl

In This Chapter

- Nailing down the basics of building Perl programs
- Writing statements
- Inserting comments
- Assigning variables
- Understanding literals

It's time get your hands dirty and dig into the basic elements of a Perl program. This chapter describes what a Perl program looks like and how you enter programs on your computer. Perl programs have a certain structure, and knowing how the elements of the structure fit together gives you the ability to put together programs that are super short, really long, or anything in between.

By the time you're finished with this chapter, you'll also know how Perl handles the kind of data that are most commonly used in programs. Consider this chapter as a sort of anatomy lesson on the inner workings of a program.

Step One: Grab Yourself a Text Editor

When it comes right down to it, Perl programs are just plain text files. You can write these files using just about any text editor that's handy. UNIX folks usually use *vi* and *emacs,* two popular editors that come with most UNIX systems. Windows users can use the Notepad or WordPad programs that come with Windows, or even the EDIT program that's part of MS-DOS, but many other better editors are available. Macintosh users can use the SimpleText program that comes on the Mac, but, again, many superior editors are available from a variety of sources. The freeware BBEdit Lite and commercial BBEdit Pro editors are particularly useful for Mac programmers.

Feel free to use the text-editing program of your choice to create and edit your Perl programs. However, if you end up doing lots of programming in Perl, definitely consider getting an editor that has extra features for programmers (my favorites are TextPad on Windows and BBEdit Pro on the Macintosh). If you're new to programming with Perl, you can use just about any text editor because your first programs will probably be fairly simple and easy to enter.

Examining Some Basic Components of a Perl Program

This section of the chapter describes a few basic steps in creating a Perl program. Here, and in the rest of the chapter, I use a number of short *code fragments*, which consist of a line or two from a complete Perl program. (The fragments are culled from a program that is described in Chapter 4, but you don't need to see the whole program to understand how the fragments work.)

Executing a statement

When Perl runs a program, it starts at the top of the program and reads downward line by line, *executing* each statement that it comes to. A *statement* in Perl is like a command in English: It tells Perl what to do. As in the line

```
print "For the file $TheFile:\n";
```

`print` is the statement, and the rest of the line tells Perl what to print. Perl contains dozens of kinds of statements. Relating statements to what they can do is the essence of understanding Perl. It's fairly easy to follow what's going on in a Perl program. Just start reading from the top and go down. (You can read more about statements later in this chapter in the section "Statements: The Stuff Perl Programs Are Made Of.")

Making a loop

Perl doesn't always follow a straight line, however. Some statements define *loops,* which are sets of lines that Perl repeats over and over until told to stop. The following example illustrates a single loop. The loop consists of the lines between the `while` statement and the `loop` statement. After Perl leaves a loop it starts reading the program again at the next line after the loop.

```
while(<INFILE>) {
```

and

```
} # End of while(<INFILE>) loop
```

In Chapter 8, you find out what happens in loops and how to tell Perl when it should stop looping. For now, all you need to know is that when you leave a loop, Perl starts executing statements right after the loop one at a time, just as it did before the loop.

Inserting a comment

In a typical Perl program, only about half of its lines really do anything. The other half are *comments,* stuff that Perl ignores. You may be thinking, "What!? Half of my program is going to be ignored by Perl!? Why bother writing it then?" I'll give you two very good reasons that hold true for every programming language:

- Comments help you read your program later so that you can fix things or use the program for new purposes.
- Comments enable other people who, for some reason down the road, have to read your program to figure out what the heck you meant when you wrote it.

Writing programs is a bit like arranging the junk in your garage: The organization makes perfect sense when you're stashing the stuff away the first time, but six months later you can't remember why you put things where you did. Comments are notes to yourself about what's going on in a program so that when you examine your program at a later date, you can make some sense of what you intended in the first place. And, by leaving comments in your program, you provide clues to other people who also have to understand your program in order to work with it.

Hopefully, you now feel a bit better about what comments are and why they take up half your program. Every line that starts with a # character is a comment. (By the way, there is not a globally accepted name for this character. In the United States, the symbol is usually called the "pound" character, but in other countries, it's often called the "hash" character.)

A comment tells Perl to ignore everything from the # character all the way to the end of the line. For example, the following lines are all comments:

```
#!/usr/bin/perl -w
# counter1.pl: one way to count the characters, words, and
#    lines in a text file.
```

You can also start a comment on the same line with other Perl statements. When Perl sees a # in the middle of a line, it again assumes that everything from the # character all the way to the end of the line is a comment and ignores it. Therefore, in the line

```
$TheLine = $_;  # Save the line's contents
```

Perl only pays attention to the text up to the ; (semicolon) and ignores the comment.

By the way, you may have noticed that program code is loaded with blank lines. Blank lines are also comments, in a way. Perl ignores blank lines so you can have as many or as few of them as you want. You can use blank lines wherever you want in your programs to make the program easier to read. I usually put blank lines between each major section of a program so that when I glance at the program as a whole, I can see where each section starts. For most programmers, blank lines act like part separators. For more information, check out "Keeping Tabs on Statements: Indenting and Spacing" later in this chapter.

Statements, the Stuff Perl Programs Are Made Of

Perl determines what you want to do with your program through the *statements* that you write. Each statement is constructed like a declarative sentence that tells Perl what to do next. Like in English, some of these "sentences" are short, others are long, and some just go on and on.

Every Perl statement falls into one of the following three categories:

- A statement containing an "active verb" that calls for immediate and definite action on the part of the program, such as "display this text" or "add these numbers"
- A *conditional* test, such as, "if such-and-so is true, then do this"
- A loop, such as, "keep doing this set of things until I tell you to stop"

Almost every Perl program has a combination of direct action statements and conditionals, and many also have loops. Trust me, before you know it, you'll be comfortable with all these statement options.

The majority of statements that you see in Perl programs are direct-action statements, such as the following:

```
open(INFILE, $TheFile) or die "The file $TheFile could " .
    "not be found.\n";
    $LineCount = $LineCount + 1;  # This is the easy part!
```

In this example, the actions to be taken are `open`, `die`, and =. The = statement is used a great deal in Perl. It's called the *assignment statement,* and you use it to set variables. The = statement may not look like an action verb, such as `open` or `die`, but it functions like one. It literally means, "Set the variable on the left of the = to the value on the right of the =". (Assignment statements and variables are covered in this chapter in the section "Variables and Literals.")

Statement endings

Perl has an easy way to tell where one statement ends and the next one begins: when it spots a semicolon (;). That's why you see so many semicolons in the code examples in this book. For example,

```
$CharCount = 0;
```

is a single statement that ends with the semicolon.

You do not need to squeeze an entire statement into a single line. In fact, it's often impossible. Perl keeps reading until it finds a semicolon and then goes back and checks to see that the whole glob reads like a single statement.

Perl enables you to have more than one statement on a line. For example, the following three statements:

```
$CharCount = 0;
$WordCount = 0;
$LineCount = 0;
```

can all fit nicely on one line:

```
$CharCount = 0; $WordCount = 0; $LineCount = 0;
```

In the previous example, the semicolons essentially act as line breaks. (By the way, the reason I put the three statements on separate lines in the first place is so that they're easier to read when you scan the program. When the choice is between clarity and saving a few lines on a page, opt for clarity.)

Blocks

Conditional and loop statements enable you to include lots of other statements within them. Each set of additional statements is called a *block*. You can recognize a block because it is enclosed within curly braces ({ and }). You can think of a block as a single set of statements that always hangs together, like a mini-program.

So that you know what I'm talking about when I mention certain punctuation marks in statements, "parentheses" refer to (and); "curly braces" or just "braces" refer to { and }; "angle brackets" refer to < and >; and "square brackets" refer to [and].

Conditional statements employ blocks to tell Perl what to do if a certain condition is true. For example, consider the sentence, "Unless you phone me before 4 o'clock, I will pick up Chris from the day-care center and start dinner." The condition in the sentence is the phrase "Unless you phone me before 4 o'clock," and the block of statements that follows is "I will pick up Chris from the day-care center and start dinner." The same would be true in Perl: The two things will happen in order, and they won't happen unless the conditional statement is true.

Loops also use blocks. A loop stated in everyday English may say something like, "Until the tree is completely full of leaves, I'll water and fertilize it every week." The loop statement is "Until the tree is covered with leaves," and the block is "I'll water and fertilize it every week." If these were instructions given to Perl, the watering and fertilizing would cycle over and over until the tree was completely leafy.

Blocks have one feature that often confuses beginning Perl users: You don't need to insert a semicolon after the closing brace of a block. Perl knows the end of a block (that is, the }) is automatically the end of a statement. For instance, in the lines

```
if(substr($TheLine, $CharPos, 1) eq " ")
    { $WordCount = $WordCount + 1 }
```

no semicolon is included after the } because Perl knows that a block is the end of the conditional statement. Some people prefer to end their blocks with semicolons for aesthetic reasons even though they don't have to. You can end the statement with a semicolon if you want to:

```
if(substr($TheLine, $CharPos, 1) eq " ")
    { $WordCount = $WordCount + 1 };
```

Give yourself a gold star if you noticed something else odd in this example: There's no semicolon *before* the closing brace (and after `+ 1`). The reason is similar to not needing the semicolon after the }. Perl knows that if you're ending a block with a }, you're also ending the last statement in the block, and therefore it lets you skip the semicolon to close out the last statement in the block. If you want to add it, you can. For example,

```
        if(substr($TheLine, $CharPos, 1) eq " ")
            { $WordCount = $WordCount + 1; }
```

Recognizing blocks within blocks

A block is a set of statements. Single statements can have blocks within them. Therefore, a block can have blocks within it.

In the following example, the first block is the one associated with the `while` statement. Within that statement there's an `until` statement that contains another block, an `if` statement:

```
while(<INFILE>) {
    $TheLine = $_;  # Save the line's contents
    . . .
    until($CharPos == $LineLen) {
        if(substr($TheLine, $CharPos, 1) eq " ")
            { $WordCount = $WordCount + 1 }
        $CharPos = $CharPos + 1;
    }  # End of until
}  # End of while(<INFILE>) loop
```

Keeping track of nested blocks

It's often tricky for even advanced programmers to keep lots of nested blocks straight in their heads. As you soon see, you can organize blocks by indenting any that fall under another block (see "Keeping Tabs on Statements: Indenting and Spacing" later in this chapter).

If indentation fails to help you keep track of your blocks, you can always determine which brace goes with which block in the same way that Perl does. You can find the right (ending) brace that matches a particular left (beginning) brace by counting all the left and right braces that follow it — each left brace counts +1, and each right brace –1. When you get to zero again after counting the first left brace, you found the match.

In the preceding example, if you want to find which of the right braces matches the left brace on the `while` line, you can go through the rest of the program, adding 1 for each left brace and subtracting 1 for each right brace. Here's the same code, with comments added to show you the process:

```
while(<INFILE>) {   ###Start at 1
    $TheLine = $_;
    . . .
    if($TheLine eq "") { next };  ###+1, -1: total is 1
    . . .
    until($CharPos == $LineLen) {   ### +1: total is 2
        if(substr($TheLine, $CharPos, 1) eq " ")
            { $WordCount = $WordCount + 1 }
           ###+1, -1: total is 2
        $CharPos = $CharPos + 1;
    }  # End of until  ### -1: total is 1
}  # End of while(<INFILE>) loop  ### -1: total is 0
```

You can see that the last brace, which took the count to 0, is the match of the first one.

Operators and functions

You need to know about two other kinds of Perl items before delving further into the language. *Operators* are symbols that enable you to perform actions on data, such as adding two numbers together. In the following statement

```
    $LineCount = $LineCount + 1;  # This is the easy part!
```

the + is an operator that tells Perl to add 1 to the value of $LineCount.

Functions are statements that act like operators, but they have alphabetic names, such as chomp, instead of symbolic names, such as =. The following line describes chomp:

```
    chomp($TheLine);  # Get rid of the line break
```

Functions have *arguments,* usually shown in parentheses, to tell Perl what the function is operating on. Many functions have more than one argument, and if they do, the arguments are separated by commas. For example, the following line contains the substr function with three arguments:

```
substr($TheLine, $CharPos, 1)
```

Throughout the book, I mix the terms "functions" and "statements." In Perl programming, there is no important distinction between the two, so you can use the two terms interchangeably.

Keeping Tabs on Statements: Indenting and Spacing

Every line in a Perl program doesn't necessarily start at the left margin, as in this example:

```
open(INFILE, $TheFile) or die "The file $TheFile could " .
    "not be found.\n";
```

The indentation of the second line is completely optional. Just as it disregards comments, Perl ignores spaces at the beginning of lines.

Indentation is a good way to make your Perl programs more readable. In the preceding example, the indentation is used to show that the `die` statement does not finish on the first line. If you have to continue a statement to a new line, indenting the run-over text makes it easier to see at a glance that the line should be read as a single unit.

To see how indentation comes in handy, compare the following two lines to those in the previous example:

```
open(INFILE, $TheFile) or die "The file $TheFile could " .
"not be found.\n";
```

If you were scanning down a page and spotted the unindented sample, you might think that the chunk in quotation marks on the second line was a separate statement, when in fact it's part of the statement from the first line.

Indenting blocks

Indentation is also useful when it comes to managing blocks. Most programmers like to indent every line in a block so that it's easy to see where Perl goes after the block finishes.

The following example illustrates how useful indentation can be in formatting the statements in your programs. The `until` statement has a block as its argument, and that block is indented four spaces farther to the right than the `until` statement. Inside the `until` block is an `if` statement, and that also has a block, which is indented another four spaces:

```
until($CharPos == $LineLen) {
    if(substr($TheLine, $CharPos, 1) eq " ")
        { $WordCount = $WordCount + 1 }
    $CharPos = $CharPos + 1;
}
```

This last example also demonstrates another nice feature of Perl: The option of indenting. You can indent however you like, and if you do it "wrong," you can still count on a perfectly functional (but possibly hard to read) program.

Perl goes even further in its lenience: You can also start and end a block wherever you want to. You can also put the beginning and ending braces on a line with the rest of the block, or on lines of their own. For example, you can choose to have the block in the following `if` statement look like this:

```
if(substr($TheLine, $CharPos, 1) eq " ")
            { $WordCount = $WordCount + 1 }
```

Or, you may choose to place the braces so that the block looks like it does in the following example:

```
        if(substr($TheLine, $CharPos, 1) eq " ") {
             $WordCount = $WordCount + 1;
        }  # End of if(substr
```

Some programmers insist that the second option is better than the first because all your blocks will then look the same. That is, the opening { will always be at the end of the line that precedes the block, and the closing } will be on a line by itself (or followed by a comment). To me, the first option is better because it saves on the number of lines in your program and is easier to read. If a block is one statement long, I usually enter it as one line with its braces on that same line. As you gain experience with Perl, you'll probably develop a preference for one style or the other.

In fact, you can even put the whole preceding `if` statement and its block on one line (which I would have done here were it not for the space limitations of an 8½ x 11 page). Not even my computer screen is wide enough to show the entire statement: The line would be more than 80 characters long. This is why it's nice that Perl enables you to break up lines as needed for such nonprogramming reasons as "it won't fit in the book" or "it won't fit on my screen" or "I just feel that way right now, so there."

Adding extra spacing for the fun of it

By the way, Perl also ignores extra spacing between each part of a statement. For instance, Perl sees the following three statements exactly the same:

```
$CharCount = 0;
$CharCount=0;
$CharCount   =      0      ;
```

A Five-Minute Guide to Numbers and Text

Your programs can have many different kinds of data, such as numbers, text, lists, files, and so on. For now, the two most important types of data you need to think about are numbers and text. (Actually, you deal mostly with three specific types of data — real numbers, integers, and strings — which I get to in a moment.)

Ah, numbers. Remember how much *fun* math was when you were a kid? To this day, I'm still not sure how educators made it so miserable, even for those of us who wanted to enjoy it. Probably 80 percent of all adults still have a mild (or heavy) dislike for math, even though we all use numbers every day in many ways.

Perl happens to love numbers. It can handle all sorts of numbers — and make your use of them a breeze. The two types of numbers that you need to care about most are *integers* and *real numbers*. In case your high school math is too distant a memory, here's a refresher: Integers are numbers that do not have anything following the decimal point, while real numbers are numbers that, well, do have something following the decimal point. (This may be a bit different than the strict definition used by mathematicians.) Therefore, 3 is an integer, and 3.5 is a real number. (You can read more about numbers and Perl in Chapter 6.)

But the world of data consists of much more than just numbers. There's also text, plus a few other types of data. Text is made up of individual *characters*. Anything you can type on the keyboard is a character, such as the letter a, the letter b, a word space, the digit 7, a hyphen (-), and so on.

In Perl, text appears in strings. A *string* is a gang of characters. An example of a string of five characters is `abcde`; another one is `a2-@c`. Perl is especially great with text. You can ask Perl to do things like "Tell me the fifth character in this string" or "Find the first place in this string that has the letter 'j', and tell me everything that comes after it" or "Split this string into two strings: the stuff before the first space, and the stuff after it" or even "Split this string into a bunch of little strings, each one being the stuff that is between the tab characters." Perl responds with aplomb!

Variables and Literals

Here's a $64,000 question: If you've scanned the sample programs in this book, did you notice all the words with a dollar sign (`$`) in front of them? Those dollar signs indicate Perl *variables*. If you're familiar with any other programming language, you already know about variables because every language has variables or something just like them. If Perl is your first language, don't worry; variables are fairly easy to understand.

A *variable* is a place to store a value. Think of a variable as a box with a label on it. The box can hold exactly one thing (the variable's value), and it has exactly one name on the label (the variable's name). You can put anything you want in the box, but it's important to remember that the box can contain only one item. You can have as many boxes (variables) in your program as you desire.

A *literal,* on the other hand, is simply a value and literals don't have names. The number 47 is a literal: It means 47 and that can never change. The number doesn't have a name; it's just the value 47. The string `Cedar` is a literal: It can never be anything other than this one set of characters — `C`, `e`, `d`, `a`, and `r` — in exactly that order with no other characters involved.

In Perl, you can tell what is and isn't a variable by looking for the `$`. Anything with a `$` at the beginning of it is a variable name. For example, `$TheFile` and `$TheLine` are variables.

Variable names can be as long or as short as you want them to be, but they cannot have any spaces in them. They can have uppercase and lowercase letters in them, as well as digits, but they cannot start with a digit. You can also use the underscore (_) character in your variable names. The following strings are more examples of variable names:

- `$Bill1`
- `$BoyIsThisALongVariableName`
- `$I_BET_this_IS_hard_TO_type`

Perl variable names are *case-sensitive,* meaning that uppercase and lowercase letters in variable names are important to properly identifying the variable. Therefore, the name $FirstCar and the name $firstcar identify two different variables. When you edit programs, be sure to keep in mind how you're entering uppercase and lowercase letters.

You can do two things with a variable: examine its value or change its value. The first time you use a variable, you assign a value to it, usually by using a literal. For example, the following statement

```
$TheFile = "sample.txt";
```

says to Perl

> "Give the variable called `$TheFile` a value of "sample.txt"

When you make an assignment statement such as this one, Perl ignores whatever was in the variable before. If you have not used the variable before, Perl creates it; if you *have* used the variable before, Perl wipes out its old value and inserts the new value.

Going back to the box analogy I used at the beginning of this section, making an assignment is like telling Perl,

> If there isn't already a box with the name `$TheFile` on it, create the box and put the literal `sample.txt` into it. If there is a box with the name `$TheFile` on it, dump out its contents and put the literal `sample.txt` into it.

In addition to changing the value of variables, you can take a look at their values. For instance, examine the following statement:

```
    if($TheLine eq "") { next };
```

This statement means

> Look at the value that's in the variable named `$TheLine`, and see if that value equals "". If so, do what's inside the block.

Here's another statement that looks at the value of a variable:

```
print "For the file $TheFile:\n";
```

This statement means

> Print the literal `For the file` (including the space after `file`) and then look at the value that's inside the variable named `$TheFile`. Next, print that value, then print the character `:`, and then go to a new line.

Here's an example in which Perl both looks at one variable, `$TheLine`, and changes another (`$LineLen`):

```
$LineLen = length($TheLine);
```

This line means

> Look at the variable called `$TheLine`, find its length, and put the value of its length in the variable called `$LineLen`.

Your statements can have a combination of assignments, commands that tell Perl to look at the current value of a variable, and literals, all in the same statement. The following example is typical of such a statement:

```
$WordCount = $WordCount + 1;
```

At first, this statement may be a tad perplexing, but it can make good sense. It means

> First, look at the value of the variable named `$WordCount`. Next, take that value, add `1`, and then place that new value into the variable called `$WordCount`.

Here's that statement again, this time with its relevant parts underlined.

First, look at the value of the variable named $WordCount.

```
$WordCount = $WordCount + 1;
```

Next, take that value, add 1,

```
$WordCount = $WordCount + 1;
```

and then place that new value into the variable called $WordCount.

```
$WordCount = $WordCount + 1;
```

This amounts to a long-winded way of saying, "Make the $WordCount variable 1 higher than it already was."

Why you always assign variables first

Get ready, because I'm about to inform you of the Number One, classic, absolutely supreme mistake that most programmers make at one time or another. The technical term for this goof is "using an unassigned variable," and it's one of the more difficult errors to unearth in a program.

A problem with unassigned variables occurs when you either examine or change a variable that you have not already assigned a value. For example, consider the statement

```
$LineLen = length($TheLine);
```

This statement makes sense if you assume that $TheLine has been assigned, because then the length function is working on a known object. However, if $TheLine has not been assigned, such as in a previous statement that has already been executed, then Perl doesn't know what it's taking the length of. So, Perl silently makes a guess about what you wanted in $TheLine, and that guess is almost always wrong.

How can you avoid this all-too-common mistake of unassigned variables? Always check your Perl programs with the -w command line option (covered in Chapter 2). One of the great blessings of using -w is that it can find almost every instance in which you look at or change a variable without having first given the variable a value. Perl is one of the few languages that has this kind of built-in feature, and the result is that if you write a program that uses unassigned variables, you can catch it early and fix it.

Perl's special variables

You have literals, whose values never change, and your own variables, whose values change when you tell Perl to change them. And you now know beyond a shadow of a doubt that you need to assign your variables before you put them to use in a program. Just when you're comfortable living with this strict warning, now you can meet a class of variables that comes with values already assigned.

Perl's *special variables* are those that Perl gives pre-assigned values. You can treat these special variables like any other variable in a Perl program: You can examine them or assign them values. For example, the variable called `$0` contains the name of the program that you're running.

Perl contains dozens of special variables, most of which are of little interest to novices (or even advanced users). I cover a few of them in this book, but if you want the complete list of special variables, turn to Appendix B.

Default arguments

Many Perl functions enable you to skip having to specify some of their arguments (see "Operators and functions" earlier in this chapter for more on arguments). If you don't specify an argument, the function uses its *default* value. This speeds up the typing of your programs but it also makes your programs harder to read because you have to remember the defaults for each function. For this reason, I rarely use the default arguments. Nevertheless, you probably need to know a little bit about default arguments because lots of other programmers use them all the time, so you can expect to see them in Perl programs that others have written.

Almost all the functions that enable you to use default arguments fill in the gaps with the Perl special variable `$_`. Many statements put values in this special variable, such as reading from a file line by line or performing a pattern search. Perl enables you to skip including `$_` as an argument in some functions because it's so often the argument of the function.

For example, the `lc` function, which changes text to lowercase, normally takes one argument: the text that will be changed to lowercase. If you have no arguments to `lc`, the function returns the lowercase version of the value in `$_` instead. Therefore, the following three lines all have the same result:

```
lc($_);
lc();
lc;
```

Although it's easier to enter the second or third statement, the first seems much clearer when you review the program later.

Chapter 4

A Perl Program Tour, Times Two

In This Chapter

- Examining two sample Perl programs and how they work
- Running programs on various operating systems
- Processing text files
- Accepting user prompts
- Identifying simple (and common) text-entry goofs

One of the best ways to begin programming, in my opinion, is to examine a model program that features many of the elements you can expect to use when you write your own programs. But why stop at one? This chapter takes you on a journey through two real, working Perl programs.

As you check out the two examples in this chapter, you can see the steps involved in creating a Perl program. Even a short Perl program created with a handful of steps can turn out to be surprisingly powerful.

Examining the Inside of a Sample Program

In Listing 4-1 you can find a program called counter1.pl. It's a typical-looking Perl program, about 40 lines long and designed to count the number of characters, words, and lines in a text file. (Bits and pieces of this program are excerpted in Chapter 3 in order to demonstrate some basic elements of programming with Perl.) After I dissect the program, in the next section of this chapter I show you what it looks like when it runs.

Incidentally, you don't have to enter the counter1.pl program by hand in order to experiment with it (I can hear the collective "Whew!" from the audience). All the sample programs featured in this book are included on this book's companion CD-ROM. You can enter a program and save it to disk, or you can copy it from the CD-ROM to your hard drive.

Listing 4-1: counter1.pl (a program that counts characters, words, and lines in a text file)

```
#!/usr/bin/perl -w

# counter1.pl: one way to count the characters, words, and
#    lines in a text file.

# The name of the file that will be counted
$TheFile = "sample.txt";

# Open the file but quit if it doesn't exist
open(INFILE, $TheFile) or die "The file $TheFile could " .
    "not be found.\n";

# Initialize the counters
$CharCount = 0;
$WordCount = 0;
$LineCount = 0;

while(<INFILE>) {
    $TheLine = $_;  # Save the line's contents
    chomp($TheLine);  # Get rid of the line break
    $LineCount = $LineCount + 1;  # This is the easy part!
    $LineLen = length($TheLine);
    # We now know how many characters (minus the line
    #    break) are on this line
    $CharCount = $CharCount + $LineLen;

    # Do the tricky stuff for counting words on the line

    # The line is empty, so we're done
    if($TheLine eq "") { next };
    # The line has at least one word on it
    $WordCount = $WordCount + 1;
    # Now loop through each character on this line
    #    to look for words
    $CharPos = 0;  # Position we are in the line
    # Check for line end; if not, check for a space
    until($CharPos == $LineLen) {
        if(substr($TheLine, $CharPos, 1) eq " ")
            { $WordCount = $WordCount + 1 }
        $CharPos = $CharPos + 1;
    }  # End of until
}  # End of while(<INFILE>) loop

# All finished, so print out the results

print "For the file $TheFile:\n";
```

```
print "Number of characters  $CharCount\n";
print "Number of words       $WordCount\n";
print "Number of lines       $LineCount\n";
#!/usr/bin/perl -w
```

The very first line in Listing 4-1 tells UNIX Perl where to find the Perl language. This special comment is optional for Windows and Macintosh users, but must appear for UNIX users. (This comment is described in Chapter 2.) Basically, the first part tells UNIX that the program is a Perl program, and the `-w` says that Perl should provide warnings if it notices that the program has questionable syntax.

```
#!/usr/bin/perl -w
```

The next set of lines is a comment to myself about the program's purpose and why I wrote it. As silly as it may seem, ten years from now when you're trying to figure out what a particular program does, having an explanation right at the top of the file will prove to be a great time-saver.

```
# counter1.pl: one way to count the characters, words, and
#    lines in a text file.
```

The following lines initialize the `$TheFile` variable. Because counter1.pl is supposed to examine a file, you need to tell the program the name of the file to examine.

```
# The name of the file that will be counted
$TheFile = "sample.txt";
```

The `open` statement that follows makes the file named in `$TheFile` available to Perl. In this case, opening the file makes it readable for use in the program. (Chapters 11 and 12 describe the process of opening files in Perl programs.) The `open` function takes two *arguments* (that is, pieces of information for the function to work with) — `INFILE` is the "handle" that you use for the rest of the program and `$TheFile` is the name of the file. Later in the program, when you refer to the file, you use its handle instead of its name.

The second part of the `open` statement is a `die` statement. In essence, the lines mean "Try to open the file or die if you can't," which is exactly what you want Perl to do when you open files. The `die` statement tells the program to stop running and display the message on the screen just before it stops.

```
# Open the file but quit if it doesn't exist
open(INFILE, $TheFile) or die "The file $TheFile could " .
    "not be found.\n";
```

You should initialize all your variables before using them. The following lines contain counters that (you guessed it!) count characters, words, and lines. They keep a running total for the whole file.

```
# Initialize the counters
$CharCount = 0;
$WordCount = 0;
$LineCount = 0;
```

The next section in the counter1.pl program (see Listing 4-1) is the `while` loop. A `while` statement takes an argument and evaluates if it is true or false. If the argument is true, Perl goes through the steps in the loop and then tests the argument again. If the argument is false, Perl skips to the first statement after the loop's block.

The following statement notes the beginning of the loop. In this case, the argument is `<INFILE>`, which to Perl means "Read a line from the file that was opened with the handle called `INFILE`. If you've read to the end of the file, return false." Thus, the loop keeps going as long as lines are in the file, and skips to the end of the block when no more lines exist.

```
while(<INFILE>) {
```

`$_` is a special variable that means "the stuff you just read." The following statement in essence says, "Take the line you just read from `INFILE` and put it in the `$TheLine` variable."

```
$TheLine = $_;  # Save the line's contents
```

When you read a line, you also get a *line terminator,* which is a character or characters that tell your computer "this is the end of a line." The `chomp` function removes the line terminator from the end of the variable so that all that's left is the text that was on the line, minus the end bit.

`chomp` is available only in Perl 5 and later versions. The `chop` function in Perl 4 accomplishes pretty much the same thing, however.

```
chomp($TheLine);  # Get rid of the line break
```

Because `$LineCount` keeps track of how many lines are in the file, I added 1 to the count in the following lines from the program because Perl just read another line. The first time through, Perl assigns `$LineCount` to the sum of 0 (the value set before the loop) plus 1 — which is, of course, 1. The next time through the loop, Perl sets `$LineCount` to the sum of 1 (the value from the last round through the loop) plus 1, which adds up to 2. In short, this statement just keeps adding 1 to the previous value of `$LineCount`.

```
$LineCount = $LineCount + 1;  # This is the easy part!
```

The `length` function (in the following line of the program) looks in a text variable and tells you how many characters are in it.

```
   $LineLen = length($TheLine);
```

Because `$CharCount` (in the next statement) keeps track of the total number of characters, you want to add the length of the line you read from the file (minus the line terminator) to the total count. `$CharCount` is one more kind of counter. Instead of adding 1 each time as you do with `$LineCount`, you add the length of the line. For example,

```
 # We now know how many characters (minus the line
     #    break) are on this line
     $CharCount = $CharCount + $LineLen;
```

The more comments (such as the following) that you use in your programs, the better! Comments help you recall the specifics of your own programs later on, and can certainly help someone else who is reading your program to know what your intentions were.

```
 # Do the tricky stuff for counting words on the line
```

The following statement tests whether a line has any text in it. Like the `while` statement, the `if` statement takes one argument, a test that evaluates to `true` or `false`. Here, we test whether `$TheLine` equals no text at all; if so, the block executes. In that block, the `next` statement tells Perl to "skip all the rest of the lines in the current enclosing block," meaning that Perl should go back and try the `while` test again.

```
 # The line is empty, so we're done
     if($TheLine eq "") { next };
```

If Perl gets this far, then the line has something on it (otherwise, the previous `if` test would have prevented Perl from getting to this point). Therefore, at least one word is on the line, so the following statement updates the `$WordCount` variable.

```
 # The line has at least one word on it
     $WordCount = $WordCount + 1;
```

The third line of the next chunk of code initializes the variable `$CharPos`, which tells you which character on a line you are on.

```
 # Now loop through each character on this line
     #    to look for words
     $CharPos = 0;  # Position we are in the line
```

The next statement walks through the line one character at a time, looking for spaces. The `until` loop (in the second line of the following chunk of code) is the exact opposite of `while`: It causes Perl to execute a block in a loop only if its argument is `false`. Here, the test is: "Am I at the end of the line I read from the file yet? If not, do the block again; otherwise, skip to the end of the block." The end of the block is also the end of the `while` loop.

```
# Check for line end; if not, check for a space
    until($CharPos == $LineLen) {
```

Inside the `until` loop, the following statement tells Perl to use the `substr` function to see whether the character it's looking at is a space character. The three arguments to `substr` mean "look in `$TheLine`, starting at the position `$CharPos` from the left side of the string, and look at `1` character." If the character is a space character, then Perl adds `1` to `$WordCount` because one space is after each word.

Note that the word count is based on the number of spaces that the program sees. At first, this makes good sense, but it can lead to highly inaccurate word counts. What if you have two spaces after some words? What if you have space characters at the end of some lines? What if you indent some lines with spaces? Any of these situations can make the reported word count much higher than what actually appears in the text file.

```
if(substr($TheLine, $CharPos, 1) eq " ")
            { $WordCount = $WordCount + 1 }
```

The following statement tells Perl to add `1` to the variable holding the line's character position.

```
        $CharPos = $CharPos + 1;
```

The next statement is the closing brace for the `until` loop.

```
}  # End of until
```

And, the following statement is the closing brace of the `while` loop that began much earlier in the program.

```
}  # End of while(<INFILE>) loop
```

I admit what follows isn't the most earth-shattering comment, but it at least tells you that you're almost done with the program.

```
# All finished, so print out the results
```

`print` statements (such as the following) tell Perl to display text on your screen. (Actually, `print` can do much more than that; see Chapter 5 for more on reading and writing files with the `print` statement.) Here, `print` displays the text `For the file`, followed by a space, followed by the value of the variable `$TheFile`, followed by a colon. The `\n` indicates that after printing this text, Perl displays the next text in the string on the next line of your screen. Printing `\n` is like pressing the Enter key in a word-processing program.

```
print "For the file $TheFile:\n";
```

The next three lines are similar to the first `print` statement: They tell Perl to print some text, the value of a variable, and then go to the next line.

```
print "Number of characters  $CharCount\n";
print "Number of words       $WordCount\n";
print "Number of lines       $LineCount\n";
```

Now, you're done! Wait, you say you want to actually do something with this program now, like run it? Of course! You don't write programs just for the fun of it: You also want to do some real work with them.

Running the counter1.pl sample program

Because the counter1.pl program I presented in the previous section of this chapter counts characters, words, and lines in a text file, you need to have a text file on hand in order to see how the program works. You can create a file called sample.txt by entering the following chunk of information (which, incidentally, is lifted from another *...For Dummies* book of mine, *Netscape and the World Wide Web For Dummies,* from IDG Books Worldwide, Inc.), or you can use any old text file of some length you happen to have around.

You can also pull sample.txt off of the CD-ROM that comes with this book. If you choose to type it yourself, be sure to use the same exact line endings as shown here:

```
The Internet is a collection of thousands of computers that
communicate through certain methods that have been agreed
on for many years. The Internet started about 25 years ago
with a small handful of computers run by a few people as an
experiment. The initial results were successful; the
network was useful, so it grew.
In fact, the Internet was partially intended to be an
experiment for how to design a network that could grow
easily, with very little central control. That concept is
still considered radical today, and you find few networks
as loose as the Internet.
```

Okay, I admit it's not the most breathtaking prose in the world. You just need a short text file to measure.

After you create your own sample text file (or use the one supplied here), the next step is to run the program, which I describe in the next section.

Because the readers of this book may be using any one of a number of operating systems, in the following sections I explain how to run Perl programs on UNIX, Windows 95/98 or Windows NT, and MacOS. By the way, if Perl finds errors when it checks your program, skip to the end of this chapter where I describe how to decipher Perl's error messages.

Running the program on UNIX

First off, to run the counter1.pl program shown in Listing 4-1 (or any other Perl program for that matter), be sure that the first line of the program actually points to the location of Perl on your system. If it doesn't, edit that line; otherwise, UNIX hands you a confusing error message. If you're not sure about Perl's location on your system, see Chapter 2 for information on installing Perl on UNIX.

To check the program for errors (such as a forgotten semicolon or quotation mark), enter the following command at the UNIX command prompt:

```
perl -c counter1.pl
```

To run the program, enter this command:

```
./counter1.pl
```

This run command tells UNIX to "run the counter1.pl program from the current directory."

Running the program under Windows 95/98 and Windows NT

To run the sample counter1.pl program (or any other Perl program under Windows), first make sure that you have opened an MS-DOS window and are in the Perl directory (for information on how to do that, see Chapter 2). To check the program for errors (such as if you misspelled a function name), enter the following command:

```
perl -c counter1.pl
```

To run the program, enter this command:

```
perl counter1.pl
```

Running the program on a Macintosh

To run the sample program, or any Perl program, on a Macintosh, launch MacPerl as you do any other Mac program by double-clicking on its icon in the Finder. To check the program for errors (such as if you forgot a parenthesis), choose Script ⇨ Syntax Check. To run the program, choose Script ⇨Run Script.

Viewing the program results

Assuming that you copy the sample.txt program from the CD-ROM to your hard disk (or, if you type it by hand, that you entered everything correctly), you see the following on your screen after you run the counter1.pl program:

```
For the file sample.txt:
Number of characters  562
Number of words       98
Number of lines       12
```

After these four lines are displayed, the program exits. On UNIX, Windows 95/98, or Windows NT, the operating system prompt appears. On the Macintosh, MacPerl still runs, waiting for you to give a command from one of the menus.

Note that the numbers shown in the figure may not match exactly what Perl reports to you. If you added extra spaces or lines, or possibly spelled things differently than in the example, the numbers will be slightly different.

Your Second Program, with More Features

If you were intrigued by the sample program in Listing 4-1, I have another program you may want to peruse to help you get the hang of working with Perl. The program, empdata1.pl, is shown in Listing 4-2; you can also find the program on this book's companion CD-ROM.

The structure of empdata1.pl is somewhat similar to counter1.pl (the first sample program in this chapter), but it serves a different purpose. The empdata.1 program enables you to look through a small text database in order to search for certain records. It is representative of the kind of programs you will write to look through a file for particular information (the employee database I use here is, of course, fictitious). I list the program in its entirety first, and then cover some of its components later.

Listing 4-2: The empdata1.pl program, which lets you query a sample employee database.

```
#!/usr/bin/perl -w

# empdata1.pl: a very simple employee database application.
#    This program reads a text file that is an employee
#    database and lets you query it by ID number.
#
#    Each record is on a single line. Each field in the
#    record is separated by a single tab character
#    ("\t"). The database has four fields:
#    - Last name
#    - First name
#    - ID number
#    - Telephone extension

# The name of the database file
$TheDB = 'edata.txt';

# Open the database file but quit if it doesn't exist
open(INDB, $TheDB) or die "The database $TheDB could " .
    "not be found.\n";

while(1) {  # Loop forever
    print "\nDo you want to search by employee ID (I), " .
        " or quit (Q): ";
    $DoSearch = <STDIN>;
    chomp($DoSearch);
    $DoSearch =~ tr/A-Z/a-z/;
    # Check if they want to quit
    if($DoSearch eq 'q') { last }
    # Check if they did *not* say i or I
    unless($DoSearch eq 'i') {
        print "You must enter either I or Q.\n";
        next;  # Go out to the while loop
    }

    # Ask them what ID they want to search for
    print "Search for ID number: ";
    $SearchFor = <STDIN>;
    chomp($SearchFor);
    # Go to the top of the database in case this isn't
    #    the first time they are searching
    seek(INDB, 0, 0);
    # Reset the count of successes
    $SuccessCount = 0;
    # Loop through the records in the file
    while(<INDB>) {
```

```
        $TheRec = $_;
        chomp($TheRec);
        ($LastName, $FirstName, $ID, $Tel) =
            split(/\t/, $TheRec);
        if($ID eq $SearchFor) {
            $SuccessCount = $SuccessCount + 1;
            print "$ID: $FirstName $LastName, ext. ".
                "$Tel\n";
        }  # End of if
    }  # End of while(<INDB>)
    if($SuccessCount == 0) { print "No records found.\n" }
    else { print "$SuccessCount records found.\n" }
}  # End of while(1)

print "Program finished.\n";
```

The database used in the program, edata.txt, is a simple text file shown as follows:

```
Anastasio     Trey     12  143
Manzanera     Phil     15  156
Stewart       Dave     17  154
Thompson      Richard  20  112
```

The four columns in the data file list each employee's last name, first name, ID number, and telephone extension.

Even though it's short, you may want to copy the edata.txt file from this book's CD-ROM. If you do type it in, be sure to use a single tab between each column. (Don't use spaces, and don't use more than one tab, or else the empdata1.pl program won't work.)

The gist of the program is that it prompts you for employee numbers and then prints out the information on those employees from the database. It lets you go through this "ask a question, get an answer" loop as many times as you want. After you finish, type **q** or **Q** and the program exits.

Breaking down the sample program

The following preamble that tells UNIX Perl where to find the Perl language is needed only on UNIX computers, but because it is a comment, it doesn't hurt to include it if you're working in Windows or on a Mac.

```
#!/usr/bin/perl -w
```

The following lines are comments that describe in detail what the program does. Whenever you're writing a program that calls for a data file in a particular format (such as four columns with tabs between them), you should indicate that in the comments right at the top of your Perl program.

```
# empdata1.pl: a very simple employee database application.
#    This program reads a text file that is an employee
#    database and lets you query it by ID number.
#
#    Each record is on a single line. Each field in the
#    record is separated by a single tab character
#    ("\t"). The database has four fields:
#     - Last name
#     - First name
#     - ID number
#     - Telephone extension
```

I named the file with its own variable (as you can see in the following lines of code) so that it's easy to change it later. Astute readers may notice that the filename in this program is in single quotation marks instead of the double quotation marks in the `open` statement in the counter1.pl program earlier in this chapter. (In Chapter 5, you can discover the difference between single quotation marks and double quotation marks in Perl.)

```
# The name of the database file
$TheDB = 'edata.txt';
```

The following lines tell Perl to open the file or quit the program with a helpful message if it can't find the file.

```
# Open the database file but quit if it doesn't exist
open(INDB, $TheDB) or die "The database $TheDB could " .
     "not be found.\n";
```

The following statement may seem a bit strange, but you may have times when you want Perl to run a loop forever (the value `1` always means `true`). Of course, the loop won't really go "forever," but you don't want to insert the test for when it should stop in the `while` statement. Instead, examine the program a few lines down to determine how to get out of the loop (hint: it's the `last` statement).

```
while(1) {  # Loop forever
```

The following lines tell Perl to print a prompt on your screen. Notice that the prompt doesn't end with `\n`; this enables you to enter text on the same line as the prompt.

```
print "\nDo you want to search by employee ID (I), " .
      " or quit (Q): ";
```

Perl waits for you to type a line and puts whatever you type into the variable $DoSearch (such as in the next line).

```
$DoSearch = <STDIN>;
```

The following line tells Perl to remove the end-of-line character(s) from $DoSearch.

```
chomp($DoSearch);
```

The next line from the program does a neat little trick: It translates any uppercase characters in $DoSearch into lowercase letters. For example, if you type HOWDY, it changes to howdy. Therefore, if your program tells users to enter I or Q, for instance, they may use either uppercase or lowercase letters. Instead of blasting them with an error message for not capitalizing the letters, the program simply doesn't care.

```
$DoSearch =~ tr/A-Z/a-z/;
```

If users type q or Q, the while loop stops. The last statement at the end of the following lines of code tells Perl to "Jump out at the bottom of the block you're in." The last statement differs from the next statement found in the counter1.pl program (see Listing 4-1) that causes Perl to start the block again at the top. Using last is the best way to tell Perl to break out of an infinite while loop.

```
# Check if they want to quit
    if($DoSearch eq 'q') { last }
```

If the user doesn't type q or Q or i or I here, he or she must have entered something incorrectly. The next statement in the last line of the following chunk of code restarts the loop.

```
# Check if they did *not* say i or I
    unless($DoSearch eq 'i') {
        print "You must enter either I or Q.\n";
        next;  # Go out to the while loop
    }
```

The user ends up at the next chunk of code if he or she enters an i or I; at this point the program asks the user which ID number he or she wants.

```
# Ask them what ID they want to search for
    print "Search for ID number: ";
```

Perl then waits for the user to type something on the keyboard but this time puts the results in `$SearchFor` (instead of `$DoSearch`, as it did earlier in this example program) . Don't forget to munch off the end-of-line stuff with `chomp`.

```
$SearchFor = <STDIN>;
    chomp($SearchFor);
```

In the counter1.pl program (see Listing 4-1), you examine the text file from top to bottom, just once. In the empdata1.pl program, covered in this section of the chapter, you want to examine the file each time a user types an ID number. Therefore, you need to tell Perl to "stop reading the file where you are and start at the top again." The `seek` statement (which you can see in the following lines from the program) lets you tell Perl where in the file to start; in this case, the instruction is to start at the top.

```
# Go to the top of the database in case this isn't
          #    the first time they are searching
    seek(INDB, 0, 0);
```

Assume you want to know how many records are found for each request. The database currently being used in this sample program has one person per ID number. Because you may want to have more than one person per ID later on, counting the number of successes can be useful.

```
# Reset the count of successes
    $SuccessCount = 0;
```

The following `while` loop reads each record of the database. The program reads a record, assigns it to a variable, and applies the `chomp` function to remove the end-of-line character or characters from the line. After Perl reads the last record, it jumps outside of the `while`'s block.

```
# Loop through the records in the file
    while(<INDB>) {
        $TheRec = $_;
        chomp($TheRec);
```

The `split` function splits a string into many other strings, based on a separator string. The `/\t/` special string tells Perl to look for tab characters. The following statement then tells Perl to fill in the four variables `$LastName`, `$FirstName`, `$ID`, and `$Tel` with the four fields from the record you just read from the database file.

```
($LastName, $FirstName, $ID, $Tel) =
           split(/\t/, $TheRec);
```

The `if` statement compares the field from the record with the field the user is looking for. If they match, the block executes. The following statements add `1` to the `$SuccessCount` variable and print out the record.

```
if($ID eq $SearchFor) {
            $SuccessCount = $SuccessCount + 1;
            print "$ID: $FirstName $LastName, ext. ".
                "$Tel\n";
        }  # End of if
```

The following statement marks the end of the inner `while` block, which means that no additional records are in the database.

```
}  # End of while(<INDB>)
```

Next, the program prints the number of records found. The `else` is part of the `if` statement, and executes only if the `if` statement is false.

```
if($SuccessCount == 0) { print "No records found.\n" }
    else { print "$SuccessCount records found.\n" }
```

The program ends up at this point after they enter `q` or `Q`.

```
}  # End of while(1)
```

It's always polite to say goodbye when you leave. That's true in programming as well, so this program prints a nice message as it is about to finish.

```
print "Program finished.\n";
```

Running the empdata1.pl sample program

You can start the empdata1.pl program the same way you start the counter1.pl program, or any Perl program for that matter. (See "Running the counter1.pl sample program" earlier in this chapter for the details.)

At the program's first prompt, type `I` or `i` and press Enter or Return.

A side note: The key above the right Shift key on your keyboard may be labeled either one of two ways: Enter or Return. In this book, whenever I say "press Enter," I mean to press the key above the right Shift key, not the key on the extreme right of the keyboard on the numeric keypad. This problem is frightfully confusing for many novice computer users, and even advanced folks get it wrong from time to time as well.

The program then prompts you with

```
Search for ID number:
```

and waits for you to enter something. For this example program, you type 15 and press Enter. The program finds the record for ID number 15 (that record starts with "Manzanera"), and gives you the original prompt again.

Play around with the program by entering different characters after the various prompts — and watch the results. Some interesting messages are displayed when you enter something that the program does not expect. To leave the program, just type q or Q when the program prompts you.

Avoiding the Most Common Oversights

Entering a typo or two during the course of writing a Perl program is not uncommon. But when you attempt to run a program containing a text-entry slip-up, Perl can get confused and tells you so by reporting an error. The natural reaction for most people, even those with years of programming experience, is to get worried or angry or both when an error message pops up.

Don't panic. Take a deep breath. Take another slow, deep breath. Seriously, you won't be able to get to the root of the problem if you're all tense and bothered. Trust me, no matter how many years you program, you always end up finding some errors in the code you're written.

So, now that you are (hopefully!) a bit calmer, you can start to appreciate the fact that Perl has more helpful error messages than almost any other programming language. The messages aren't always right on the money, but they can get you pretty close to the spot where the problem lies with minimal searching on your part.

Perl has myriad error messages, but a few definitely crop up more than others owing to some common typos that everyone seems to make. The following errors are produced by minor text-entry goofs that can be easily avoided. (The examples in this section are taken from the counter1.pl program shown in Listing 4-1, with a few errors added to it.)

Forgetting a semicolon

Probably the most common error message you see when programming in Perl looks something like this:

```
# syntax error, near "open"
File 'counter1.pl'; Line 10
# Execution aborted due to compilation errors.
```

You can look and look at Line 10, the one with the `open` statement, and you won't see anything wrong with it. The trick here is to examine the statement that comes *before* the `open` statement and see whether it ends with a semicolon. (Perl knows that a statement ends only when it encounters a semicolon.) In this case, the error is caused by a missing semicolon at the end of Line 7 of the program:

```
$TheFile = "sample.txt"
```

Forgetting a quotation mark

The following sort of error message can be extremely frustrating if you don't know of a quick fix:

```
# Bare word found where operator expected, near
# "open(INFILE, $TheFile) or die "The"
#  (Might be a runaway multi-line "" string starting on
#  line 7)
File 'counter1.pl'; Line 10
```

This error is similar to forgetting a semicolon; instead, it's a quotation mark that's accidentally omitted:

```
$TheFile = "sample.txt;
```

In this case, Perl did a good job of guessing what is wrong, suggesting that a `runaway multi-line "" string` on Line 7 is the problem, which is precisely right.

Entering one parenthesis too many or too few

When you have loads of opening and closing parentheses in a program, it's easy to slip an extra one in by accident. If that's the case, you may see a message from Perl that reads something like this:

```
# syntax error, near ") eq"
File 'counter1.pl'; Line 38
# syntax error, near "}"
File 'counter1.pl'; Line 42
```

Here, Perl can't determine where the error is exactly, but it actually got it right on the first guess: Line 38 contains an extra right parenthesis:

```
        if(substr($TheLine, $CharPos, 1)) eq " ")
```

Having one parenthesis too few in a Perl program can cause harder-to-find problems:

```
# Can't use constant item as left arg of implicit ->,
# near "1 }"
File 'counter1.pl'; Line 39
# Scalar found where operator expected, near "$CharPos"
File 'counter1.pl'; Line 40
# (Missing semicolon on previous line?)
# syntax error, near "$CharPos "
File 'counter1.pl'; Line 40
```

Yarp! All of this was produced because the last parenthesis on Line 38 is missing:

```
        if(substr($TheLine, $CharPos, 1) eq " "
```

Here is another good lesson in hunting down typing errors: Start where Perl says it found an error. If you don't find the error there, go up a line or two and see if the problem started earlier.

A final word of advice: Trust Perl to find the simple typos for you (where it can), and remember that it's giving you all the help it can, which is more than you can say for many programming languages.

Part II
The Basic Perl Programming Ingredients

"This part of the interview tells us whether or not you're personally suited to the job of systems administrator."

In this part . . .

Perl is a fairly easy programming language to learn. By the time you finish the five chapters in Part II, you'll have absorbed much of what you need to know to write a fully working program in Perl. This part contains information about working with text and numbers, and some programming features that only Perl offers.

Chapter 5
Terrific Text

In This Chapter

- Using the `print` statement
- Understanding strings
- Using special characters
- Quoting text
- Putting strings together and pulling them apart
- Changing parts of strings

If you've been reading along from the beginning of this book, you've seen only a smattering of what Perl can do. If you haven't, that's okay, although you might want to check out the two examples I present in Chapter 4 — they introduce about two dozen different Perl statements, functions, and operators. This chapter and Chapters 6 through 8 examine the major types of data Perl works on and show you how to use Perl to handle that data. In this chapter in particular, I describe one of Perl's strongest features, text handling.

Even the dweebiest of dweebs among us (yes, even us Perl programmers) use considerably more text than numbers in our daily lives. We talk, we read, we jot down notes, and so on, all day long. In computer terms, you can accomplish four basic tasks with a Perl program in terms of managing text — reading text, writing text, searching through text, and changing text.

I base some of the examples in the following chapters on the two programs I present in Chapter 4. (Again, you may want to give that chapter a go if you haven't already.) I give some examples in which I change one or the other of the two programs from Chapter 4 to do something different or more interesting. I also include many other examples to give you a small taste of how to use Perl's many text-handling features.

Checking Your Work: The `print` Statement

One of the most common Perl statements — one you use over and over when you work with Perl — is the `print` statement. This statement is the best one to use when you're experimenting with Perl features. And checking your work as you proceed is just one use of the `print` statement; it's actually used for all kinds of display and output of information.

The `print` statement takes many forms, but the main one includes the statement followed by an *argument* (a string of text or numbers), as in the following example:

```
print "This is a string!";
print 72;
```

In addition to strings and numbers, you can use a *list* as an argument. (I cover the topic of strings in the next section of this chapter and lists in Chapter 7.) Another interesting use of the `print` command is writing to a file .(I tell you how to do that in Chapter 11.)

At any time, you can use the `print` statement to see the end results of what you're doing. Assume that you just found out how to add two numbers together with the + operator (see Chapter 6); you can test that operator with a one-line program, such as this one:

```
print 2+3;
```

As you would expect, the program displays the numeral 5.

You can also get the same result with a two-line program, such as the following:

```
$a = 2 + 3;
print $a;
```

Perl prints `5` on your screen.

Defining Strings

Text items in Perl are called *strings.* A string is zero or more characters put together in a single chunk. A *character* is anything that you can type, such as letters, digits, punctuation, and spaces. Strings appear in variables and just as themselves, in which case they are called *string literals*. An example of a one-character string literal is the letter *d*. An example of a five-character string is *vbn59*. Perl variables (which I define in Chapter 3) can hold strings or numbers.

The length of a Perl string is practically unlimited. That's right, you can make Perl strings as long as you want. Then again, you don't have to give them any length at all. A zero-character string is as a *null string*. "A textless string, that's odd!" you say? Here's how that works:

If you have a variable called `$Short`, for example, and that variable has a value that is one character, you can remove the single character from the variable and get a smaller value that has zero characters in it. The variable doesn't disappear because Perl knows to how remove characters while retaining the variable. Similarly, if you want to add to a variable character by character, you can start with no characters and build from there.

Visible Characters versus Character Values

You probably think of characters as the entries you see on the screen of your computer or that are printed on the page of this book, but computers (by necessity) have a much more liberal view of what constitutes a character. A computer recognizes many other kinds of characters that don't appear on screen or on printouts, or appear differently on different computers.

In the world of Perl, a *character* is an eight-bit byte. A bit is a single unit of information, a 1 or a 0. A byte is the chunk of information that the computer processes. So, how does this bits-and-bytes definition fit your notion of characters?

How values translate to characters

Each byte can have a value in it. The values range from 0 to 255, and standards exist for how some of the values correspond to letters, digits, and punctuation. The standards say stuff like: "The value 65 means A" or "The value 97 means a." So, if a computer thinks that it is supposed to display a byte and that byte has the value 65, the computer knows that it should display a capital A.

One problem with this scheme is that the computer cannot display certain character values. A simple example is the value 20, which translates to the "space" character. (As far as a computer goes, when you press the spacebar on your keyboard, you enter a character and not just a space.)

A more complicated example is the value 13, which means "carriage return." On a computer screen, it can be interpreted as "this is the end of the line." Other examples of nonprinting characters are the value 7 ("beep"), value 12 ("form feed"), and value 24 ("cancel"). A slew of such values represents valid characters, even though they do not result in anything being displayed on screen.

Which values are defined and which aren't

The original standard for characters, ASCII, is now a relic, even though it is the basis for all other subsequent character standards. ASCII defined equivalents only for the values 0 to 127, and as you've just seen, not all the equivalents can be viewed. Because characters can have values from 0 to 255, ASCII leaves 128 to 255 undefined.

Well, computer geeks hate to leave anything undefined, so they have specified what the other 128 values should signify. Unfortunately, different standards groups define the values differently. Every group thinks that its set of value-to-character mappings is best and tries to force other people to go along. So far, no one has been successful in creating a consensus on the matter.

For example, when the IBM PC came out in 1981, IBM decided to make its own set of definitions. It decreed that the value 128 meant a capital C with a cedilla underneath it (Ç), 129 meant a lowercase u with an umlaut over it (ü), and on and on. Apple, on the other hand, defined 128 as a capital A with an umlaut over it (Ä), 129 as a capital A with a circle over it (Å), and so on.

The 93 standard visible characters

The thing to remember here is that, with computers, characters are really just numeric values between 0 and 255, and only 93 of them (the values 33 through 126) have standard representations. The 93 visible characters are A through Z (in both uppercase and lowercase), 0 through 9, and these guys:

```
!"#$%&'()*+,-./:;<=>?@[\]^_'{|}~
```

Listing 5-1 shows program code that is designed to display all 93 of the standard visible characters. It uses the `%` operator (which I explain in Chapter 6), the `for` loop statement (which I describe in Chapter 8), and the `sprintf` function (which I demonstrate in Chapter 9). The program generates two handy tables that display the characters and their corresponding values, as shown in Figure 5-1.

The upshot of all this is that text strings can contain any kind of characters, not just the ones that you can type. This is useful in many circumstances. For example, maybe you want to display a character that you can't type.

Listing 5-1: This program produces the character-value/output tables shown in Figure 5-1.

```
# chartabl.pl: A program to display character tables

$Column = 1;
$Out = '';
for ($i = 33; $i<=126; $i++) {
    $Out .= sprintf("%3s", $i) . "=" . chr($i) . "  ";
    if(($Column % 10) == 0) { $Out .= "\n" }
    $Column += 1;
}

$Out .= "\n\n";
$Column = 1;
for ($i = 33; $i<=126; $i++) {
    $Out .= chr($i). "=" . sprintf("%3s", $i) . "  ";
    if(($Column % 10) == 0) { $Out .= "\n" }
    $Column += 1;
}
print $Out;
```

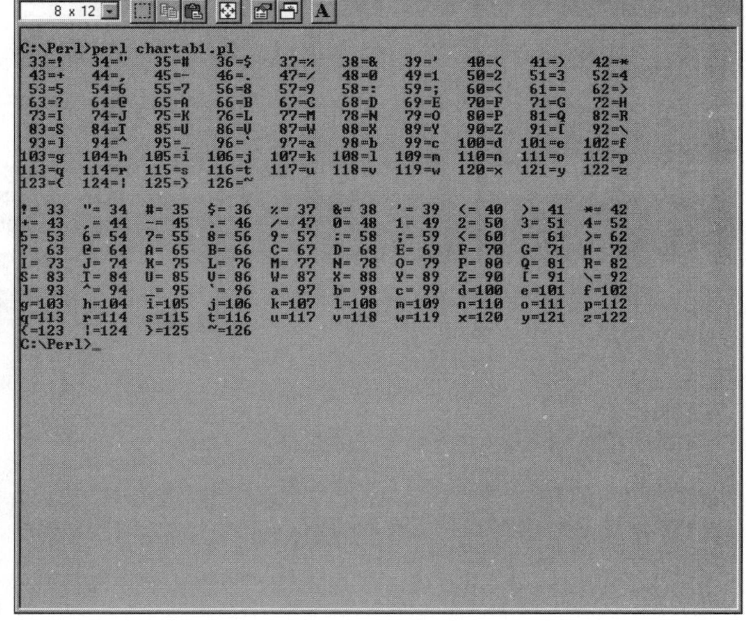

Figure 5-1: Character-value tables output by the chartab1.pl program shown in Listing 5-1.

Special characters in text

Many characters exist that you can type but that you won't see in regular text. Perl defines special character combinations (see Table 5-1) that make it possible to enter these "invisible" characters within a string.

MacPerl users should be aware that `\n` means the same thing as the character whose ASCII value is 10, as opposed to the character whose ASCII value is 13 that UNIX Perl users are familiar with. The technical reasons for this difference aside, it can be a real puzzler when you convert programs from one operating system to the other.

Table 5-1 Special Characters in Strings

Character	*Meaning*
`\n`	Newline
`\r`	Carriage return
`\t`	Tab
`\f`	Formfeed
`\b`	Backspace
`\v`	Vertical tab (Perl 5 and later versions)
`\a`	Bell or beep
`\e`	Escape

The actions that the print statement takes when displaying these characters varies from operating system to operating system. The only character that works universally the same way is `\n`, which always (as far as I know) causes the print statement to go to the left margin of a new line.

For example, the statement

```
print "This is on line one.\nThis is on line two.\n";
```

displays

```
This is on line one.
This is on line two.
```

And, the statement

```
$Blue1 = "Sapphire";
$Blue2 = "Azure";
print "$Blue1\n$Blue2\n";
```

displays

```
Sapphire
Azure
```

For those of you out there who like (okay, need) to count in hexadecimal or octal, you also can use special backslash formats to indicate characters in these number systems. (The *decimal* number system is based on ten digits; the *hexadecimal* system uses 16 digits, and *octal* has only 8.) You can use `\x` followed by two characters that are the hex value you want, or you can use just `\` with an octal value. For instance, you can represent the letter B as `\x42` in hexadecimal or `\102` in octal.

These special characters do *not* work in strings with single quotation marks. Look what happens when you use single instead of double quotes:

```
print 'This is on line one.\nThis is on line two.\n';
```

Executing this statement displays

```
This is on line one.\nThis is on line two.\n
```

Not everything inside single quotation marks is output exactly as you enter it. The two exceptions in Perl are `\'` and `\\`. Perl converts a `\` inside single or double quotation marks to a single quotation mark and a `\\` combination inside either single or double quotation marks to a backslash. This makes sense: You need some way to indicate an apostrophe (`'`) or a backslash (`\`) inside single quotation marks. For example:

```
print 'Here\'s a backslash: \\.';
```

This program displays

```
Here's a backslash: \.
```

Here are two more tricks you can use with double quotation marks. (***Note:*** These don't work with single quotation marks.) If you want to put a double quotation mark inside your text, use `\"`.

```
$Shout = "Help me!";
print "And then he shouted \"$Shout\" very loudly.\n";
```

When you run this program, Perl displays

```
And then he shouted "Help me!" very loudly.
```

And to prevent Perl from trying to interpret a dollar sign inside double quotation marks, enter it as `\$`, as in

```
$Sweet = "sugar";
print "\$Sweet is $Sweet.";
```

This displays

```
$Sweet is sugar.
```

Perl also gives you a way to specify a character by its value. Earlier in this chapter, I note that each character has a value from 0 to 255. If you know the value of the character you want to display, you can use the `chr` function, whose argument is the value. The `chr` function takes a number as its argument and returns the character associated with that value. For example,

```
=$CapB = chr(66);
print "The letter after A is $CapB.\n";
```

displays

```
The letter after A is B.
```

Quoting Text

When you want to tell Perl to use a literal string, you use *quoted text.* You enter quoted text in two main ways: with single quotes or double quotes. For example, you can assign the characters "Help me!" to the variable `$Shout`, using either of the following statements:

```
$Shout = 'Help me!';
```

```
$Shout = "Help me!";
```

Both of the preceding methods produce the same result (you get `Help me!` on screen); but under some circumstances, whether you use single or double quotes can make a huge difference. Understanding how to use quotation marks is a critical aspect of handling text in Perl.

Single versus double quotes

To summarize the main difference between single and double quotation marks: *Single quotation marks do not interpret, and double quotation marks do.* That is, if you put something in single quotation marks, Perl assumes that you want the exact characters you place between the marks — except for the slash-single quote (\') combination and double-slash (\\) combination, which I talk about in "Special characters in text," earlier in this chapter. If you place text inside double quotation marks, however, Perl interprets variable names. Perl also interprets special characters inside double-quoted literal strings.

Take a look at the following short program, which uses single quotes in its `print` statement:

```
$Book = 'Perl For Dummies';
print 'The title is $Book.';
```

When you run the program, Perl displays

```
The title is $Book.
```

Now change the single quotes to double quotes in the `print` statement:

```
$Book = 'Perl For Dummies';
print "The title is $Book.";
```

When you run the program now, Perl displays

```
The title is Perl For Dummies.
```

In the first program, the single quotes tell Perl not to interpret anything inside the quotation marks. In the second program, Perl sees the double quotes, interprets the variable `$Book`, and then inserts that into the text.

Note that the period at the end of the `print` statement appears immediately after the value of `$Book`. After interpreting the variable `$Book`, Perl starts looking for text again, finds the period, and prints it.

You can have as many variables as you want inside double-quoted strings. For example:

```
$Word1 = "thank";
$Word2 = "you";
$Sentence = "I just wanted to say $Word1 $Word2.";
print $Sentence;
```

These lines print

```
I just wanted to say thank you.
```

Perl interprets each variable and places it directly in the variable `$Sentence`. Notice that when the `print` statement displays the contents of `$Sentence`, it inserts a space between the two quoted words, just as it should, and the period at the end. Perl picks out just the variables and substitutes for them but leaves other characters, such as spaces, exactly as you enter them.

Functions for quoting text

Although quoting text with single and double quotation marks is easy, having a function to do the same comes in handy in some situations. Perl has two such functions: `q` and `qq`. The `q` function quotes its argument like single quotation marks, and the `qq` function quotes its argument like double quotation marks. The main purpose of these functions is to enable you to use single and double quotation marks within strings without having to use the `\'`, `\\`, and `\"` special characters.

For example, you may want to use `q` if you have a string that has a bunch of apostrophes. Compare

```
$ISaid = 'This isn\'t Bill\'s shirt, I\'m sure.';
```

with

```
$ISaid = q/This isn't Bill's shirt, I'm sure./;
```

Both lines assign the same string to `$ISaid`, but the second one is much easier to read (and type).

You can use any character for the beginning and ending quote. The slash (/) character is common, as is the vertical bar (|):

```
$ISaid = q|This isn't Bill's shirt, I'm sure.|;
```

You also can use parentheses, square brackets, angle brackets, and curly braces for the delimiters. If you use the left member of any of these character pairs, Perl knows to look for the right member as the one that signifies the end of the quoted text:

```
$ISaid = q(This isn't Bill's shirt, I'm sure.);
```

```
$ISaid = q<This isn't Bill's shirt, I'm sure.>;
```

When you have a lot to say

Another way to quote text is with a *here document,* which is particularly useful if you have many lines in a string. Instead of putting a quotation mark at the beginning and end of the string, you start a here document with << and a string (with no space between the << character combination and the string) and then terminate the quote by putting the string by itself on a line at the end of the quote.

Here's an example that puts four lines of text into a variable called `$TheLongString`, using the string `BLARG` as the delimiting string:

```
$TheLongString = <<'BLARG';
This is the first line,
And this is the second,
Which is followed by the third,
And so on, ad nauseum.
BLARG
```

The type of quote that you use for the string tells Perl whether to interpret any variables. If you use `<<"BLARG"` (instead of `<<'BLARG'`) in the preceding code, Perl substitutes any variable names you include in the quote into `$TheLongString`.

Manipulating Strings

Perl features operators that let you perform operations on strings that are similar to addition, multiplication, and subtraction. These operators don't do math, but they manipulate strings in ways that resemble some basic math functions.

Combining strings

"String addition," for example, is simply a matter of taking one string and adding its text to the end of another string. The technical term for string addition is *concatenation;* Perl's concatenation operator is a period.

The following line, for example, displays `window` on-screen:

```
print "win" . "dow";
```

You can use concatenation in string assignment as well:

```
$Name = "Susan";
$Sentence = "Ask ". $Name . " about the goldfish pond.";
print $Sentence;
```

The result:

```
Ask Susan about the goldfish pond.
```

The need for string concatenation comes up often in Perl programs. It's a handy way to take information from different places and bring it all together into a single string. If you're often using double-quoted strings, though, you probably don't need to use string concatenation. For example, the following two lines have the exact same result:

```
$Sentence = "Ask ". $Name . " about the goldfish pond.";
$Sentence = "Ask $Name about the goldfish pond.";
```

The first line in this example concatenates three strings; the second line uses substitution within a single string.

You also can use string concatenation to accomplish mundane tasks, such as making sure your program lines don't get too long. For example, consider the statement

```
print "$ID: $FirstName $LastName, ext. ".
             "$Tel\n";
```

I use concatenation here to avoid running over the end of the line. Instead of printing just one string, Perl prints two concatenated strings together.

Perl even gives you a way to concatenate a string to the end of an existing string while saving on some typing. Assume that you have the string `$AllNames`, to which you keep adding names. You may have the statement

```
$AllNames = $AllNames . $CurrentName;
```

A shorter way to express the same thing in Perl is

```
$AllNames .= $CurrentName;
```

The `.=` operator concatenates the string on the right to the end of the string on the left.

Making lots of copies

Just as you can add strings, you can multiply them. The not-so-technical term for this is *repetition*. Perl uses the x operator for repetition. You use a string on the left of the x and a number on the right, and Perl repeats the string that many times. For example,

```
print 'Q'x10;
```

displays 10 Qs in a row:

```
QQQQQQQQQQ
```

Zapping the end of a string

A simple form of string subtraction is to hack the last character off the end of a string. That's when you use the chop function. The function changes the string into the string minus its last character but returns a value of what got chopped off, which can be tricky. Here's an example:

```
$SixLet = "TUVWXY";
$A = chop($SixLet);
print "\$SixLet is now $SixLet and \$A is now $A.";
```

This displays

```
$SixLet is now TUVWX and $A is now Y.
```

Programmers typically use chop to remove the newline character from the end of multiple-line input. For example, many programs throughout this book read lines in from a file. The lines always end with the computer's line-ending character. You can use chop to get rid of that character.

The chomp function works like the chop function except it knows that some computers have two-character line endings and therefore "chomps" the correct number of characters. You rarely need to worry about this difference, but if you're munching the ends of lines, using chomp is safer than using chop. (The chomp command is not available to Perl 4 users.)

Simple String Transformations

Perl lets you do more than just shove strings together. Many functions let you change the actual contents of a string. I cover the basic functions here.

Letters come in two varieties: lowercase and uppercase. The `lc`, `lcfirst`, `uc`, and `ucfirst` functions enable you to force specific cases in your text. The `lc` and `uc` functions affect the case of an entire string; the `lcfirst` and `ucfirst` functions change just the first letter. (Sorry, Perl 4 users. These functions are available only in Perl 5 and later versions.)

The following code, for example

```
$Name1 = "AbCdEf";
$Name2 = "GhIjKl";
print lc($Name1) . " -- " . uc($Name2) . "\n";
print lcfirst($Name1) . " -- " . ucfirst($Name2) . "\n";
```

Generates this result

```
abcdef -- GHIJKL
abCdEf -- GhIjKl
```

If you really like using backslash characters instead of functions, you can use special characters to achieve much the same effect as the four upper-case/lowercase functions. The special characters `\l` and `\u` put the next letter in a string in lowercase or uppercase, respectively, which serves the same purpose as the `lcfirst` and `ucfirst` functions. For example,

```
$Name1 = "AbCdEf";
print "\l$Name1\n";
```

displays

```
AbCdEf
```

The `\L` and `\U` special characters tell Perl to make all letters that follow them lowercase or uppercase, respectively, until Perl sees the special character `\E`, which indicates the end of the `\L` or `\U`.

```
$Name1 = "AbCdEf";
print "\L$Name1 AND THEN\E \U$Name1\U\n";
```

displays

```
abcdef and then ABCDEF
```

Getting Information from Strings

Two string functions (`length` and `ord`) that I cover in this section return information about a string. The `length` function returns the number of characters in a string. For example,

```
$LineLen = length($TheLine);
```

The following is another example of the `print` function at work:

```
$TodaysWord = 'equilibrate';
print length($TodaysWord);
```

This command displays

```
11
```

The `ord` function tells you the numeric value of a character (the opposite of the `chr` function, which converts a numeric value into a character — see the section "Special characters in text" earlier in this chapter). For example,

```
print ord('C');
```

displays

```
67
```

If the string you use as an argument to `ord` is longer than one character, Perl only looks at the first character in the string when determining the value.

Chapter 6

Nifty Numbers

In This Chapter

- Differentiating integers and real numbers
- Using Perl's basic math operators
- Employing counters for incrementing and decrementing values
- Assigning values to variables
- Examining numeric functions
- Turning numbers into strings

Part of the reason that computer programs are so good with math is that computers themselves are pretty darn good with math. So people who create programming languages have it pretty easy when it comes to adding a zillion math functions to their programs.

You'll be happy to know that Perl will do a whole lot for you in terms of math besides addition, subtraction, multiplication, and division, and it does it with less muss and fuss than languages like C or Java. Unlike those other languages, you don't have to spend as much time rigidly defining your numeric variables and making sure that you are only combining two variables of the same type. You can just use a number and go.

Integers and Real Numbers

Computers handle two kinds of numbers: *integers* and *real numbers* (also known as *reals* or *floating-point numbers*). The basic difference between these two in Perl is that integers have no decimal point or fractions and real numbers do.

If I were writing about almost any programming language other than Perl, I would have to follow the previous paragraph with pages and pages of description of how the language stores integers in the CPU, how it handles real numbers differently, and so on — enough to make most novice programmers run away screaming or break down in heaving sobs. Fortunately, this book is about Perl.

Perl stores all numerical values internally as real numbers in whatever way that best suits the operating system and CPU. Perl uses floating-point math, which simplifies programming because you can forget about the different number systems that you have to worry about when you program in most other languages.

Perl can figure out when you probably want to think in terms of integers instead of reals. When you specify a number without a decimal point, Perl knows that it needs to try to operate as if the number were an integer.

You specify integers as numbers without decimal points:

```
$Count = 43;  # An integer
```

You specify reals as numbers with a decimal point:

```
$Temperature = 43.955;  # A real
```

You also can specify numbers by using scientific notation. In Perl, scientific notation consists of the letter E and a number preceding it and following it. (Whether the E is uppercase or lowercase is not important.) The value on the left is multiplied by 10 raised to the power of the number on the right. For example, the Perl scientific notation for the following variable $Temperature is equivalent to the real-world scientific notation of $.43955 \times 10^2$:

```
$Temperature = .43955E2  # A real in scientific notation
```

In other words, don't sweat the difference between integers and reals (that is, unless you're also absorbing some other programming language, too). In Perl, a number is a number is a number, and they work just fine in all the math you do.

Perl's Basic Math Operators

First things first. A number of math operators get the most mileage when you're programming with Perl.

Operators for simple calculations

The Perl operators for the simple math operations of addition, subtraction, multiplication, and division are +, -, *, and /, respectively. For example, you may want to get the product of 93 and 46:

"True" and "false" are numbers, too

Perl, like most programming languages, lets you use mathematical logic to handle values of "true" and "false." The if statement takes one argument, which is either true or false. If the argument is true, the if statement executes the statements in its block. (I cover logic in Chapter 8, describing all the statements that use logic, including if statements.)

The main reason I mention if statements here is to demonstrate one essential part of logic: how Perl handles true/false situations. As you may guess (because numbers are one of the main topics of this chapter), Perl uses numbers for true and false values. A false value is the same as the number 0 (zero), and a true value is any value other than 0.

Therefore, when a statement checks whether an argument is true, it actually checks whether it equals the number 0 or the string "0". If it equals either of these values, it's false; otherwise, it's true.

Besides the number 0, a null string ("") can stand in as a false value, but Perl programmers rarely do that. Thinking of false as 0 and true as everything else is much simpler.

```
$BigNum = 93 * 46;
print $BigNum;
```

As you can figure out with your calculator, this displays

```
4278
```

Parentheses and algebraic calculations

If you know basic algebraic notation, you know that you can use parentheses to force certain operations to happen first in an equation, as you can see from the following example:

```
$a = (5 + 2) - (4 * 9) + (3 / 7); print $a;
```

That's five plus two, minus the product of four times nine, plus the division of three by seven. And that produces

```
-28.5714285714286
```

Always use parentheses in your mathematical statements so that you can easily see what kind of math you're doing to the numbers and variables in your statements. Perl maintains a list of operators that take precedence over other operators in case you don't use parentheses, but it's easy to forget which operator does what. For example, the equation `5 + 2 - 4 * 9 + 3 / 7` may mean exactly what you intend it to, but then again, it may not. In your mind, it may mean `(((((5 + 2) - 4) * 9) + 3) / 7)`, which comes out to 4.28571; while in someone else's mind it may mean `(5 + 2) - (4 * 9) + (3 / 7)`, which comes out to –28.57143. Why risk doing it wrong when you can definitely do it right?

Positive and negative value operator

As you're aware, you can use a minus sign to make a positive number negative and a negative number positive. For example, –3 means negative three, and –(–4) means positive four. The same is true in Perl; when you put a minus sign in front of a variable, it inverts the variable's positive or negative value. Observe:

```
$Count = -2;
$InverseCount = -$Count;
print $InverseCount;
```

This code generates a value of positive 2 on screen:

```
2
```

Exponential calculations operator

Perl uses the `**` operator to raise the number on its left to the power of the number on its right. Therefore, to raise 2 to the power of 10, you would enter

```
$b=2**10; print $b;
```

Which gives you a result of

```
1024
```

Modulo arithmetic calculator

Modulo arithmetic involves dividing one number by an integer and returning the remaining value. To get the remainder for a division operation in Perl, you use the % operator in place of the division operator (/). For example, the following code generates the remainder of 8 divided by 3:

```
$c=8 % 3; print $c;
```

The result is

```
2
```

If the operation were regular division instead of modulo arithmetic, it would look like this:

```
$c=8 / 3; print $c;
```

And, it would display this:

```
2.66666666666667
```

Doing Math and an Assignment at the Same Time

Sometimes you want to change a variable based on that variable's current value. For example, you may want to double the value of `$d`. In English, you would say, "Take the current value of `$d`, double it, then make `$d` equal to that new value." In this case, you can use the following statement:

```
$d = $d * 2;
```

Perl lets you compress the `$d = $d * 2;` statement a bit by putting the desired operator before the = and skipping the variable on the right side of the equation. In which case, the statement can be written as

```
$d *= 2;
```

Though it may seem confusing, some programmers prefer the second method because it means less typing, and some think it looks better.

Another example of changing a variable based on that variable's current value is adding `1` to the variable `$e`, as

```
$e += 1;
```

Autoincrementing and Autodecrementing

A common numbers-based feature in programming is the *counter*. A counter is a variable that you set to increase a value incrementally with each iteration of a *loop* (a set of instructions that are repeated until a desired action occurs). When you use a counter in this way, you're either *autoincrementing* or *autodecrementing* a value.

Using loops with autoincrementing and autodecrementing is very common in Perl programs. In your regular, non-programming life, you often read instructions such as "put four teaspoons of salt into the water" or "take this medicine three times a day." In your head, you keep a counter that you increment each time you do the task, and you check that counter against the instructions you were given. "Okay, there's one teaspoon; is that four? No. Okay, there's two teaspoons; is that four? No. Okay, . . ."

The following example shows a counter in action:

```
$SuccessCount = $SuccessCount + 1;
```

That's one way to express the statement in Perl. Another way is to use the compressed method I describe in the preceding section of this chapter:

```
$SuccessCount += 1;
```

Counters are so common in programming, however, that Perl's creators included a special construct that lets you shorten the line even more than by using `+=` . The *autoincrement operator*, `++`, adds 1 to the value. You can write the preceding example as

```
$SuccessCount++;
```

You can decrement a number (that is, subtract 1 from it) in the same way by using the *autodecrement operator* (`--`). For example,

```
$SuccessCount--;
```

The `++` and `--` operators only add or subtract 1 to your variable. To add or subtract other numbers, you need to use `+=` and `-=`.

Perl programmers like to get fancy with these special counting operators, but they sometimes instead get cryptic and therefore make mistakes that are difficult to identify later. The autoincrement and autodecrement operators can be used in the middle of an assignment, and Perl interprets the code that uses ++ and -- differently depending on whether you place the operator before or after the variable.

If the operator appears before the variable name, Perl increments the variable and returns the incremented value. If the operator appears after the variable name, Perl returns the original value of the variable and increments the variable.

The following shows what happens when you place the operator *after* the variable:

```
$f = 7; $g = $f++;
print "Using \$f++, \$g is $g and \$f is $f\n";
```

The result is

```
Using $f++, $g is 7 and $f is 8
```

Here, Perl assigns the initial value of `$f` (which is 7) to `$g` and then increments `$f` by 1 (which now makes `$f` 8). The position of the ++ operator determines when the variable increments. When you place the operator after `$f`, it doesn't increment until the actual occurrence of the ++ operator.

A different example shows what happens when you place the operator *before* the variable:

```
$f = 7; $g = ++$f;
print "Using ++\$f, \$g is $g and \$f is $f\n";
```

The result is

```
Using ++$f, $g is 8 and $f is 8
```

Here, Perl assigns `$f` a value (7), increments the value `$f` by 1 (so `$f` now equals 8) and then assigns the value of `$f` to `$g` (making `$g` 8 as well). The key lies in the position of the operator. You can see why most Perl programmers need to look closely at code that involves the ++ or -- operators to make sure that the statement does what they want it to do.

Truth be told, using += 1 and -= 1 is much clearer than ++ and --, but feel free to use whichever method works for you.

Simple Numeric Functions

The makers of Perl included several functions for simple math. These functions are as easy to use as operators, even though explaining them involves a world of technical terms. The `sqrt` function returns the square root of the function's *argument* (the value or statement that is processed by the function), the `log` function returns the *natural logarithm* (a logarithm with *e* as its base) of its argument, and `exp` returns *e* raised to the power of its argument. The following statements are examples of all three:

```
print "The square root of 121 is " . sqrt(121);
print "The log of 121 is " . log(121);
print "e raised to 121 is " . exp(121);
```

The `abs` function returns the absolute value of the argument, meaning that it returns a positive value whether the value of the argument is negative or positive. The `int` function returns the integer portion of the argument. Examples of these two functions are

```
$ThePosValue = abs($SomeValue);
$MyWhole = int($SomeValue);
```

You should know this about the `int` function: It rounds down for positive numbers but rounds up for negative numbers. The following is an example of what I mean:

```
$h = 3.4; $i = int($h); print "$i\n";
```

```
$h = -3.4; $i = int($h); print "$i\n";
```

These statements display, respectively

```
3
```

```
-3
```

Converting Numbers into Strings

Perl makes converting numbers into strings more convenient than most other programming languages. You don't have to do anything special because Perl "understands" that when you use numbers for string-like purposes, you want it to treat the numbers as a string. For example, you may want to make a variable that consists of a number plus a text label.

Here's an example of converting a number to a string.

```
$Ann = 5; $Ann += 1;
$Ann = $Ann . "bcd";
print $Ann;
```

The result is

```
6bcd
```

In the first line, `$Ann` is a number (6). In the second line, `$Ann` is changed from a number to a string (`6bcd`). From this point on, `$Ann` is a string, and you shouldn't treat it as a number.

After you convert a number variable into a string, you should treat that variable like a string. Technically, you *can* treat strings like numbers, but predicting the results accurately is next to impossible. For example, you can use the * operator to multiply two strings together. Perl tries hard to find numbers in the strings and do the "right thing" with them, but you cannot always guess what that right thing is. Don't risk it: Always use math functions and operators exclusively with numbers.

Counting in Numbering Systems Other Than Decimal

If you like to count by using either the *hexadecimal* numbering system (one based on 16 digits) or the *octal* numbering system (one based on 8 digits), you can use them easily in Perl. To specify a number in hexadecimal (sometimes called *hex* for short), you preface it with the characters `0x`. To specify a number in octal, you use a leading zero (`0`). For example,

```
$Mask = 0xFF00;
$SomeOctal = 0177;
```

Perl provides two functions for converting numbers from these two systems to decimal values. The `hex` and `oct` functions take strings that represent numbers in their respective formats and return decimal numbers. For example,

```
$Address = 'FFFF';
$Location = hex($Address) + 12;
```

If you use the hexadecimal system, the following program shows how to create a decimal-to-hex conversion chart. It uses some of the math operators shown in this chapter, as well as some of the list processing that I talk about in Chapter 7.

```
# hexchart.pl: Prints a decimal-to-hex conversion chart.
@HexD = ('0', '1', '2', '3', '4', '5', '6', '7', '8',
     '9', 'A', 'B', 'C', 'D', 'E', 'F');
for($i = 0; $i <= 255; $i += 1) {
     printf("%3s=$HexD[int($i / 16)]$HexD[$i % 16]  ", $i);
     if(($i % 8) == 7) { print "\n" }
}
```

The output of the chart generated by this program is 32 lines long, so it won't all fit on a standard-size computer screen. Figure 6-1 shows how the output looks under Windows 95 with a larger-sized MS-DOS window.

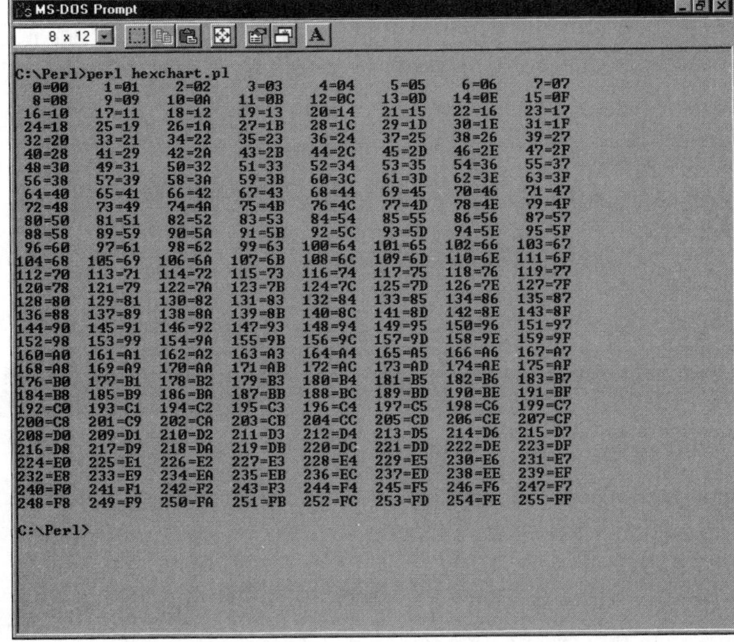

MS-DOS Prompt
8 x 12
C:\Perl>perl hexchart.pl
0=00 1=01 2=02 3=03 4=04 5=05 6=06 7=07
8=08 9=09 10=0A 11=0B 12=0C 13=0D 14=0E 15=0F
16=10 17=11 18=12 19=13 20=14 21=15 22=16 23=17
24=18 25=19 26=1A 27=1B 28=1C 29=1D 30=1E 31=1F
32=20 33=21 34=22 35=23 36=24 37=25 38=26 39=27
40=28 41=29 42=2A 43=2B 44=2C 45=2D 46=2E 47=2F
48=30 49=31 50=32 51=33 52=34 53=35 54=36 55=37
56=38 57=39 58=3A 59=3B 60=3C 61=3D 62=3E 63=3F
64=40 65=41 66=42 67=43 68=44 69=45 70=46 71=47
72=48 73=49 74=4A 75=4B 76=4C 77=4D 78=4E 79=4F
80=50 81=51 82=52 83=53 84=54 85=55 86=56 87=57
88=58 89=59 90=5A 91=5B 92=5C 93=5D 94=5E 95=5F
96=60 97=61 98=62 99=63 100=64 101=65 102=66 103=67
104=68 105=69 106=6A 107=6B 108=6C 109=6D 110=6E 111=6F
112=70 113=71 114=72 115=73 116=74 117=75 118=76 119=77
120=78 121=79 122=7A 123=7B 124=7C 125=7D 126=7E 127=7F
128=80 129=81 130=82 131=83 132=84 133=85 134=86 135=87
136=88 137=89 138=8A 139=8B 140=8C 141=8D 142=8E 143=8F
144=90 145=91 146=92 147=93 148=94 149=95 150=96 151=97
152=98 153=99 154=9A 155=9B 156=9C 157=9D 158=9E 159=9F
160=A0 161=A1 162=A2 163=A3 164=A4 165=A5 166=A6 167=A7
168=A8 169=A9 170=AA 171=AB 172=AC 173=AD 174=AE 175=AF
176=B0 177=B1 178=B2 179=B3 180=B4 181=B5 182=B6 183=B7
184=B8 185=B9 186=BA 187=BB 188=BC 189=BD 190=BE 191=BF
192=C0 193=C1 194=C2 195=C3 196=C4 197=C5 198=C6 199=C7
200=C8 201=C9 202=CA 203=CB 204=CC 205=CD 206=CE 207=CF
208=D0 209=D1 210=D2 211=D3 212=D4 213=D5 214=D6 215=D7
216=D8 217=D9 218=DA 219=DB 220=DC 221=DD 222=DE 223=DF
224=E0 225=E1 226=E2 227=E3 228=E4 229=E5 230=E6 231=E7
232=E8 233=E9 234=EA 235=EB 236=EC 237=ED 238=EE 239=EF
240=F0 241=F1 242=F2 243=F3 244=F4 245=F5 246=F6 247=F7
248=F8 249=F9 250=FA 251=FB 252=FC 253=FD 254=FE 255=FF
C:\Perl>

Figure 6-1: The output from a decimal to hexadecimal conversion program.

Chapter 7
Learning to Love Lists

In This Chapter

- Constructing lists
- Adding and removing list elements
- Slicing lists
- Splitting strings and returning them into lists
- Distinguishing scalar context from list context

In addition to the two basic kinds of data — text and numbers (which are covered in the preceding two chapters of this book) — Perl uses a third type of data called *lists.* When a Perl function returns more than one value, it always returns those multiple values as a list. Perl also uses lists to gather its own internal data, which helps you and your programs to work more efficiently. Plus, understanding how to use lists is crucial to your taking full advantage of Perl's most powerful features, such as its ability to organize large chunks of data into a manageable whole.

What's on the List for Today?

A *list* is an ordered gang of *elements* (or *items*), each of which is usually a number or a string. A list follows a definite order: The first element is always first, the second element is always second, and so on. Note that "ordered" doesn't mean "sorted" as with other programming languages. The order of the items in the list doesn't change unless you tell Perl to change it. A list also has a definite length, so you can always tell how long a list is. The length of a list can change, however, as you add or subtract list items.

In addition to numbers and strings, lists can also be in the form of *references.* The subject of references falls under some advanced topics I cover in Chapter 16 and Chapter 19.

Incidentally, Perl programmers also use the term *array* when referring to a list. For all practical purposes, "list" and "array" mean the same thing and can be used interchangeably (which I do in this book to add a bit of variety).

Perl programmers use another special term to refer to anything that is a string or a number and nothing else — they call them *scalars*. Keep in mind that a scalar is never a list, and a list is never a scalar. You'll soon see why the term "scalar" came to be: To repeatedly say "strings or numbers" can get really tedious.

Basic list construction

A Perl list is constructed somewhat like a grocery list:

```
juice
bread
paper towels
asparagus
```

This list contains individual elements, it follows a particular order, and the list as a whole can be thought of as one item ("my shopping list").

If you keep track of your car's gas mileage, you may end up with a list that looks something like this:

```
23.4
23.6
23.4
22.9
```

Both the mileage list and the grocery list are perfectly valid lists for Perl.

The elements in a single list can include both text data and number data. For example, you may have a list that looks like this one:

```
juice
bread
9
juice
```

Although it's difficult to imagine what kind of logic went into the ordering of this list, it is nevertheless a valid list as far as Perl is concerned.

Literal lists

A *literal list* in Perl is almost always shown as a series of elements with a comma (`,`) between each. Typically, literal lists are also enclosed within parentheses. The parentheses are not absolutely required, but you can end up with some difficult-to-diagnose problems if you leave them off, so I recommend always using them so that Perl doesn't misinterpret your intentions. Lists often appear on a single line, but they can span multiple lines as well. For example, the grocery list from the preceding section of this chapter may look like this:

```
('juice', 'bread', 'paper towels', 'asparagus')
```

This list contains four string *literals*. (See Chapter 5 for a discussion of literals.) You always use quotation marks around a string literal so that Perl will know where the string starts and ends.

Variable names

Many of the variable names you see in this book start with a dollar sign ($). Perl uses another symbol to begin the variable names of lists: the at-sign (@). For example, examine the following assignment in which multiple values are stored in the variable `@Shop`:

```
@Shop = ('juice', 'bread', 'paper towels', 'asparagus');
```

This statement tells Perl, "The list called `Shop` is assigned to be four elements long; the first element is `'juice'`, the second element is `'bread'`, the third element is `'paper towels'`, and the fourth element is `'asparagus'`."

List variable names start with `@`, and scalar variable names start with `$`. When you see a variable name such as `@Shop`, you know you have a list on your hands; when you see a variable name such as `$Shop`, you've identified it as a string or a number.

Null lists

Not all lists contain elements. A list that consists of no elements is called an *empty list* or *null list*. You can specify a list to have no values with an assignment like the following in which you make `@Shop` an empty list:

```
@Shop = ();
```

The `()` in the previous statement is actually a list: It's a list with no elements between the `(` and `)`. You can also specify an empty list with one or more spaces between the parentheses because you still have no elements in it:

```
@Shop = ( );
```

Specifying Slices of Lists

What happens if you want to address just one element of a list, and not the list in its entirety? Because lists are ordered, you can refer to each element by its numbered place in the list. You can then say to Perl, "Set the variable `$Dub` to the value of the third element of the list `@Music`." For example,

```
$Dub = @Music(2);
```

If you're thinking that the preceding statement should say `@Music(3)` and not `@Music(2)`, remember that Perl counts list elements starting at 0, and not at 1. Therefore, the first element of a Perl list is always element number 0, the second element is element number 1, and so on. (If you've used other programming languages, such as C and Pascal, you're probably already familiar with this programming quirk.) If Perl is your first programming language, be sure to drill this into your brain: "Perl counts items in lists beginning at 0."

You can refer to a part of a list as a *slice*. You specify a slice by putting the element number(s) of the slice in square brackets (`[` and `]`). If you are talking about a slice with a single element, that slice is a *scalar slice,* and you must place a `$` at the beginning of the list's variable name.

For example, if you want to print the first element of the `@Shop` list, you enter

```
@Shop = ('juice', 'bread', 'paper towels', 'asparagus');
print $Shop[0];
```

which would display

```
juice
```

You can assign scalar slices to scalar variables, such as

```
$Third = $Shop[2];
```

This statement assigns the string `paper towels` (element number 3 in the list designated by `[2]` in Perl-speak) to the variable `$Third`.

You may be wondering why you change the symbol for a slice from `@` to `$` when discussing a slice that's only one element. That's because the values in a list are always scalars and are never lists. For example, the value in `Shop[0]` is a scalar, not a list. Thus, its name should start with `$`, the symbol for a scalar variable.

Slices of lists can contain more than one element. Multielement slices are themselves lists, and thus their variable names start with @. For example, a slice of the @Shop list that consists of the second and third elements can be assigned with something like this:

```
@TwoEls = @Shop[1,2];
```

You can also place list slices on the left side of assignments. This is commonly done to change the value of one element without redefining the whole list. For example,

```
@Shop = ('juice', 'bread', 'paper towels', 'asparagus');
$Shop[1] = 'muffins';
```

turns the list in @Shop into

```
('juice', 'muffins', 'paper towels', 'asparagus')
```

Perl makes it easy to find out how many elements are in a list without having to count each of them. The variable $#listname is the number of the last element in a list. So, for the four-element shopping list I've been using in this chapter, entering

```
print $#Shop;
```

displays the number

```
3
```

Note that this is *not* the length of the list; it is the number of the last element. The length of the list is actually that number plus 1.

When Perl doesn't know your list

Perl has what I consider to be a nasty feature that supposedly exists for the sake of programming friendliness. You can have a list variable and a scalar variable with the same name that are completely unrelated. For example, you can have a program that has both @Shop and $Shop, and the two variables may have nothing to do with each other.

This can create confusion when you're first learning how to use single-element array slices. If you forget to put the square brackets and the element number in the variable name, you can easily miss the fact that you're using a scalar variable that has nothing to do with the list variable.

To keep your sanity, never purposely use a scalar variable with the same name as a list variable. If you have a list called @Shop, do not use a scalar called $Shop; call it something else like $ShopNum.

Using Lists to Simplify Basic Tasks

Perl's list-handling abilities simplify a number of programming tasks. For example, assume that you want to compare a single string against a lengthy set of strings in a dictionary to determine if the test string matches any in the set. Further assume that your test string is in the variable `$Test` and consists of the following words:

```
. . .
interest
interested
interesting
interface
interfaith
interfere
interferon
intergenerational
. . .
```

Without using lists, your program would have to look something like the following:

```
. . .
if($Test eq 'interest') { print "A match was found.\n" }
if($Test eq 'interested') { print "A match was found.\n" }
if($Test eq 'interesting') { print "A match was found.\n" }
. . .
```

Creating such a program can be sheer tedium. Furthermore, if you want to perform some different action if the test is successful, updating every line of the program is subject to human error because you have to enter that action into every line by hand.

This task can be made simple by using a list. You first create a list whose elements consist of all the words to test against the dictionary, and then you *loop* through the list, as in the following example. (I cover loops in Chapter 8.)

```
. . .
@WordList = (
    'interest', 'interested', 'interesting', 'interface',
    'interfaith', 'interfere', 'interferon',
    'intergenerational');  # Line breaks are ignored
$ListPos = 0;  # Start at position 0
# Loop until you go off the end of the list
until($ListPos > $#WordList) {
```

```
    if($Test eq $WordList[$ListPos])
        { print "A match was found.\n" }
    $ListPos += 1;
}
. . .
```

You now have just one place where the action is given (the `print` statement), which makes updating the program faster and easier.

Using lists simplifies more than just the process of updating a program. For example, what if you don't know which list you're testing against until you run the program? This frequently happens because lists are kept in text files that are updated separately from the Perl program. With lists, getting this information is a cinch. Instead of assigning the list at the beginning of the program, you can write two or three lines of Perl code (which I describe in Chapter 11) that read lines from the text file and add each line to the list. The loop in the program remains identical; only the source of the list changes.

Using the `print` Statement with Lists

Many functions take lists as *arguments* (values entered after the function to modify the operation of the function). The most widely used example of a function that takes a list is the `print` statement. The `print` statement takes one argument — a list. It is common for that list to have a single element. For example,

```
$Color = "mossy teal";
print $Color;
```

displays

```
mossy teal
```

You can also print a list in exactly the same fashion by specifying a list instead of a single value. For example,

```
@Color = ('mossy teal', 'burnt umber', 'bone white');
print @Color;
```

displays

```
mossy tealburnt umberbone white
```

The print statement runs the elements together, rather than separating them with a space as it does with the words in each element, because the list is simply a gang of items. You can print the elements individually by entering the following statement

```
print $Color[0] . ' ' .  $Color[1] . ' ' . $Color[2];
```

which displays the string

```
mossy teal  burnt umber  bone white
```

In the preceding example, you print a list that consists of a single string which is formed from five strings — the first slice, the string that is a single space, the second slice, the string that is a single space, and the third slice. You can also print a list of five elements with a statement such as

```
print ($Color[0], ' ', $Color[1], ' ', $Color[2]);
```

which displays the string

```
mossy teal burnt umber bone  white
```

Note that this is a true list with five elements: the first slice, a string, the second slice, another string, and the third slice.

Adding and Removing List Elements

You don't have to construct your lists by using assignments. In fact, it's common practice to build up a list by starting with a null list and adding elements one by one.

The push and unshift functions

The two functions you use to add elements to a list are push and unshift. push adds one or more elements to the end of a list, whereas unshift adds elements to the beginning of a list. Each of these functions takes two arguments: the name of the list to which you want to add elements and the list of elements you want to add. The following lines show push and unshift in action:

```
@SomeList = (8, 'eight', 9, 'nine');
@TenList = (10, 'ten');
push(@SomeList, @TenList);
unshift(@SomeList, "The Big Seven");
```

Given the previous lines, the list @SomeList becomes

```
('The Big Seven', 8, 'eight', 9, 'nine', 10, 'ten')
```

The shift *and* pop *functions*

You can also remove an element from the beginning or end of a list with the shift and pop functions, respectively. These functions take one argument — the name of the list — and return the value that was removed. For example,

```
@SomeList = (8, 'eight', 9, 'nine');
$Removed = shift(@SomeList);
print $Removed;
```

displays

```
8
```

and the list @SomeList now contains only three elements:

```
('eight', 9, 'nine')
```

The functions I just described enable you to alter the two ends of a list to make it expand and shrink as you desire. Table 7-1 shows you these functions at a glance.

Table 7-1 Functions for Adding or Subtracting Elements from the Ends of Lists

Function	*Result*
push	Adds items to right side of list
pop	Removes items from right side of list
unshift	Adds items to left side of list
shift	Removes items from left side of list

The splice *function*

Perl, being the lenient and flexible language that it is, also has a function that lets you add or remove elements from any part of a list. The splice function removes some elements and adds others in their place. It takes four arguments:

- The list to modify
- The position (element number) that indicates where to start replacing
- The number of elements to remove
- The list of elements to insert

The following example illustrates each of the `splice` arguments

```
@Nums = (1, 2, 3, 4, 5);
splice(@Nums, 3, 1, ('dog', 'cow'));
```

and results in this:

```
(1, 2, 3, 'dog', 'cow', 5)
```

You don't have to remove any elements in order to add elements with `splice`. If you set the third argument (the number of elements to remove) to `0`, then you're simply adding elements to the list. For example, if you enter the following

```
@Nums = (1, 2, 3, 4, 5);
splice(@Nums, 3, 0, ('dog', 'cow'));
```

the `@Nums` list equals

```
(1, 2, 3, 'dog', 'cow', 4, 5)
```

Note that when you don't remove any elements, the new elements go *before* the element indicated by the second argument.

You can also use `splice` to remove elements by using a null list. (See the section "Null lists" earlier in this chapter for more information.) For example, the following entry

```
@Nums = (1, 2, 3, 4, 5);
splice(@Nums, 3, 1, ());
```

results in this:

```
(1, 2, 3, 5)
```

Perl allows you to leave off the fourth argument if it's a null list. The equivalent `splice` statement without a null list would be

```
splice(@Nums, 3, 1);
```

When you use `splice` to remove items, Perl returns those items. (Returning values from a function is described in Chapter 3.) For example,

```
@Nums = (1, 2, 3, 4, 5);
$GotOne = splice(@Nums, 3, 1);
print $GotOne;
```

displays

```
4
```

If you are removing more than one item, return the items into a list. For example,

```
@Nums = (1, 2, 3, 4, 5);
@GotSome = splice(@Nums, 3, 2);
```

The `@GotSome` list now equals

```
(4, 5)
```

Two nifty list operators

There's more to lists than functions. Perl also has two useful operators that operate on lists to make list creation easier. In Chapter 5, I describe how the `x` operator repeats strings. That same operator can also be used to repeat lists. Given the following statement

```
@h = (883, 895) x 3;
```

`@h` now equals

```
(883, 895, 883, 895, 883, 895)
```

Perl also makes it easy to create lists that consist of sequential integers (and not real numbers, such as 3.45 or 8.76) by using the *range operator,* which consists of two periods ("..") between the starting and ending values, as follows:

```
@n = (3 .. 8);
```

The result is the list

```
(3, 4, 5, 6, 7, 8)
```

You must list the smallest number in the range first when using the range operator; you can't use the range operator, for example, to create the list `(8, 7, 6, 5, 4, 3)`. You can also use the range operator with characters. For example, to create the list `('a', 'b', 'c', 'd', 'e', 'f')`, you can enter the following:

```
('a' .. 'f')
```

The `push`, `unshift`, `shift`, and `pop` functions pretty much boil down to special cases of `splice` that you can use interchangeably. Table 7-2 shows the functions and their splice equivalents:

Table 7-2 How `splice` Relates to `push`, `unshift`, `shift`, and `pop`

Function	*`splice` Equivalent*
`push(@r, @s)`	`splice(@r, $#r+1, 0, @s)`
`pop(@r)`	`splice(@r, $#r, 1)`
`unshift(@r, @s)`	`splice(@r, 0, 0, @s)`
`shift(@r)`	`splice(@r, 0, 1)`

Doing the Splits with the `split` Function

As I mention frequently throughout the book, Perl is a superb text-handling language. The `split` function is one of the greatest text-handling tools in Perl.

After you work with lists, you can see why `split` is the greatest thing since, um, split bread. `split` looks at a string and splits it apart, returning a list of strings. For example, you can use `split` to examine a sentence and return a list of each word in the sentence. Or, if you have a tab-delimited text file that is a database (such as the empdata1.pl program described in Chapter 4), `split` can split the lines in the file into fields in a single function.

Unless you use the `split` default arguments in Perl (and I recommend against this practice because it makes your programs difficult to read), `split` takes two or three arguments. If you want to create a list of all the split-out strings in your program, you use two arguments: the pattern to use as the *delimiter* (the indicator of the end of one thing and the beginning of the next) and the string to search. Later in this section of the chapter, I tell you how you can use three arguments with `split`.

String patterns are among the more advanced topics in Perl. I cover them in more depth in Chapter 13, but for now, I show you some very simple patterns. The patterns I show you here start and end with a slash (/) character and contain the exact character you want to split between the slashes.

For example, to split a sentence that is in a string into a list of words (using the space as the delimiter), you would use

```
$Sentence = "It is time for our tea, Sir.";
@Words = split(/ /, $Sentence);
```

The @Words list now looks like this:

```
('It' , 'is' , 'time' , 'for' , 'our' , 'tea,' , 'Sir.')
```

Splitting by tab characters is just as easy. For example, consider the following lines:

```
        ($LastName, $FirstName, $ID, $Tel) =
            split(/\t/, $TheRec);
```

The first argument in the preceding split statement is the pattern for a tab character (\t). Because each record has four fields, instead of splitting the $TheRec string into a named record, you can split it directly into a list of variables. This process is somewhat akin to (but much simpler than) entering the following:

```
@TempList = split(/\t/, $TheRec);
$LastName = $TempList[0];
$FirstName = $TempList[1];
$ID = $TempList[2];
$Tel = $TempList[3];
```

If you need just the first few items in a string and don't care about the rest, you can use a third argument in split to say how many elements should be in the resulting list. In the preceding example, if the only data you want to use are the first names and last names, you can enter

```
        ($LastName, $FirstName, $RestOfLine) =
            split(/\t/, $TheRec, 3);
```

In this case, $RestOfLine may or may not have tab characters in it. split stops looking for more elements after the second tab character and stuffs whatever remains into the last element of the array on the left side of the assignment. In the preceding example, the remainder of the record is put into $RestOfLine.

You can probably find many uses for split as you write your own Perl programs. For example, you may have a text file that contains lines like this:

```
Temperature=28.3
Size=large
Color=crimson
Texture=rough
```

For each line, you want to know what the attribute on the left is, as well as the value on the right. In a line-by-line loop of the program, you can use

```
($Attribute, $Value) = split(/=/, $TheLine);
```

You can then do some testing based on `$Attribute`.

Using Scalar Variables

The list-creation assignments in previous sections of this chapter all use *literals* for their values. But you can also use scalar variables in your list assignments just as easily. (See Chapter 3 for definitions of literals and scalars.) For example, examine the following lines:

```
$LakeName = "Mammoth";
$LakeLen = 1291.3;
@Lake[8,9] = ($LakeName, $LakeLen);
```

The previous statements cause `$Lake[8]` to become the string `Mammoth` and `$Lake[9]` to become the number `1291.3`.

Employing Existing Lists

You can also use existing lists when defining new lists. When you name a list while assigning a new or existing list, Perl expands the list inside the assignment to all its elements. The following is a quick way to insert the elements from one list into another. For example, if you use the following statements

```
@a = (12, 24, 36);
@b = ('Dozens', @a);
```

`@b` is set to

```
('Dozens', 12, 24, 36)
```

Perl behaves like this because list elements cannot be lists themselves. If you try to make a list an element of another list, Perl politely pulls out all the elements of the inner list and replaces them in the list at the left side of the assignment.

Distinguishing Context Types

Perl operates in two *contexts:* scalar (anything in the form of strings or numbers) and array. ("Array" and "list" are synonymous.) Perl uses the context of an expression to determine what kind of output a function or operator will produce. You can determine which context you're in by looking at what kind of assignment is being created. Consider the following example:

```
$a = somefunction($b);  # scalar context
@c = somefunction($d);  # array context
($e, $f) = somefunction($g);  # array context
```

The general rule is that if the item on the left of an assignment is a scalar, you're in scalar context; if the item on the left of the assignment is a list, you're in array context. Note that in the third line of the preceding example, even though scalar variables are shown, they are in a list, so the statement is in array context.

Most of the time, you don't have to be bothered with which context a function is in because the function returns the same result in either case. However, some Perl functions give you completely different results depending on the context. A few Perl operators also change their output depending on the context.

In the previous examples shown in this chapter, the `split` function is in an array context — that is, the left-hand side of each assignment is always a list. If the left-hand side of an assignment were a scalar, however, `split` returns the number of elements that it finds. For example, in the following case

```
$x = "This has exactly five words.";
@y = split(/ /, $x);
$z = split(/ /, $x);
```

`@y` is set to the list

```
('This', 'has', 'exactly', 'five', 'words.')
```

However, `$z` is set to

```
5
```

The two varying results I just noted, both of which come from the same function call of `split(/ /, $x)`, are due to the differences in the context.

And, here's a place where Perl can get really confusing. If you use the name of a list in a scalar context, Perl interprets the name as the length of the list. This little bit of shorthand can be confounding to even advanced programmers, unless the statement with that shorthand is carefully examined to see why the particular results were achieved. For example, you can say something like

```
@h = ('A', 'short', 'list', 'of', 'words');
$ListLen = @h;
print $ListLen;
```

and Perl will display

```
5
```

Using `$#h+1` to get a list length is always less confusing than using `@h`.

From time to time, you may want to force Perl to evaluate a function in a scalar context. You can use the `scalar` function to do this. If you must use `@` to get a list length, you can use `scalar` to make your program less confusing when reading it later. For example,

```
@h = ('A', 'short', 'list', 'of', 'words');
print scalar(@h);
```

prints

```
5
```

Without the `scalar` function in this case, Perl prints out all the elements of the list.

Chapter 8

Cool Conditionals and Lovely Loops

In This Chapter

- Using comparison operators
- Exploring conditionals
- Looking at loops
- Stepping through list elements

Almost every Perl program you write contains an `if` statement. The `if` statement offers two simple choices: If such-and-such is true, do A, otherwise do B. Another very common programming instruction says: Loop around while such-and-such is true. (For example, "as long as there are more lines in this file, do this" or "while elements still exist in this list, do that.") Perl's `while` statement makes looping easy because your program checks to see if a loop is done every time it goes through a block of statements.

In this chapter, I explore the means to create highly useful conditional `if` statements and looping `while` statements by using the powers of Perl. A *conditional statement* is one that tests a condition (for example, determining if it is true or not) and then decides what should be done based on the result of the test.

A Little about Logic: If/Then Statements and Value Comparisons

Before delving too far into the intricacies of `if` statements, you need to know a little about Perl logic. The `if` statement takes one argument: a logical value. Given this, the simple format of the `if` statement is

```
if(LOGICAL) { BLOCK }
```

The preceding statement means that if the argument is true, execute the block of statements; otherwise, just go on to the next statement after the `if` statement. A slightly less simple form of this statement is

```
if(LOGICAL) { BLOCK1 } else { BLOCK2 }
```

This line means that, if the argument is true, execute `BLOCK1`, otherwise execute `BLOCK2`.

Perl uses 0 (zero) for logical false and every other value for logical true. In order to generate a true or false value, you typically use Perl's comparison operators to compare two items. (The true-false comparison operators you use in Perl are shown in Table 8-1.) For example, by using these operators, you can test if one numeric variable is larger than another, or whether a certain variable equals a specific value, or whether a string variable is equal to `'finished'`, and so forth.

It is a good idea to place comparisons within parentheses so that you can readily see what's going on in a statement.

Table 8-1 True-False Comparison Operators

Comparison	*Math operators*	*String operators*
Equal to	`==`	`eq`
Not equal to	`!=`	`ne`
Less than	`<`	`lt`
Greater than	`>`	`gt`
Less than or equal to	`<=`	`le`
Greater than or equal to	`>=`	`ge`

When you do a comparison, Perl returns a 0 if the comparison is false or a value other than 0 if the comparison is true.

The following example compares the values 5 and 3 using one of the math operators listed in Table 8-1. When given the following instructions

```
$T1 = 5;
$T2 = 3;
if($T1 > $T2) { print "$T1 is greater than $T2\n" };
```

Perl displays

```
5 is greater than 3
```

If you change the values for `$T1` and `$T2` to 4 and 6, respectively, you get different results — namely, Perl doesn't print anything because 4 is not greater than 6 and therefore the block with the `print` in it is not executed.

A common mistake made with numeric comparison operators is to compare two numbers with the = operator instead of the == operator (two equal signs with no space between them). You must use the == operator in comparisons because = almost always returns true because it's not comparing anything. For example,

```
$a=3;
if($a = 7) { print "It's true!\n" }
else { print "It's false!\n" }
```

always prints

```
It's true!
```

If you replace the `if($a = 7)` with `if($a == 7)`, the program works as you expect it to.

To compare strings, you must use the comparison operators listed in the third column of Table 8-1. For example,

```
if($Time eq 'early') { print "It is early!\n" };
```

Most of the time, you use the `eq` and `ne` string comparison operators. However, you can also use the other operators to determine which string comes first in a comparison of the character values in two strings. (For example, 'a' is less than 'b', 'ad' is less than 'ae', and so on.) The ranking of each character is derived from ASCII standards, which are covered in Chapter 5.

Perl compares two strings until it finds a letter in the same position that is not equal in each, and it bases its result on that different letter. For example, in comparing 'abcd' to 'abxy', it would find that the first two letters were identical and would make the comparison based on comparing 'c' (from the first string) to 'x' (in the second string).

Perl also features a comparison operator that returns three different values. This operator, sometimes called a *three-value compare,* is `<=>` for numbers and `cmp` for strings. The operator returns -1, 0, or 1 if the value on the left is less than, equal to, or greater than, respectively, the value on the right. For example, if `$a` is set to `4`, `3 <=> $a` would return -1, `4 <=> $a` would return 0, and `5 <=> $a` would return 1. For strings, if `$b` is set to `Frank`, `'Bob' cmp $b` would return -1 because 'B' is less than 'F', `'Frank' cmp $b` would return 0, and `'Fred' cmp $b` would return 1 because 'e' is greater than 'a'. (The first two letters are the same.)

You can link conditional tests together in Perl just as you would in a conventional English sentence. For example, you may say to yourself, "If I am hungry and cashews are in the cupboard, I will have a snack." This means that only if both statements "I am hungry" and "cashews are in the cupboard" are true will you have a snack; if either statement is false, you won't. Another example is "If it is Mickey or Billy on the phone, I'll take the call." In this case, if either of the two statements "Mickey is on the phone" or "Billy is on the phone" is true, then you will take the call.

Perl can handle this kind of multipart logic with ease. The two most common operators you use for if/then statements are `and` and `or`, just as you may expect. You place these operators between logical tests, and the result is another logical value. Again, you should always use parentheses to make your programs easier to read.

The following example uses an `and` expression:

```
if(($Hunger >= 8) and ($Cupboard[4] eq 'cashews'))
    { print "OK, OK, you can have a small snack.\n" }
```

The following example uses `or`:

```
if(($Caller eq 'Billy') or ($Caller eq 'Mickey'))
    { print "Answer the phone already!\n" }
```

You can also use the `not` operator to invert the meaning of the comparison tests. That is, the `not` operator changes the result of a test from false to true or from true to false. For example, you may say, "If it's not Saturday night, you cannot have a fever." You can write such a statement in Perl like this:

```
if(not($Night eq 'Saturday'))
    { print "No fever tonight!\n" }
```

You can use `&&` instead of `and`, `||` instead of `or`, and `!` instead of `not` if you wish. In fact, if you're using Perl 4, you have to use `&&`, `||`, and `!` because the `and`, `or`, and `not` operators were introduced in Perl 5.

If you are a Perl 5 user, you can also use the `xor` operator. This operator returns true if the two items being compared have different truth values but returns false if they have the same truth value. (See Table 8-2.)

Table 8-2 The Results of the xor Operator

If A is	*And B is*	*Then A xor B is*
True	True	False
True	False	True
False	True	True
False	False	False

`xor` isn't all that useful in daily life, but some programs have a need for it, so it's nice that Perl 5 provides it.

If You Like Conditionals Like I Like Conditionals . . .

As I mention at the top of this chapter, a *conditional statement* is one that tests a condition and then decides what the outcome should be based on the result of the test. In this section, I cover a few conditional tests that get a lot of mileage in Perl.

The `else` and `elsif` statements

As I note earlier in this chapter, an `if` statement can look something like this:

```
if(LOGICAL) { BLOCK }
```

Now, take a look at the following statement:

```
if(LOGICAL) { BLOCK1 } else { BLOCK2 }
```

If you have the second statement and the `else` block starts with another `if`, you can use an `elsif` clause, which means "otherwise, if this is true, execute the next block." The format of `elsif` may look like this:

```
if(LOGICAL1) { BLOCK1 } elsif(LOGICAL2) { BLOCK2 }
          else { BLOCK3 }
```

In the example just listed, if the first comparison is true, Perl executes `BLOCK1` and ignores the rest. If the first comparison is false but the second one is true, Perl executes `BLOCK2` but not `BLOCK1` and `BLOCK3`. If neither of the comparisons is true, Perl executes `BLOCK3`. In short, regardless of the form of the `if` statement, Perl executes only one of the blocks.

By the way, you can group a number of elsif clauses:

```
if(LOGICAL1) { BLOCK1 }
            elsif(LOGICAL2) { BLOCK2 }
            elsif(LOGICAL3) { BLOCK3 }
            elsif(LOGICAL4) { BLOCK4 }
            else { BLOCK5 }
```

You don't have to use an else statement if you've used elsif, but it's always good programming style to end with an else because you're assured that all possible situations are covered.

Note: elsif is not spelled with a second *e*. Do not use elseif or else if; Perl will give you an error message if you do.

The unless statement

If your conditional test in the if statement starts with not, you can use unless instead of if. unless is exactly the same as if not. For example,

```
if(not($Flavor eq 'banana'))
          { print "Excuse me, but I ordered banana.\n" }
```

is the same as

```
unless($Flavor eq 'banana')
          { print "Excuse me, but I ordered banana.\n" }
```

Using unless makes programs a bit clearer, particularly if the logic inside the argument is already convoluted enough without the not statement.

Conditional operators

When you have an if statement that is used to determine an assignment, you may want to use the ? operator as shorthand. The ? operator always has a test preceding it — if the test is true, it returns the result to the right of the ? expression; if it's false, it returns the result that is to the right of the following : operator. That is, the ? operator returns the value before the : operator if the test is true and returns the value after the : operator if the test is false.

For example, if you are testing "if the texture is smooth, you should use paint, otherwise you shouldn't use paint," you can write something like

```
if($Texture eq 'smooth') { $PaintVal = 'yes' }
else { $PaintVal = 'no' }
```

which you can then turn into

```
$PaintVal = ($Texture eq 'smooth') ? 'yes' : 'no';
```

Although the second version is a more-compact way to structure this statement, it's more difficult to read. Therefore, you may want to avoid using it for general aesthetic principles, because even if it works, you may not be able to remember what it does when you reread the program later.

Going Around in Loops

The `if` statement is useful when you want to conduct a test, execute one block of code if the test is true, and then move on after executing that block. However, the `if` statement can't help much if you want to loop around and keep trying the test. For example, you may want to create a program that does something like the following:

```
Look for any corners that have dirt in them. If you find
one, clean it. Keep looking and cleaning until you don't
find any more dirty corners.
```

The following is a similar example, with more of a computer bent:

```
See if there are any characters left in the string; if so,
cut off a character, do some more processing, and then
go back and see if there is anything left in the string.
```

Looping with the `while` statement

Perl makes it easy for you to create the kind of loops I just described. The format of the `while` statement looks like this:

```
while(LOGICAL) { BLOCK }
```

The first time Perl comes across a `while` statement in a program, it looks to see if the argument of the statement is true. If it is true, Perl executes the statements in the block. When it reaches the end of the block, Perl checks the `while` argument again; if the argument is true, Perl executes the block once more, and so on.

Avoiding infinite loops

You may be thinking, "Why in the world would I write a program that keeps looping around forever?" Good question, and the answer is, "You wouldn't." Perl terminates `while` loops whenever one of the following actions occurs:

- Something inside the loop causes the logical test to change from true to false.
- The last statement in the loop is executed.

Commonly, a conditional statement inside a `while` loop affects the test on which the `while` loop is based. For example,

```
$Counter = 3;
while($Counter > 0) {
    print "$Counter  ";
           $Counter -= 1;
}
print "\nI made it to zero.\n";
```

displays

```
3  2  1
I made it to zero.
```

In this example, Perl changes the `$Counter` variable inside the loop and performs the test each time with a new value.

Incidentally, an `until` statement is exactly like a `while` statement followed by "not" or a similar negative expression. The relationship of `until` and `while` is just like that of `unless` and `if`. The preceding program written with an `until` statement (and with the > operator changed to <=) looks like this:

```
$Counter = 3;
until($Counter <= 0) {
    print "$Counter  ";
           $Counter -= 1;
}
print "\nI made it to zero.\n";
```

Loop hopping: `next` and `last` statements

Another method for getting out of a loop is the `last` statement. A `last` statement basically says, "Jump to the end of the loop, to right after the closing brace." You can use a `last` statement instead of using a logical test in the `while` statement. For example,

```
$Counter = 3;
while(1) {  # This is always true!
    print "$Counter  ";
           $Counter -= 1;
    unless($Counter > 0) { last }
}
print "\nI made it to zero.\n";
```

displays

```
3  2  1
I made it to zero.
```

The `next` statement tells Perl to jump up to the top of the loop and perform the test in the conditional again. You often use `next` to avoid executing the rest of the lines in a block.

Another similar statement, `redo`, is rarely used. Like `next`, it causes Perl to jump to the top of a block but not go through the logical test, whereas `next` always results in a test. You're best off using `last` to get out of a loop at the end of a block or `next` to jump back up to the top.

Yet another form of the `while` loop exists, but it's rarely used:

```
while(LOGICAL) { BLOCK1 } continue { BLOCK2 }
```

In this case, `BLOCK2` is executed after `BLOCK1` but before the `LOGICAL` is tested a second time. The value of constructing a statement such as this is that `BLOCK2` gets executed even if you use `next`. You can use this treatment if you want some steps that are executed after a `next` or at the end of `BLOCK1`, such as some "cleanup" steps or steps that check to see if any more data is left to process.

Souped-up loops: The `for` statement

Although `while` loops are pretty useful, they aren't the end-all-be-all loop mechanism. For example, if you have a counter that increments in your loop and you use that counter for the conditional test, it may be desirable to put the test and the incrementing together in a single statement so that they are easier to see. For that task, Perl offers the `for` statement.

The format of a `for` loop looks like the following:

```
for(INIT; LOGICAL; REINIT) { BLOCK }
```

In the preceding line, INIT is a statement that is executed once before the loop begins, LOGICAL is a test just like that in a while loop, and REINIT is a statement that is executed just before LOGICAL is tested after each round through the loop (except the first).

For example, a for loop may say to Perl

```
for($i = 0; $i <10; $i +=1) { print "$i " }
```

This displays

```
0 1 2 3 4 5 6 7 8 9
```

The for loop acts exactly like the while loop but is more compactly built. For example, the format

```
for(INIT; LOGICAL; REINIT) { BLOCK }
```

is identical to

```
INIT;
while(LOGICAL)
    { BLOCK }
continue
    { REINIT }
```

To get a better idea of how the for loop works, examine the following chunk of code:

```
# hexchart.pl: Prints a decimal-to-hex conversion chart.
@HexD = ('0', '1', '2', '3', '4', '5', '6', '7', '8',
    '9', 'A', 'B', 'C', 'D', 'E', 'F');
for($i = 0; $i <= 255; $i += 1) {
    printf("%3s=$HexD[int($i / 16)]$HexD[$i % 16]  ", $i);
    if(($i % 8) == 7) { print "\n" }
}
```

In this block, the for loop is used to count from 0 to 255, and the block itself is designed to display data. The printf statement in the block uses the value of the counter $i in its calculations, and the if statement uses $i to decide where to put in line breaks.

Perl's for loops really come in handy when you need to cycle through a limited set of values and execute a block on each. It is an efficient way of defining a loop in a single argument and allowing the associated block to do the basic processing work.

For and more: The foreach statement

At times, you may want to use the data in a list to do some element-by-element processing. For example, if the list is a set of words in a sentence, you may want to look at each word to determine if it matches some specific value. Or, if the list is a set of numerical measurements, you may want to determine which items in the list exceed a certain test value.

You can use `while` and `for` statements to step through each element in a list, but Perl offers you a simpler way to accomplish the same task — the `foreach` statement — which looks like this:

```
foreach $VARIABLE (LIST) { BLOCK }
```

This statement says that for each item in the list, Perl sets `$VARIABLE` to the value of the element and executes the `BLOCK`. For example:

```
@StartTimes = (25.6, 34.0, 26.7, 30.8, 32.7);
@LowTimes = ();
foreach $i (@StartTimes) {
     if($i < 30 ) {
          print "$i is a low time.\n";
          push(@LowTimes, $i);
     }
}
```

The previous block results in the following output

```
25.6 is a low time.
26.7 is a low time.
```

and the list `@LowTimes` ends up with the value `(25.6, 26.7)`.

If necessary, a `foreach` statement can contain a `continue` statement, such as the following:

```
foreach $VARIABLE (LIST) { BLOCK1 } continue { BLOCK2 }
```

For added convenience: The map statement

Another function, `map`, offers even more convenience than `foreach` in some cases. The `map` function returns a list based on executing either a Perl expression or an entire block on each element of a list. Note that `map` does not change the list in its argument: It returns a different list. (This function is available only with Perl 5 and later versions.)

If you have a single expression that you want to execute on each element of a list, you can use

```
map(EXPRESSION, LIST);
```

For example, if you want the lowercase equivalent of every string in a list, you can use

```
@LCWords = map(lc, @Input);
```

Or if you want a list that is the logarithm of all the numbers in another list, you can use

```
@Logs = map(log, @Measurements);
```

If you have a block that you want to execute on each element of a list, you would use a different format for `map`:

```
map { BLOCK } LIST;
```

At the beginning of the `BLOCK`, the Perl special variable `$_` is set to the value of the element being examined. (The `$_` variable is described in more detail in Chapter 14.) For example, if you want to create a list of elements and put them all in lowercase, you can use

```
@AllLC = map { if(lc($_) eq $_) { $_ } } @Input;
```

You can even make this example a bit more interesting by returning the elements that are all lowercase and returning the string `error` for every element that isn't lowercase. To do that, you'd use

```
@AllLC = map
    { if(lc($_) eq $_) { $_ } else { 'error' } }
    @Input;
```

Using Expressions as Logical Values

The conditional and loop statements listed to this point in the chapter all use comparison statements in their arguments. Perl does not require that you use comparisons in conditional and loop statements, however. You can put anything in the argument to `if` or `while`, for example. Comparisons make the most sense to beginners because they are simple to construct, but Perl *expressions* can be used as well.

Every Perl expression returns some value. If you use an expression as an argument to a conditional or loop statement and the expression returns a value of 0 or a null string, the expression is treated as "false" and any returned value other than 0 is treated as "true."

Using expressions in the arguments of conditional statements is a good way to make your programs more compact, although doing so sometimes affects the readability of the program. For example, if you have the conditional statement

```
if($Counter != 0) { ... some statements... }
```

you can replace it with

```
if($Counter) { ... some statements... }
```

In this case, `$Counter` being not equal to 0 is the same as `$Counter` being true, and therefore you can simply use its value in the argument to `if`.

Some Perl functions return a true value if they are successful and a false value if they are not. You can use those functions in `if`, `while`, and other statements instead of comparisons. (In Chapter 14, I describe how to write subroutines, which return values, so you can also use subroutines as logical values.)

The `open` function

The `open` function is used to open text files. (You can find more on `open` in Chapter 4.) Programs return true if they successfully open a file and false if they don't (such as when a file can't be found). Armed with this knowledge, you can write a program like this:

```
$CheckOpen = open(DATA, "datafile.txt");
unless($CheckOpen)
    { die "The file datafile.txt could not be opened." }
```

The `unless` statement looks to see whether `open` returned a false value, and if so, `unless` causes the program to quit with the `die` statement. The previous three lines can be shortened to

```
unless(open(DATA, "datafile.txt"))
    { die "The file datafile.txt could not be opened." }
```

Short-circuit logic: and *operators and* or *operators*

In Perl, the `or` and `and` operators (and their Perl 4 equivalents of `||` and `&&`) "short-circuit" the evaluation of a statement. Perl evaluates only statements that are strung together with `or` or `and` if it must in order to determine the result of the logical expression.

The `or` operator and `and` operator are not exactly the same as `||` and `&&`, but they're close enough. Serious Perl programmers will tell you that `or` and `and` take "lower precedence" than `||` and `&&` and lower precedence than many other operators. *Precedence* refers to the order in which operators are evaluated if they aren't placed within parentheses. Therefore, avoid using `or` and `and` in places in which you aren't surrounding your function arguments with parentheses. Always use parentheses to prevent any misunderstanding, regardless of the operators and functions you use.

The `or` comparison is true if either the statement to the left of the `or` operator is true or the statement to the right of the operator is true. Therefore, the statement

```
STATEMENT1 or STATEMENT2
```

means "Evaluate `STATEMENT1`; if it is true, ignore `STATEMENT2`."

In the following `open` statement, Perl first evaluates `open(INFILE, $TheFile)`. If that expression returns true, Perl doesn't even evaluate the expression on the right side of the `or` operator. So, a true value "short-circuits" Perl's examination of whatever is to the right of the `or` operator (in this case, the `die` statement).

```
open(INFILE, $TheFile) or die "The file $TheFile could " .
    "not be found.\n";
```

"Short-circuiting" Perl by using the `and` operator has similar results. Because an `and` comparison is true only if both sides of the comparison are true, no reason exists for Perl to look at the right side if the left side is false. Therefore, the statement

```
STATEMENT1 and STATEMENT2
```

means "Evaluate `STATEMENT1`; if it is false, ignore `STATEMENT2`." You can use this statement when you are sure you don't want Perl to execute a second statement unless the first one returns a true value.

Caveat Emptor: Jumping around Programs by Using Labels

Perl, like most programming languages, allows you to jump around your programs at will. In this chapter, you can see how to do that with conditional and loop statements. *Labels,* by comparison, allow you to jump to a named part of your program.

Using labels is generally a bad idea. I'm not saying that you should completely avoid using labels; but in general, you're better off using other Perl mechanisms because labels make your program difficult to read. Nevertheless, you may see them in programs written by people who disagree with me, and you may want to use them yourself, but I find that they're more trouble than they're worth.

In Perl, a label is indicated by a single word followed by a colon. By tradition, labels are shown in all uppercase, but mixed case is also allowable. A label can appear before a loop statement (such as `while`, `until`, `for`, and `foreach`), or it can appear by itself before a block.

Perl programmers commonly use labels to avoid using a loop. The `last` or `next` statements inside a block redirect Perl to the beginning or end of the block, just as they do in loop statements. The `last` and `next` statements, when used with labels that tell the program where to jump to, are useful for determining if a certain value is one of many different values and then doing something different based on each outcome.

For example, assume that the variable `$CheckID` holds the ID number of a product. If that ID is one of three special values, then you'll want to print one of three different messages; otherwise, you just want to put that ID into the end of a list for later searching. This sort of program makes use of a `last` statement, and the program may look like this:

```
ID1CHECK: {
       if($CheckID == 101) {
          print "Supervisor's signature required.\n";
          last ID1CHECK;
       }
       if($CheckID == 121) {
          print "Backordered.\n";
          last ID1CHECK;
       }
       if($CheckID == 131) {
          print "Import duties apply.\n";
```

(continued)

(continued)

```
            last ID1CHECK;
        }
        #  Here if everything is OK
        push(@OnHold, $CheckID);
}
```

You can also use Perl labels with the `goto` statement. The `goto` statement causes Perl to jump from wherever the statement is to the label. Some programmers will tell you to never, ever use `goto`. A decade or so ago, many professional programmers began to claim that unsystematic jumping with `goto` (or its equivalent in other languages) was inherently evil and counter-productive, and they tried to get everyone to agree. They're probably right to some degree, but I'm not absolutely set against it. Nevertheless, I recommend against using `goto` statements.

Another bad idea is the `reset` statement, which can be used in loops to reset the values of variables to their initial state. Because it's so troublesome, I'm not even going to tell you how to use a `reset` statement. If you see it used in somebody else's Perl program and are curious about what `reset` does, you can find out in Appendix B. But don't even think about using it yourself. Really.

Chapter 9

Operators and Functions for Doing More-Advanced Stuff

In This Chapter

- Locating text in strings
- Formatting text
- Using random numbers
- Checking the time
- Programming for Y2K
- Handling bits one at a time
- Turning lists into strings
- Sorting lists

If you've perused the previous chapters in this part of the book, you should have a pretty solid grounding on Perl's basic string, numeric, and list operators and statements. In this chapter, I delve into intermediate-level Perl features on a wide variety of topics that let you spread your wings a bit and explore additional programming possibilities.

Using Undefined Variables

A basic rule for constructing statements in Perl is that you should always define your variables before using them on the right side of an assignment. Doing so prevents Perl from inserting default values for undefined variables.

You may, however, have some good reasons for using undefined variables. For instance, the `pop` function covered in Chapter 7 returns an undefined value if you are trying to `pop` from an empty list. This is preferable to its returning a false value because false is a perfectly reasonable value for an item in a list.

Because some functions return an undefined value, you want to be able to determine if an undefined value was in fact returned. That's when you can make use of the `defined` function. The `defined` function takes one argument, an expression, and returns true if the argument is defined and false if that argument is undefined. For example,

```
unless(defined($Yummy = pop(@Bonbons)))
      { print "There are no more bonbons left." }
```

After executing the preceding statements, the variable `$Yummy` contains the value popped off the `@Bonbons` list. But, if the list is empty, the `defined` function will return false, Perl will print the message about the depleted supply of bonbons, and `$Yummy` will hold the undefined value.

Looking for Strings within Strings

As I note in Chapter 5, strings are groups of characters. At times, you may want to examine a *substring,* a string that is part of a larger string.

Using the `substr` function

The `substr` function lets you view just a part of a string in many different ways. The `substr` function returns a string that is a substring of a larger string. Its format is

```
substr(FULLSTRING, POSITION, LENGTH)
```

The first character is at position 0, the second character at position 1, and so on. If you want to count from the right side of the string instead of from the left side, use a negative number for the position.

For example

```
$Small = substr("This is a long string", 5, 4);
print $Small;
```

displays

```
is a
```

because `is a` are the four letters (a space is also a letter) that start from position 5 from the left side of the string. However,

```
$Small = substr("This is a long string", -5, 4);
print $Small;
```

displays

```
trin
```

because `trin` are the four letters that start from the fifth position from the right side of the string.

You do not have to include a length argument with the `substr` function. If you leave the argument off, Perl returns everything from the position specified in the second argument to the end of the string. For example,

```
print substr("This is a long string", 5);
```

displays

```
is a long string
```

You can also use the `substr` function on the left side of an assignment to add a substring into a string. In that case, the first argument is the name of the string variable you want to change, and the length is the number of characters you want to delete from the full string at the position that the substring is being added. You can probably understand this function better by examining a few examples, so here goes.

To add a substring without removing anything that's already there, set the length argument to 0. For example, if you tell Perl

```
$TestStr = "Long string";
substr($TestStr, 4, 0) = "er";
print $TestStr;
```

Perl displays

```
Longer string
```

To delete some characters as you add others, set the length argument to the number of characters you want to delete:

```
$TestStr = "Long string";
substr($TestStr, -3, 3) = "ange trip";
print $TestStr;
```

displays

```
Long strange trip
```

If you are using Perl version 5.005 or later, the `substr` function has a fourth argument that lets you specify a replacement string right in the `substr` function. So, if you're working with Perl 5.005 or a later version, the previous example can be written as:

```
# Works in Perl 5.005 or later only
$TestStr = "Long string";
substr($TestStr, -3, 3, "ange trip");
print $TestStr;
```

and the result would be the same.

Using the `index` function

Instead of looking in a string by location, you may want to look into a string to see if a particular substring lurks inside of it. The `index` function works great for this purpose. The format of the function is

```
index(FULLSTRING, SUBSTRING, POSITION)
```

The previous statement tells Perl to look for the substring in the full string, starting at the given position. If you do not fill in that position, Perl starts at the left side, position 0.

Perl returns the first position at the point where the beginning of the substring is found. If the string isn't found, Perl returns -1, the position before the first position. For example,

```
print index("Will call", "ll");
```

displays

```
2
```

But note that

```
print index("Will call", "L");
```

displays

```
-1
```

Using the `rindex` function

The `rindex` function is the complement of the `index` function: It returns the position of the last (that is, the rightmost) match for the string:

```
print rindex("Will call", "ll");
```

displays

```
7
```

Applying Some Fancy Formatting to Text and Numbers

The `print` statement (described in Chapter 5) is very flexible, but it isn't good at restricting what it prints. For example, you may want to print a column of numbers, some of which are two-digit numbers and some of which are three-digit numbers. The following is an example of that:

```
for($i = 98; $i <= 101; $i += 1) { print "$i\n" }
```

This statement displays

```
98
99
100
101
```

However, you may want the right side of the numbers to all line up nicely, like this:

```
 98
 99
100
101
```

No easy way exists to right-align a column of numbers with the `print` statement. However, `print` has a cousin called `printf` that lets you specify a format for each argument you print. The function looks like

```
printf(FORMAT, LIST)
```

where the format is a string that tells Perl the format of the output, and the list is a list of items that will be formatted using that string.

An almost-identical function to `printf`, the `sprintf` function, is used for assigning strings. `sprintf` returns what `printf` would have printed so that you can then assign the returned value to a string variable.

The `printf` function is very powerful and gives you lots of flexibility in how you format your strings and numbers. Unfortunately, the strings used in formatting are not all that easy to remember. To be honest, they're downright complicated, and many Perl programmers have to look in the Perl online manual every time they use format strings. Nevertheless, you should find out how to use strings for formatting because the results are worth it.

Each format string starts with a percent sign (%). The format string consists of four parts, the first three of which are optional:

- A flag to indicate what will come before the output
- The minimum field width
- The precision
- The field type

It actually makes sense to examine the parts of a format string in reverse order because the last segments are the most important ones.

- The *field type* tells Perl the type of format to use. The field type options are listed in Table 9-1.

Table 9-1 Field Type Options

Option	*Description*
s	String
d	Integer
f	Real number
g	Compact real number
u	Unsigned integer
x	Hexadecimal (lowercase)
X	Hexadecimal (uppercase)
o	Octal
e	Scientific notation (lowercase)
E	Scientific notation (uppercase)
c	Single character (by value)
ld	Long integer
lu	Long unsigned integer
lx	Long hexadecimal
lo	Long octal

- The *precision,* which is optional, is expressed as a period (.) followed by a number. For real numbers and scientific notation, the precision is the number of digits shown after the decimal point in the resulting string. For strings, it consists of the maximum number of characters extracted from the beginning of the string.
- The *minimum field width* tells Perl that it should pad a number or string to a certain width, which is quite useful for getting columns to line up. For example, if you have a column of two-digit and three-digit numbers, you would set the minimum field width to 3 to get the padding on the left of the two-digit numbers. Note that if the number doesn't fit in the minimum field width given, Perl will use additional characters as needed to print the number correctly.
- The *flag* can be one of five values. The flags are used mostly with numbers, rather than strings and characters. Table 9-2 explains the meaning of each flag.

Table 9-2 Flag Values and What They Mean

Flag	Meaning
+	A + or - should always appear in the output.
-	Left-adjust the output (this also works with strings).
0	Pad the number with zeros instead of spaces, if needed.
#	Use the alternate form. In hexadecimal, this flag causes 0x or 0X to be placed before the number; for octal, this flag causes a 0 to be put before the number.

In addition to the flag values shown in Table 9-2, one more flag can be used. A *blank space* inserts a space before positive numbers so that they line up with negative numbers.

Got all that? Don't worry if you haven't. It becomes clearer when you see some examples. For instance, the following shows how to format a real number so that only two decimal places show:

```
$TestNum = 283.357;
printf("%.2f", $TestNum);
```

This displays

```
283.36
```

Note that Perl correctly rounded the number before truncating the extra digits. The following is a similar example, using scientific notation:

```
$TestNum = 283.357;
printf("%.2E", $TestNum);
```

This displays

```
2.83E+02
```

A format string can have text other than the actual format string in it. As long as your other text doesn't have any percent signs (%), Perl interprets the other characters as text to be displayed. For example,

```
$TestNum = 283.357;
printf("The answer is %.2f, give or take.", $TestNum);
```

displays

```
The answer is 283.36, give or take.
```

If you want to display a percent sign, you must use two percent signs together:

```
printf("Two thirds is about %.3f%%.", ((2/3)*100));
```

This displays

```
Two thirds is about 66.667%.
```

The examples so far in this section of the chapter have just a single formatted number. However, a format string can specify many values with different formats. The following statements,

```
$Str = "Two thirds is about ";
$Num = (2/3)*100;
printf('%s%.3f%s', $Str, $Num, '%.');
```

are another way of displaying the string in the previous example:

```
Two thirds is about 66.667%.
```

The `sprintf` function works just like `printf`, except that it returns strings instead of printing them. For example, you may use it in a statement such as the following:

```
$Answer = sprintf("The answer is %.2f.", $TestNum);
```

The program in Listing 9-1 shows you all the different permutations of the various formats. The output of those formats is shown in Listing 9-2. The program shows a way to use `printf` to get two columns of text to line up when the length of the material in the first column changes. By using `printf` with a format of `%-29s`, the program forces the second column to start in position 30, regardless of what was in the first column. The program also uses a *subroutine,* which I cover in Chapter 10.

Note: Some versions of Perl may output slightly different answers than those you see in Listing 9-2.

Listing 9-1: Here you see the entire printf.pl program, which is designed to output the formatting examples you can see in Listing 9-2.

```
$Str = 'Dummies';
$Num = 3.141593;
$Int = 4142;
@StrFmts = ('s', '4s', '.4s', '4.4s', '10.4s',
    '10.9s', '-10.9s' );
print "The original string is \"$Str\"\n";
&OutList(@StrFmts, $Str);
@NumFmts = (
    'd', '4d', '.4d', '4.4d', '10.4d', '10.10d',
    '-4.4d', '+4.4d', ' 4.4d', '04.4d',
    'f', '4f', '.4f', '4.4f', '10.4f', '10.10f',
    '-10.4f', '+10.4f', ' 10.4f', '010.4f',
    'e', '4e', '.4e', '4.4e', '10.4e', '10.10e',
    '-10.4e', '+10.4e', ' 10.4e', '010.4e',
    'g', '4g', '.4g', '4.4g', '10.4g', '10.10g',
'-10.4g', '+10.4g', ' 10.4g', '010.4g',
);
print "\nThe original number is $Num\n";
&OutList(@NumFmts, $Num);
@HOFmts = ('x', 'X', '3x', '.3x', '3.3x', '10.3x',
    '10.10x', '#x', 'o', '#o' );
print "\nAnd a few hexa and octal examples on $Int.\n";
&OutList(@HOFmts, $Int);

sub OutList {
    local($TestStr) = pop(@_);
    local(@TestFmts) = @_;
    local(@OutFmts, $Fmt);
    foreach $Fmt (@TestFmts) {
        unshift(@OutFmts, sprintf("%s%$Fmt%s", ("%$Fmt=|",
            $TestStr, "|")));
    }
    until(@OutFmts == 0) {
        printf('%-29s%-29s%s',
        pop(@OutFmts), pop(@OutFmts), "\n");
    }
}
```

Listing 9-2: The output of the printf1.pl program shown in Listing 9-1.

```
The original string is "Dummies"
%s=|Dummies|                      %4s=|Dummies|
%.4s=|Dumm|                       %4.4s=|Dumm|
%10.4s=|      Dumm|               %10.9s=|   Dummies|
%-10.9s=|Dummies   |

The original number is 3.141593
%d=|3|                            %4d=|   3|
%.4d=|0003|                       %4.4d=|0003|
%10.4d=|      0003|               %10.10d=|0000000003|
%-4.4d=|0003|                     %+4.4d=|+0003|
% 4.4d=| 0003|                    %04.4d=|0003|
%f=|3.141593|                     %4f=|3.141593|
%.4f=|3.1416|                     %4.4f=|3.1416|
%10.4f=|    3.1416|               %10.10f=|3.1415930000|
%-10.4f=|3.1416    |              %+10.4f=|   +3.1416|
% 10.4f=|    3.1416|              %010.4f=|00003.1416|
%e=|3.141593e+00|                 %4e=|3.141593e+00|
%.4e=|3.1416e+00|                 %4.4e=|3.1416e+00|
%10.4e=|3.1416e+00|               %10.10e=|3.1415930000e+00|
%-10.4e=|3.1416e+00|              %+10.4e=|+3.1416e+00|
% 10.4e=| 3.1416e+00|             %010.4e=|3.1416e+00|
%g=|3.14159|                      %4g=|3.14159|
%.4g=|3.142|                      %4.4g=|3.142|
%10.4g=|     3.142|               %10.10g=|  3.141593|
%-10.4g=|3.142     |              %+10.4g=|    +3.142|
% 10.4g=|     3.142|              %010.4g=|000003.142|

And a few hexa and octal examples on 4142.
%x=|102e|                         %X=|102E|
%3x=|102e|                        %.3x=|102e|
%3.3x=|102e|                      %10.3x=|      102e|
%10.10x=|000000102e|              %#x=|0x102e|
%o=|10056|                        %#o=|010056|
```

Keeping Track of the Time

All computers are good at keeping time, and Perl gives users easy access to the current time through four functions. You can include these functions in your programs for displaying the current time and date, determining how long something takes to run, displaying the age of a file, and other neat tricks.

The `time` function, which has no arguments, is the number of non-leap year seconds since January 1, 1970. (In MacPerl, it is the number of seconds since January 1, 1904.) You use this function with the `localtime` and `gmtime` functions to find out the month, day, and so on.

By itself, the `time` function isn't all that useful. For example,

```
print time;
```

prints

```
904500209
```

(Well, that's what it printed at the time I wrote this.)

The `localtime` function takes a time as its argument and returns a list of nine elements:

- Second
- Minute
- Hour
- Day of month
- Month (January = 0, February = 1, . . .)
- Years since 1900
- Weekday (Sunday = 0, Monday = 1, . . .)
- Day of the year (January 1 = 0, January 2 = 1, . . .)
- Whether the local time zone is using daylight saving time (true or false)

The following lines demonstrate one common way to use the `localtime` function to receive information on the current time:

```
 ($Second, $Minute, $Hour, $DayOfMonth, $Month, $Year,
    $WeekDay, $DayOfYear, $IsDST) = localtime(time);
$RealMonth = $Month + 1;
print "$RealMonth/$DayOfMonth/$Year";
```

displays

```
9/13/98
```

For this program, you have to add 1 to the month before you use it in a date string. If you forget to do that (as many people do), your month will be off by 1.

The `gmtime` function returns the time as Greenwich Mean Time (as in Greenwich, England), which is the basis of standard time throughout the world.

If you want to display the date and time in a standard format (with each number in two digits), you have to use the `printf` function that I cover in the section "Applying Some Fancy Formatting to Text and Numbers" earlier in this chapter. The following statement produces that standard format:

```
printf('%02d:%02d:%02d %02d/%02d/%02d', $Hour, $Minute,
    $Second, $RealMonth, $DayOfMonth, $Year);
```

displays

```
15:40:01 09/13/98
```

If you want to use *list slices* (covered in Chapter 8) instead of explicit variable names, you can use something like the following:

```
@DayNames = ('Sun', 'Mon', 'Tues', 'Wed', 'Thur',
    'Fri', 'Sat');
@TimeArr = localtime(time);
print $DayNames[$TimeArr[6]];
```

In the chunk of code I just listed, `$TimeArr[6]` is the element that represents the current weekday and is used to pick the element out of `@DayNames` for the current weekday name.

Another time-related function is `sleep`. The argument is the number of seconds you want Perl to take a nap. For instance, if you want your program to do nothing for two seconds, you would enter

```
sleep(2);
```

Keeping Track of the Year 2000

By now, almost everyone has heard about the massive computer problems that may potentially occur come January 1, 2000. All computer programs, in any computer language, that have handled years as two-digit integers, may develop problems when the year goes from "99" to "00" if those programs are comparing the year values. This glitch has become known as the *Year 2000 bug* (or *Y2K bug* for short).

For instance, assume you store years as two-digit numbers and calculate the difference in years by subtracting the first date from the second date. You will get a negative number if the first date is in 1998 and the second date is in 2000 because you will be subtracting 98 from 00, which gives you –98, not 2 as you hoped.

Fortunately, Perl never stores years in two-digit integers unless you work really hard at making it do that (which, of course, you shouldn't). All Perl integers can have far more than two digits. But, that doesn't mean you can safely ignore the Year 2000 problem when you program. In fact, I know of a Y2K-related mistake that some Perl programmers have been making over the past few years.

When you use the `localtime` and `gmtime` functions, the year returned from those functions is the number of years since the year 1900, not the two-digit year number. This has a significant effect on the way that you program for display. Take the example from the preceding section of this chapter:

```
 ($Second, $Minute, $Hour, $DayOfMonth, $Month, $Year,
    $WeekDay, $DayOfYear, $IsDST) = localtime(time);
$RealMonth = $Month + 1;
print "$RealMonth/$DayOfMonth/$Year";
```

Assuming that you run the program in 1998, this program displays

```
9/13/98
```

However, if you run the program two years later, it displays:

```
9/13/100
```

which is clearly not what you wanted it to display.

For all your programs that display year values taken from the `localtime` and `gmtime` functions, you must take into account the fact that the year returned is the number of years since 1900. You can do that in either one of two ways:

- Display a four-digit year by adding `1900` to the value returned. This causes your displayed dates to look like `9/13/1998` and `9/13/2000`, which assures accuracy.
- Check if the value returned is greater than 100, and if so, subtract 100 from the returned value. This will always give you a one-digit or two-digit number, but you will not know whether the time period being described is 1900–1999 or 2000–2099.

I strongly prefer the first solution, because you always know which time period is being displayed. However, if you insist on using the second solution, the following is some Perl code that always returns a two-digit year:

```
($Second, $Minute, $Hour, $DayOfMonth, $Month, $Year,
    $WeekDay, $DayOfYear, $IsDST) = localtime(time);
$RealMonth = $Month + 1;
$ShortYear = ($Year % 100);  # Use modulo arithmetic
printf('%02d/%02d/%02d', $RealMonth, $DayOfMonth,
    $ShortYear);
```

When you run this program in the year 2000, you'll get a display that looks like this:

```
09/13/00
```

Picking Numbers at Random

A few programming tasks require the use of *random numbers*. For example, if you use Perl to write games, you may want to create a game that involves an element of chance, such as the rolling of dice. You may also want to generate some random numbers by picking random records from a database.

The `rand` function returns a somewhat random real number between 0 and the argument you give to the function. (I say "somewhat random" because these aren't true random numbers; I explain the difference a little later in this section.) If you don't have an argument, `rand` returns a random real number between 0 and 1. For example, the following statement produces a random integer between 1 and 10:

```
$PickANumber = int(rand(10)) + 1;
```

Because `rand` in this example chooses a number between 0 and 10, the `int` function produces integers between 0 and 9. To increase the range to between 1 and 10, you add 1 to the result.

Perl's `rand` function does not produce truly random numbers. In fact, if you don't tell Perl which seed to use, Perl produces the same series of numbers each time you run Perl. (The *seed* is the first random number in the series of random values that Perl returns.) If you want numbers that look really random, you must set the seed for the random values with Perl's `srand` function.

The `srand` function takes a single argument that is used as the seed. If you do not specify an argument for `srand`, it uses the current value from `time`. For example, a program that resets the seed to the current time would look like this:

```
srand();
$PickANumber = int(rand(10)) + 1;
```

The rand function is not meant to be used in strong cryptography (that is, codes that cannot be broken even with a great deal of concerted effort) or other applications that require truly random numbers. Unless you employ a foolproof method for picking the seed for srand, a clever hacker who knows you're using Perl can figure out the random-number seed with little effort.

Shifting Bits with Bit-Level Operators

Numbers in the land of Perl are either false (with a value of 0) or true (with any value other than 0). Each bit in a byte has a value of either 1 or 0. For bits, a value of 1 translates to true and 0 translates to false. Therefore, you can think of a byte, which has eight bits, as something that holds eight true-false values. You can operate on the bits in Perl's numbers using logical operators (which I describe in more depth in Chapter 8).

The three basic bit-level logical operators for combining two numbers are | (or), & (and), and ^ (exclusive or). You always want to use these operators on integers. Perl won't let you use them on real numbers because Perl truncates a real number before using the operators (see Chapter 6 for more information on real numbers). Normally, bit-wise logic is used on hexadecimal and octal numbers. However, Perl typically displays all numbers as real numbers, so you have to use the printf function to display your results in hexadecimal. For example, the following printf statement

```
$H1 = 0xfed0; $H2 = 0xedc4;
$Result = $H1 & $H2;
printf("The 'and' of %x and %x is %x", $H1, $H2, $Result);
```

displays

```
The 'and' of fed0 and edc4 is ecc0
```

printf is necessary in order to get Perl to print hexadecimal values. If you instead use

```
print "The 'and' of $H1 and $H2 is $Result";
```

Perl displays

```
The 'and' of 65232 and 60868 is 60608
```

Perl also employs something called a *unary bit-wise negation operator*, ~ (a tilde), which turns all 1 bits into 0, and 0 bits into 1. For example, if you write the following:

```
$H3 = 0xfed0;
$H4 = ~$H3;
printf("The negation of %x (%d) is %x (%d)",
    $H3, $H3, $H4, $H4);
```

Perl prints

```
The negation of fed0 (65232) is ffff012f (-65233)
```

The negation operator (~) and the exclusive-or operator (^) work on values that are 32 bits long. Most systems that run Perl use 32-bit integers, but not all do. This means that bit-moving logic that runs fine on one operating system may not run well on another. Some versions of Unix, for example, go one way, while other versions of Unix go the other.

You can shift numbers one bit at a time with the << and >> operators. These operators move a number to the left of an operator by the number of bits to the right of the operator. As you may guess, << shifts bits to the left and >> shifts bits to the right. For example, given the following lines,

```
$H3 = 0x0f30;
$H4 = $H3 << 2;
printf("The left shift of %x (%d) by 2 bits is %x (%d)",
    $H3, $H3, $H4, $H4);
```

Perl displays

```
The left shift of f30 (3888) by 2 bits is 3cc0 (15552)
```

Converting Lists to Strings

It's relatively easy in Perl to print data that consist of numbers and text. Printing lists, however, is another matter. Consider the following:

```
@Nums = (2.7, 80, 46.2);
@Strs = ("Who's", "on", "first?");
print @Nums, "\n";
print @Strs, "\n";
```

The preceding lines of code run the values in the lists together, with somewhat unattractive results:

```
2.78046.2
Who'sonfirst?
```

Because printing lists where the values don't get squished together is desirable, Perl has a nifty way to convert a list into a string with whatever characters you want between each list item. You can accomplish this with the `join` function. The `join` function takes two arguments: the separator (which can be as many characters as you want) and the list. For example,

```
@Nums = (2.7, 80, 46.2);
@Strs = ("Who's", "on", "first?");
print join('--', @Nums), "\n";
print join(' ', @Strs), "\n";
```

gives you the following results, which read a lot better than the previous example:

```
2.7--80--46.2
Who's on first?
```

The `join` function is also handy for printing list elements on separate lines, as shown in the following example.

```
@Nums = (2.7, 80, 46.2);
print join("\n", @Nums), "\n";
```

The `join` function returns a string, so it is also useful outside of the `print` function. For example, to create a string that is a tab-delimited record, you can use

```
@Nums = (2.7, 80, 46.2);
$TheRecord = join("\t", @Nums);
```

Rearranging Lists

In Chapter 7, I explain how to put lists together, how to look at just parts of lists, how to pull items out of lists, and how to stuff (or splice) items into lists. Here, I describe how to rearrange the order of the elements in lists.

If I say to you, "Name two ways you may want to change the order of some of your lists," you might reply, "reverse the order" and "sort the items." Perl, being the versatile language that it is, has simple functions to accomplish both of these tasks.

The reverse function reverses the items in its argument. For example,

```
@Strs = ("Who's", "on", "first?");
print join(' ', reverse(@Strs));
```

displays

```
first? on Who's
```

As you may have guessed, you use the sort function to sort lists. The sort function returns the original list in sorted order. Perl also lets you define how sort will sort.

If you want to sort your list in alphabetical order, use the sort function with a single argument, namely, the list. For example, the following statement,

```
@Strs = ('cognition', 'attune', 'bell');
print join(' ', sort @Strs);
```

displays

```
attune bell cognition
```

Another more-complicated form of the sort function lets you define the method Perl uses to sort. This form has two arguments: a block or subroutine that tells Perl how you want to sort, and the list itself (Chapter 10 offers more information on subroutines). In the following example, the block compares two values, $a and $b, and returns a -1, 0, or 1 depending on how $a compares with $b. The cmp and <=> operators really come in handy here (I cover those operators in Chapter 8).

For example, assume that you want to sort a list of strings by their length and ignore their alphabetical order. You can use

```
@Strs = ('cognition', 'attune', 'bell');
print join(' ', sort { length($a) <=> length($b) } @Strs);
```

which displays

```
bell attune cognition
```

If you were using sort with subroutines, the previous example would look something like the following:

```
sub lensort { length($a) <=> length($b) }
@Strs = ('cognition', 'attune', 'bell');
print join(' ', sort lensort @Strs);
```

Part III

More of the Nuts and Bolts of Perl

"Sure, at first it sounded great – an intuitive network adapter that helps people write memos by finishing their thoughts for them."

In this part . . .

The chapters in this part describe some of the "intermediate" techniques you need to know in order to put together even more useful and versatile Perl programs. You can find out about object-oriented Perl, how Perl can process databases, and its ability to help you grab files off the Internet.

Chapter 10

Perl and CGI: Web Server Programs Demystified

In This Chapter

- Understanding how CGI works with Web servers
- Creating simple HTML documents
- Reading user requests in forms
- Processing Web forms
- Redirecting users to other sites

Unless you've spent the past few years in a cave without a battery pack and a phone hook-up, you probably have heard lots of talk (maybe too much) about the World Wide Web and the wonders that it brings to all of us. Chalk up another plus for the Web: It has done more than anything else for promoting the widespread use of Perl.

The Web has had an enormous impact on the popularity of the Perl programming language. That's because Perl can be used in tandem with Web servers to make your Web pages more interactive and informative. A large measure of the work you do using Perl and the Web involves the creation of on-screen forms designed to get information from users and then return it to you. The information generated by these forms is handled by *Common Gateway Interface (CGI)* programs, a topic that also gets a fair amount of coverage in this chapter.

The most interesting aspect of HTML as it relates to Perl is HTML forms. How to process a form after a user has completed it is a topic I just happen to cover in this chapter. If you need some brushing up on HTML, which you need to know before you do much with a Web server, check out *HTML For Dummies,* 3rd Edition, by Ed Tittel and Steve James (IDG Books Worldwide, Inc.).

Programs That Live to Serve

If you create Web sites, you can just put up pages of static and unchanging text and graphics. It's more likely, however, that the contents of your pages change depending on the needs of the person visiting your Web site. Many ways exist to determine how user interaction changes what the user sees on-screen, and all of them involve programming on some level.

This chapter shows you how you can use Perl to augment your *Web server* (the program that processes requests for documents sent over the Internet). When a user requests a Web page from a Web server, that request gets transmitted to a Web server. The Web server then determines what to do with the request.

If the request is simple (for example, "Show me this page of information"), the Web server simply retrieves that information from a disk and transmits it to the user. If the request is more complicated, such as "I just filled in this form, now do something with it," "Search for this and that text," or "Let me look at this restricted area," you need to use a program of some sort in order to determine what the user is requesting and supply exactly what it is that he or she wants.

Perl can take a Web request, even a very complex one, and break it into its individual parts fairly easily. Perl is also adept at pulling together disparate pieces of information and presenting them in a single coherent form, which is precisely what you're trying to accomplish when you build a Web page.

The dozens of different kinds of Web servers all have their own requirements for how they interact with Perl. Therefore, this chapter does not cover how to set up your server to interact with Perl, but I do tell you what to do after you follow your Web server's instructions on how to hook together the server with a programming language such as Perl. The methods for working with Web servers that I cover in this chapter are for typical Unix Web servers; but very similar programs also work with Windows and Macintosh Web servers.

The Ins and Outs of CGI and Web Servers

From the Web's earliest days, Web servers have needed a way to interact with programming languages. The early programmers who created Web servers decided to use a single, standard method for connecting programs to their servers, instead of having to use a different method for each server and each language. Using a standard method simplifies the process of running programs from a Web server. That method is called *CGI,* which stands for *Common Gateway Interface.*

How CGI works can be stated in a single sentence: CGI passes a user's request to a program using some special variables or standard file input; the program, in turn, passes information to the user using standard file output (see Chapter 11). Incidentally, CGI programs are often called *scripts*.

Your Perl program works with the Web server software, not around it. Web users coming to your Web site don't run your programs directly. Instead, they access the Web server, and the Web server software launches your programs. Therefore, your CGI programs need to be able to talk to a Web server.

The various Web servers out there have different requirements and perform different actions when you run a CGI program. For example, some Web servers require that all your CGI programs be in one directory on the server and the programs must follow certain naming rules; other servers enable you to put your programs wherever you want and give them whatever names you please.

In order to write Web server programs with Perl, you need to know two things:

- **Input** — Determining what the user requested
- **Output** — Deciding how to tell the user what you want to say

Collecting the input is more difficult than displaying the output because you have to plan for more variables when accepting input. You can create your output using a `print` statement (see Chapters 4 and 5 for the particulars of the `print` function). The input part is a bit more difficult.

For now, all you need to know is the format of the input and the kind of information in the special variables. The output you create is the same output that's normally sent by your Web server, such as HTML or plain text. In the following sections, I show you the format of the file input and the kind of information contained in the special variables used to process user input. I also provide examples of Web server file output created in HTML, the most commonly used file format on the Web.

Read the instructions that come with your Web server software before writing any CGI programs in Perl. Most Web servers are designed to simplify the process of using CGI programs; nevertheless, many programming hopefuls are unsuccessful on their first few attempts at programming CGI scripts because they don't follow the rules of the road for the Web server they're using.

Beyond CGI

In olden times (before 1994), CGI was the only game in town for interfacing Web servers and programming languages. Almost every server still supports CGI, but now the most popular servers also support their own programming interfaces, and usually to their own programming languages. For example, the Web servers from Netscape run a language called JavaScript, which interfaces to a server through a different interface than CGI.

All in all, CGI is pretty limited, even if the programming languages to which it attaches aren't. The custom *application programming interfaces*, or APIs, used by newer Web servers give you many more capabilities than plain old CGI. If you get serious about creating programs that work with your Web server and your server has its own API, consider finding out how to use the server's API. (Of course, the API may not be nearly as easy to use as Perl, but few languages are.)

If your Web server runs on Windows 95, Windows 98, or Windows NT, it may use an extended version of CGI that most Windows Web servers use. The interface is called *Windows CGI*. Although this version is much more complicated than standard CGI, it has many features not available in standard CGI.

If you're running on UNIX and using the Apache Web server, you can embed Perl directly into the server. This process greatly speeds up launching Perl scripts from your Web server. (See your Apache instructions for how to embed Perl.)

Using Environment Variables

You can obtain information from a Web server in one of two ways: through special variables called *environment variables* or through standard file input (which is described in Chapter 11). For many requests that come to your program from the Web server, you use environment variables, but for most HTML forms, you use standard file input.

The term "environment" comes from UNIX, although it also applies to Windows. Environment variables are set in the operating system and they're similar to Perl text variables. Perl can read operating system environment variables and use them just like other Perl variables. (Attention Macintosh users: The Mac doesn't really have environment variables, but MacPerl pretends to have them for use in CGI programs.)

UNIX has dozens of environment variables, but this chapter covers only those that are specific to running CGI programs. They're set by the Web server software as a way to communicate information to programming languages like Perl. The CGI standard defines many of these variables, but only a few of them are truly useful to most Perl programmers.

Getting at variables

Perl variables, like environment variables, have names. (The methods you use to view and set the values of environment variables are described in Chapter 16.) The environment variable names in CGI are in all capital letters. For example, to get the value of an environment variable with the name VARNAME, you can use the following statement:

```
$ENV{"VARNAME"}
```

For example, assume that a variable called `REMOTE_HOST` has the domain name of the computer making the request. You can set a variable `$TheUserHost` in your Perl program with the following statement:

```
$TheUserHost = $ENV{"REMOTE_HOST"};
```

Just to give you a feel for the variables' names and the typical values you may see, the following is a list of the CGI variables you may see after a Web server request:

```
GATEWAY_INTERFACE -- CGI/1.1
                HOME -- /
         HTTP_ACCEPT -- image/gif, image/jpeg, */*
           HTTP_HOST -- www.mycompany.com
     HTTP_USER_AGENT -- Mozilla/3.01b1 (Macintosh; I; PPC)
     PATH_TRANSLATED -- /usr/local/wn/scripts
        QUERY_STRING -- eastern
         REMOTE_ADDR -- 169.207.113.247
         REMOTE_HOST -- jl12.cs.cmu.edu
      REQUEST_METHOD -- GET
SCRIPT_NAME -- /telltime.cgi
         SERVER_NAME -- www.mycompany.com
         SERVER_PORT -- 80
     SERVER_PROTOCOL -- HTTP/1.0
     SERVER_SOFTWARE -- WN/1.14.2
         WN_DIR_PATH -- /usr/local/wn/scripts
             WN_ROOT -- /usr/local/wn/scripts
```

You need to use only a few environment variables to get information from a user, and rarely need to use the others. In the following sections, I describe the most important variables. Later in this chapter, under "A Few Other Environment Variables," I describe some lesser-used variables also worth knowing about.

Posing a query

After a user clicks on a link to your program, the Web server launches the program. Your program may need to know certain things about the user's request, so the Web server sets a few variables with this information.

The `QUERY_STRING` variable contains all the text after the ? in the user's request. For example, assume your home page includes the following statement:

```
<p>
To see the current time in the central time zone, choose
<a href="/amy/telltime.cgi?central">this link</a>.
To see what time it is in the eastern time zone, choose
<a href="/amy/telltime.cgi?eastern">this link</a>.
```

When the user selects the time zone link, the value of `QUERY_STRING` is either `central` or `eastern`. Therefore, your Perl program may have something in it similar to this:

```
$TheTime = time();
$DesiredTimeZone = $ENV{"QUERY_STRING"};
if($DesiredTimeZone eq 'central')
    { $TheTime += 3600 }  # Add one hour
elsif($DesiredTimeZone eq 'eastern')
    { $TheTime += 7200 }  # Add two hours
```

The query string is assigned by you in your HTML pages. To enable the user to make choices on an HTML page, you need to use HTML forms, which are described in the section "Gathering Information from HTML Forms," later in this chapter.

`QUERY_STRING` is the one variable you really need for most kinds of form processing. A raft of other environment variables are available, but they don't help much with what you really want to do, which is to figure out what the user wants so that you can supply it.

Determining the source of a request

Two environment variables can be used to log accesses to your Web site (also called "tracking hits"). These variables, `REMOTE_HOST` and `REMOTE_ADDR`, tell you which computer made a request to your Web server. ***Note:*** These variables identify the computer, not the user.

REMOTE_HOST is the *domain name* of the computer making the request (if the Web server is able to determine the domain name), whereas REMOTE_ADDR is the *IP address* of that computer. (If you're unfamiliar with domain names and IP addresses, you can find out plenty about them in *The Internet For Dummies,* 5th Edition, by John Levine, Carol Baroudi, and Margaret Levine Young, published by IDG Books Worldwide, Inc.

You may want to use the values of REMOTE_HOST and REMOTE_ADDR to determine what information is given in the Web page that is displayed to the user. For example, you may want to give more detailed information to someone on a computer you recognize than someone who's a stranger. However, this practice is incredibly unsafe. It's possible for a user to pretend to be on a certain computer by changing an address on the Internet. It's best just to ignore the values in REMOTE_HOST and REMOTE_ADDR.

REMOTE_HOST may be a null string (a string with zero characters) if your Web server can't translate the IP address that it receives with a request into a domain name. Most Web server administrators prefer to see domain names in the logs for their Web servers rather than IP addresses, so your program should check whether REMOTE_HOST has a value, and if not, use REMOTE_ADDR instead. An example of this kind of check would be:

```
# Get the host name or IP address for the log
unless($ENV{REMOTE_HOST} eq '')
    { $TheWhere = $ENV{REMOTE_HOST} }
else { $TheWhere = $ENV{REMOTE_ADDR} }
```

Gathering Information from HTML Forms

Using a *query string* (the text after the ? in a URL) is a simple, direct way to get a single piece of information from a user (see "Posing a query" earlier in this chapter). But sometimes you may need more than just one piece of information. For example, you may want to find out a user's name and address or the answers to some yes-or-no questions. If you want this sort of information, the user must fill out a *form.*

An HTML form has two components that are relevant to CGI programs: the *HTTP method* (the syntax) used in the form, and the names of the elements in the form (such as the names of the buttons). Beyond that, the rest of the form consists mostly of formatting designed to make text entry more user-friendly.

The method for submitting forms can be either GET or POST. The GET method puts any responses to a form in a query string, whereas the POST method puts the responses into the body of the HTTP reply that you can read from the standard file input (see Chapter 11 for more on file input). You can use either GET or POST, depending on which one suits your fancy.

For example, the following is the HTML that displays a short and simple form, the results of which are shown in Figure 10-1:

```
<hr><form method=POST
   action="http://www.bigstate.edu/accts/namecolor.pl">
First name: <input name=FirstName size=30><br>
Last name:  <input name=LastName size=30><br>
Favorite color: <select name=FavColor>
<option>crimson<option>apricot<option>saffron
<option>emerald<option>sapphire<option>magenta
<option>pearl<option>coal<option>chestnut
</select>
<br><input type="submit" value="Send">
</form><hr>
```

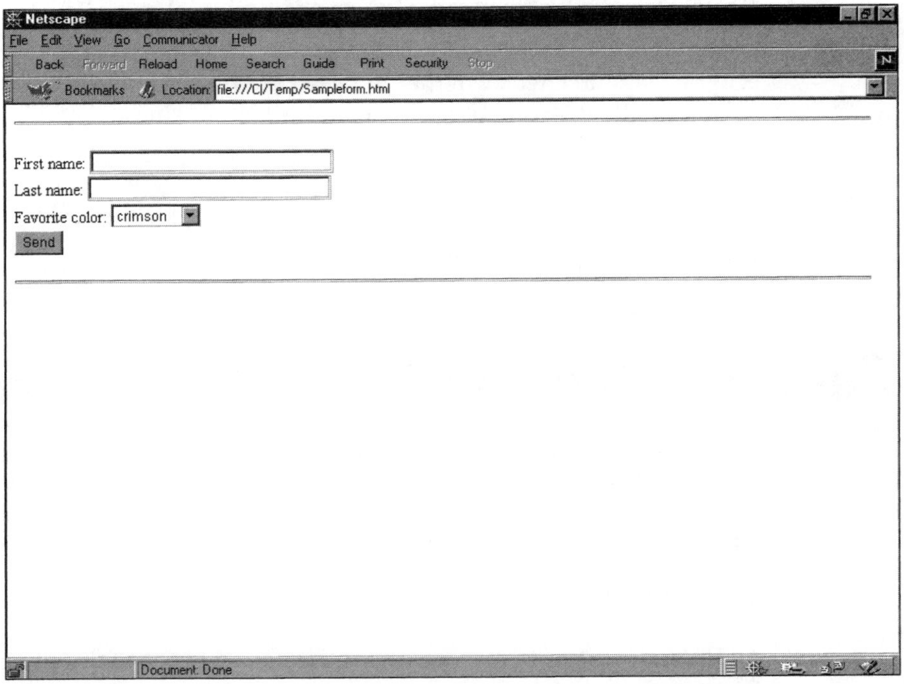

Figure 10-1: A small form designed to return values for three named elements.

The form in Figure 10-1 returns values for three named elements: `FirstName`, `LastName`, and `FavColor`. CGI returns values in a very compact yet difficult-to-decipher fashion — as a single string with each element listed as `elementname=elementvalue`, spaces in the values turned into plus-sign (+) characters, and an ampersand (&) character inserted between each element. For example, if a person named Sharon Fulton who really likes purple fills in the form, the returned string will look like this:

```
FirstName=Sharon&LastName=Fulton&FavColor=magenta
```

Determining what is in the response gets a bit more complicated than what I just described. Many special characters are encoded as a percent sign (%) followed by the hexadecimal value of the character. For example, if Sharon enters `Sharon & Pete` instead of `Sharon`, the returned string becomes:

```
FirstName=Sharon+%26+Pete&LastName=Fulton&FavColor=magenta
```

Two methods for getting the form data

As I note in the previous section, you can use either GET or POST as the HTTP method for submitting a form to your Perl program. Where you read the form data that's submitted depends on which method you use.

- With `GET`, the response comes back in the `QUERY_STRING` environment variable, which you can read with `$ENV{"QUERY_STRING"}`.
- With `POST`, the response comes in the content of the reply, which you can read from the standard file input.

The environment variable `REQUEST_METHOD` tells you whether the `GET` or `POST` method was used. To read the correct number of characters, you need to know how long the content of the request is, and then read that many characters using Perl's `read` function (the `read` function is described in Chapter 12). The environment variable `CONTENT_LENGTH` tells you how long the request is. Then, you can put the text into the variable `$TheReq` by using the following statement:

```
read(STDIN, $TheReq, $ENV{"CONTENT_LENGTH"});
```

If you want your Perl program to be *robust* (that is, capable of doing more than just simple things), check whether the request has either the `GET` or `POST` methods:

```
if($ENV{"REQUEST_METHOD"} eq 'GET')
    { $TheReq = $ENV{"QUERY_STRING"} }
else
    { read(STDIN, $TheReq, $ENV{"CONTENT_LENGTH"}) }
```

Splitting apart a strung-together response

If you read the previous sections, you know how to get a response from a user, but that response ends up being a smashed-together string of characters that looks something like the following:

```
FirstName=Sharon&LastName=Fulton&FavColor=magenta
```

Perl is great at handling data like this string. You can write a program that will split this string into pairs of items, such as FirstName and Sharon, LastName and Fulton, and so on, but hey, why bother? A program such as this for reading HTML forms is so common that one has already been written for you. The CGI_Lite program, which is on this book's companion CD-ROM, is the easiest of the programs used to get the request string because it requires just one or two statements. (It's a Perl 5 program and employs some of the object-oriented features covered in Chapter 19.)

To use CGI_Lite, you have to make it available to Perl. The best way to do that is to copy the CGI_Lite file, called CGI_Lite.pm, into one of the directories in Perl's search path. (Chapter 14 shows you how to locate these directories; they're listed in the special `@INC` list.) Then, start your Perl program by entering something like the following statements:

```
use CGI_Lite;
$InCGI = new CGI_Lite();
@FormData = $InCGI->parse_form_data();
```

In the first line of the previous chunk of code, the `use` statement tells Perl to read the `CGI_Lite` module into the program you are writing. (The `use` statement works a bit like the `require` statement described in Chapter 14, except that it has some extra object-oriented features.) For now, assume that `use` is a way to get a Perl object-oriented module into your program (modules are described in Chapter 19). The second line causes Perl to create an object described in `CGI_Lite`, and the third line tells Perl to use the `parse_form_data` method in the object. The point of all this is to create a list called `@FormData`, whose items are the names and elements returned.

Picking values to use as Perl variables

The following list describes someone named Sharon Fulton and her preference for shades of purple:

```
('FirstName', 'Sharon', 'LastName', 'Fulton',
    'FavColor', 'magenta')
```

Next, you want to do something with the values in the array, namely put them in Perl variables that you can use in your program. You can do this quickly for element names you know by looking through the array for the name you know and then picking the next item in the array for your Perl variable. For example, the following program looks for the name `FirstName` and then sets `$FormFirst` to the element after that.

```
# Fill in $FormFirst with the name given
for($i = 0; $i <= $#FormData; $i += 1) {
    if($FormData[$i] eq 'FirstName') {
        $FormFirst = $FormData[$i + 1];
        last;
    }
}
```

You do have a better way available to you to manage this data. Lists such as this one that are in the form "name, value, name, value . . ." can be handled with *associative arrays,* which are covered in Chapter 16.

Displaying Output to the User

The interesting part of using CGI is that it enables you to feed information to end users. After you find out a few rules for how to supply information, you can create your own programs to tell users whatever you desire.

Every message sent from a Web server to a Web client consists of two parts: *header information* and the *main message.* The header information may be very short, but it's essential because it contains format information that the user's Web browser must have. If it isn't included, most Web browsers assume that the main message is a plain text file.

A few servers pass their own header information to the top of the response, in which case your Perl program isn't supposed to pass any headers. Most servers pass some header information, but not the most important piece: the MIME content type. *MIME* stands for *Multipurpose Internet Mail Extension,* and it's used on the Web, as well as in Internet mail. MIME types are more properly called *Internet media types,* but the name MIME has caught on and stuck.

A MIME type tells a Web client what kind of information is in the response from the server. The Web client then uses this MIME information to decide how to show that information. For instance, a Web client reacts differently when you say "this is an HTML document" than if you say "this is a GIF image" or "this is a compressed program file."

The header that you send to the client before you start sending your own information starts with the string `Content-type:` followed by a space and then the MIME type. For example, if you're going to send back an HTML document to a user, your Perl program prints the following statement before it does anything else:

```
Content-type: text/html
```

Dozens of different MIME types exist, most of which you probably won't ever use. Table 10-1 shows the MIME types that you're most likely to send over the Internet.

Table 10-1 MIME Types for Common File Formats

MIME Type	*Description*
text/html	A regular HTML document
text/plain	A plain text file that appears exactly as you send it
application/binary	A binary file that's saved to disk
image/gif	A picture in GIF format
image/jpeg	A picture in JPEG format
audio/aiff	A sound file in AIFF format

The header information is separated from the body of the message by a blank line. Therefore, you have to insert `\n\n` at the end of your `Content-type` line.

A few servers send out the Content-type line to the client for you, which means that you shouldn't send it out yourself. (See your server's documentation for instructions on what sort of data you should be sending out in your CGI programs.)

For an example of how to send information back to the user, take a look at the following short Perl CGI program that ignores any client input and returns a brief message formatted as HTML. This program lacks the HTML header information, but it does work.

```
print "Content-type: text/html\n\n";
print "<b>Thank you</b> for running my Perl program.";
```

By comparison, the following is a longer and more complex example program called thetime.cgi. The program displays the time to the user. Note the amount of HTML that the program puts out.

```
# CGI program to tell the user what time it is.
#     The user either got here with a URL of
#     "central" or "eastern" or nothing.
$TheZone = "Pacific";
if ($DesiredTimeZone eq 'central') {
    @TimeArr = localtime(time + 3600);
    $TheZone = "Central";
}
elsif($DesiredTimeZone eq 'eastern') {
    @TimeArr = localtime(time + 7200);
    $TheZone = "Eastern";
}
$Hour = $TimeArr[2];
$Minute = $TimeArr[1];
$TimeString = "$Hour:$Minute";
print <<"EndOfStuff"
ContentType: text/html

<html><head><title>At the tone...</title></head><body>
In the <b>$TheZone</b> time zone, it is now $TimeString.
</body></html>
EndOfStuff
```

The HTML document that relates to the previous program would look something like this:

```
Which time zone do you want to see the time for?
<br>
<a href="/cgi-bin/thetime.cgi?pacific">Pacific</a>?
<br>
<a href="/cgi-bin/thetime.cgi?central">Central</a>
<br>
<a href="/cgi-bin/thetime.cgi?eastern">Eastern</a>
```

Creating an HTML Form

You can use CGI programs to take requests from users and combine them into a single response. This process is useful when the information you are sending is brief and the user wants to see many different items on a single page.

For example, assume that you have a Web page designed to sell musical instruments. You can have a master page with links to descriptions of each instrument, but that means your users who are interested in comparing several instruments have to go back and forth from the main page to each of the other pages featuring the instrument descriptions. Instead, you want them to be able to compare all the instruments they're interested in simultaneously.

To enable your users to compare many items at once, you can create an HTML form by using the following code:

```
<form method=POST action="/cgi-bin/dispguit.cgi">
Please pick the instruments from the following list. You
may choose as many as you want.
<br><input type=checkbox name=GoyaStandard>
Goya standard guitar
<br><input type=checkbox name=GoyaConcert>
Goya concert guitar
<br><input type=checkbox name=VegaArtistGrand>
Vega Artist Grand guitar
<br><input type=checkbox name=HarmonySteel>
Harmony steel guitar
<br><input type="submit" value="Show me">
</form>
```

Part of the program used to create the form looks like what you see in Listing 10-1.

Listing 10-1: A program for displaying information based on user requests.

```
#  First get the form data. CGI_Lite will only return
#    the values of checkboxes that are selected by
#    the user, so you don't have to check for "on"
#    and "off"
use CGI_Lite;
$InCGI = new CGI_Lite();
@FormData = $InCGI->parse_form_data();

print <<EndOfTop;
Content-type: text/html

<html><head><title>Guitar Information</title></head><body>
Thank you for considering our guitars. Here is the
information you requested.
EndOfTop

while(@FormData) {
    $ThisGuitar = shift(@FormData);  # The item name
```

```
        $ThisOn = shift(@FormData);  # Toss this out
        $DisplayThis = &GetData($ThisGuitar);
        print "<hr>$DisplayThis";
    }

    print "</body></html>\n";
```

Using Redirection to Link to Other Sites

Links on one Web page that point to a different Web server are commonplace, and most Web administrators want to keep track of who follows their links to other servers. For example, if you list a dozen different sites on your server, you may want to tell the administrators of a site, "I sent 100 people in your direction last week."

The typical way to send someone to another site is simply to provide a link to that site, but you won't know when or if a user accesses one of those links. A less-common method to link to other sites is *redirection,* which employs a CGI program that sends an HTTP message to the user's browser, which then links the user to the other site. By using redirection, you can also log how many times you send users to each site.

Listing 10-2 displays a program called ad-url.cgi that tracks redirections. I wrote the program for a newspaper called *MicroTimes*. The newspaper's editor wanted the *MicroTimes* Web page to list the newspaper's advertisers who had their own Web sites and also link the newspaper's site to the advertisers' sites. The first section of the program in Listing 10-2 sets up a variable, `$WebPerson`, that's used in many places within the program. The program then fills in the `$TheSearch` variable with the user's request.

The program in Listing 10-2 then checks to see if `$TheSearch` is blank, which it shouldn't be. If it isn't blank, the program opens the `AdURLs` file and reads through it one line at a time (see Chapter 11 for a description of reading from files). Each line is split into two variables, `$TheName` and `$TheURL`, and the program compares `$TheName` to `$TheSearch`. If they match, the program sets some variables and jumps out of the loop.

After the loop, the program looks to sees whether an entry in the database matched the search. If it does, the `PrintFound` subroutine prints the appropriate HTTP redirection headers; if not, the `PrintNotFound` subroutine prints an error message. The HTTP headers put out by the `PrintFound` subroutine cause most Web clients to automatically go to the specified URL; but if they don't, the text in the message enables the user to go to that URL manually.

The sections in the middle of the program in Listing 10-2 create log entries in an external log file using the `sprintf` function described in Chapter 9. The log is opened, a line is written to it, and then closed (see Chapter 11 for more on this process).

Listing 10-2: A program for redirecting Web clients.

```
$WebPerson = 'webmaster@yourcompany.com';

# Look at the string they handed to us in the URL
$TheSearch = $ENV{QUERY_STRING};

# Look in the search string
unless($TheSearch eq '') {
    $RefURL = '';  # The URL we will send them to
    # Open the database
    open(IN, 'AdURLs') or die "Could not open the URL " .
        "database. Please send mail to $WebPerson so " .
        "we can fix this.\n";
    # Read the database line-by-line
    while (<IN>) {
        $TheString = $_; chomp($TheString);
        # Split the line into two parts, based on
        #    whitespace between them
        ($TheName, $TheURL) = split(/\s+/,$TheString, 2);
        # Check if the part we just got is the same as
        #    the part in the search string
        if ($TheName eq $TheSearch) {
            # If so, set some variables and leave
            $RefName = $TheName;
            $RefURL = $TheURL;
last;
        }
    }
    close(IN);
    unless ($RefURL eq '') {   # We found a match
        &PrintFound;
    }
    else {   # We didn't find a match
        &PrintNotFound;
        # Change the $RefName for the log
        $RefName = "ErrorNotInDatabase:$TheSearch";
    }
}
else {  #The search string was empty
    print "HTTP/1.0 400 Bad Request\n";
```

```
    print "Content-Type: text/html\n\n";
    print "<head><title>Incorrect Request</title>" .
        "</head><body>\n";
    print "There was no query.\n";
    print "</body>\n";
    $RefName = 'ErrorNoRequest';  # This is for the log
}

#  We displayed what we wanted to, now make a log entry

# Get the time right now into a bunch of variables
($Second, $Minute, $Hour, $DayOfMonth, $Month, $Year,
    $WeekDay, $DayOfYear, $IsDST) = localtime(time);
$RealMonth = $Month + 1;  # Since $Month starts at 0
# Format the variables to be two digits long
$DateAndTime = sprintf("%02d/%02d/%02d\t%02d:%02d:%02d",
    $RealMonth, $DayOfMonth, $Year, $Hour, $Minute,
    $Second);

# Get the host name or IP address for the log
unless($ENV{REMOTE_HOST} eq '')
    { $TheWhere = $ENV{REMOTE_HOST} }
else { $TheWhere = $ENV{REMOTE_ADDR} }

# Open the log and write the line
open(ADLOG, '>>AdLog') or die "Could not append to the " .
    "URL log. Please send mail to $WebPerson so we can " .
    "fix this.\n";
print ADLOG "$DateAndTime\t$TheWhere\t$RefName\n";
close(ADLOG);

sub PrintFound {
        print <<"EndFound";
HTTP/1.0 302 Found
Location: $RefURL
Content-Type: text/html

<head><title>Redirection Information</title></head><body>
If you are reading this, your Web browser does not support
redirection. That's OK: simply select <a href=\"$RefURL\">
this</a> and you will be taken to the advertiser you
selected.
</body>
EndFound
}
```

(continued)

(continued)

```
sub PrintNotFound {
        print <<"EndNotFound";
HTTP/1.0 404 Not Found
Content-Type: text/html

<head><title>Incorrect Request</title></head><body>
There is no entry in the URL database for '$TheSearch'.
This may indicate an error in our database of URLs.
If you are sure you got this message by simply choosing
one of the links on our page, please send email to
<a href=\"mailto:$WebPerson\">$WebPerson</a>.
</body>
EndNotFound
}
```

In order to use the redirection program in Listing 10-2, your Perl CGI program must be the only one sending any HTTP headers. However, this program doesn't work on all Web servers because it sends out its own headers. It won't work on a server that also sends out a set of headers because a Web client can only understand one set of headers. You may find that many servers enable you to prevent those servers from sending out headers for some CGI programs using special settings. (Check your Web server documentation to determine how you can prevent the server from sending out any HTTP headers for this particular program or any CGI programs.)

The *MicroTimes* Web site I mention earlier in this section of the chapter contains pages with links to a database. A portion of the HTML for the site's pages looks like this (plus some, for the hundreds of additional advertiser's URLs):

```
<h3>Computer Systems</h3>
<a href="ad-url?ACME">ACME Micro-System, Inc.</a><p>
<a href="ad-url?AdvancedComputer">Advanced Computers
and Technology</a><p>
<a href="ad-url?Airt"> AIRT Computers</a><p>
```

The advertiser database consists of a simple text file with lines of advertisers' names and the respective URLs for their home pages:

```
ACME   http://www.acmemicro.com/
AdvancedComputer  http://www.plgrn.com/adv-comp.html
Airt    http://www.airtcomp.com/
```

Security and CGI programs

You can do lots of stuff with Perl and CGI that will make your Web pages more interesting and versatile. However, you can also do plenty of stuff that's detrimental to the security of your site. When you write CGI programs, be careful when reading and writing files on your system. Hackers who enjoy breaking into systems and wreaking havoc with them are always on the lookout for poorly written programs that are easily cracked and manipulated. After hackers break in, they may alter your Web pages (in some cases, by adding offensive material) or they can steal private corporate information such as customer records.

Keep an eye on any CGI programs that take input from a user and then use that input as a command for the Web server (some of the pitfalls of doing this are described in Chapter 18). Before you write any Perl CGI program, read the Web Security FAQ document that can be found at

```
www-genome.wi.mit.edu/WWW/
    faqs/www-security-faq.html/
```

This document lists many of the common security mistakes programmers make when creating CGI programs.

A Few Other Environment Variables

A number of environment variables, other than the ones I mention earlier in this chapter, are available to your CGI programs. Frankly, some of those other variables aren't terribly useful, but the following few are definitely worth adding to your CGI program mix.

For additional client information

The `CONTENT_TYPE` variable holds the MIME type of the form handed to the CGI program. This variable is often left blank, but it can be set in the HTML `<form>` tag with the `enctype` attribute.

Most Web clients also send a few additional HTTP headers when they make requests. These headers appear in environment variables whose names have `HTTP_` before the header name and hyphens changed to underscores. For example, the User-Agent header put out by most clients can be accessed from the `HTTP_USER_AGENT` environment variable. ***Note:*** Not all Web servers put values in every environment variable that Web clients give them.

For server information

Table 10-2 lists the environment variables that provide information about the Web server from which a CGI program is launched.

Table 10-2 Server Information Variables

Variable	*Description*
SERVER_SOFTWARE	The name and version of the Web server software
SERVER_NAME	The domain name that the server is running from
SERVER_PORT	The TCP port on which the request was made
SERVER_PROTOCOL	The version of HTTP that the server is running
GATEWAY_INTERFACE	The version of CGI that the server is using

Some Web servers also create server-specific environment variables. Unfortunately, those variables don't have standard names, so you can't find them easily. For example, my favorite Web server software on UNIX, WN, creates environment variables called WN_DIR_PATH and WN_ROOT; other servers create similar variables with their own non-standard names.

For user authentication

If your Web server supports user authentication, REMOTE_USER contains the name of the user. AUTH_TYPE is the protocol used to authenticate the user. If your Web server supports the Internet IDENT protocol, and the user's computer does as well, the REMOTE_IDENT variable holds the user's login name.

Don't rely on the IDENT protocol to provide you with any security. It is easy to fool an IDENT server into thinking that a user is someone he or she isn't.

For program information

SCRIPT_NAME is the path to the CGI program being run, in case you need to know what directory you're in.

Chapter 11

The Files Go In, The Files Go Out

In This Chapter

- Defining the two basic file types
- Opening and closing files
- Reading and writing text files
- Getting statistics on your files
- Examining standard file input/output

When you use a computer, it's easy to take seemingly simple things for granted. Consider your electronic files, for instance. You probably think of them as merely "those things on my disk." They have names, they have stuff in them, and that's about it. But, as you may suspect, the whole business of managing files is complex enough that I devoted a whole chapter of this book to it.

In the following pages, I tell you how Perl handles files and how file handling is related to lots of other areas of Perl programming. After you read this chapter, you'll be able to write programs that read text files for information and write text files that contain your program results. For instance, you may want to write a program that reads a text file and writes out the same file in a different format. With Perl, you can accomplish this task with just a few lines.

File under Definitions: Perl File Types

In general computer terms, a *file* is an ordered set of bytes stored on disk and given a filename. The bytes in a file are ordered so that you know where the beginning and end of the file are, the file is stored on disk so you can retrieve it later, and it's given a filename so that you can access the exact file you want.

For most computer users, this definition covers it. However, Perl's roots in UNIX complicate matters a bit. UNIX files don't have to reside on a disk. They can consist of any stream of ordered bytes that a program can access. You can view program output or a stream of data coming in from a network as a file in Perl. (Later in this chapter in the section "Moving File Streams in UNIX: Standard In, Standard Out, and Standard Error," you can see some pretty snazzy things you can do with special files that don't reside on disk, but for now, just think of files as disk files.)

As for what's inside a file, the bytes in a file can have any value. The contents of a file are relevant only to programs that read that file. That is, you may not care about the contents of a file that you don't read, but that file may be valuable to other programs that run on your computer.

You can divide files into two broad categories based on their contents: *text files* and *binary files.* No hard-and-fast rules exist for separating the two kinds of files, but generally a text file contains bytes whose values are displayable characters plus a few characters that don't always show up on screen, and a binary file is any file that isn't a text file.

Text files contain values that you can see on screen, such as letters, digits, and punctuation, as well as the special characters for spaces, carriage returns, line feeds and tabs. Text files are typically human readable, although many text files are meant to be read by programs. Binary files are not human readable because they contain nonprinting characters; they almost always are meant to be read solely by programs.

You should know the difference between the two kinds of files because Perl has some handy features that apply only to text files. Because so many of the files that Perl programmers need to read are text files, Perl makes text file handling as easy as possible. This isn't to say that handling binary files is especially difficult, but if you know a file is a text file, your program for reading from and writing to that file will be briefer and easier to read than a program meant to handle binary files.

Opening Files

Whether you want to read from or write to a file, you must first open it. Every operating system has a different way of opening files, but Perl takes care of the differences among Windows, Mac, and UNIX systems behind the scenes. Regardless of your operating system, you can use Perl's `open` statement in the same way. The format of `open` is

```
open(HANDLE, FILENAME);
```

Giving a file a handle

The *handle*, which is similar to a nickname, is a name that you use in a program to talk about a file. File handles are shown in Perl programs without any special characters in front of them. The naming rules for file handle names are the same as the rules for variable names (see Chapter 3). It has become a Perl convention to use all uppercase letters in file handle names.

For example, what follows is a typical `open` statement:

```
open(INFILE, 'sample.txt');
```

It's also commonplace to use a variable to hold the filename and use that variable as the second argument to `open`:

```
$TheFile = 'sample.txt';
open(INFILE, $TheFile);
```

In both these cases, the file handle is `INFILE`. This is an arbitrary choice; you can name your file handles whatever you want, as long as you follow the rules for variable names that I cover in Chapter 3.

Reading, writing, or appending: Choosing a file opening mode

When you open a file, Perl needs to know what you want to do with the file. You can open a file for reading, writing, or appending. If you want to program with files, you must understand the difference between these three tasks.

- **Opening a file for reading:** You read a file to look through it and not change its contents in any way. You can read a file in any order, but people usually move from beginning to end. Of course, you can only read from a file that already exists.
- **Opening a file for writing:** You open a file for writing when you want to enter new information into a file. You can write to a new file, which is how you create a file, or you can write to an existing file, in which case you immediately wipe out everything that's already in the file. Opening a file for writing is like starting fresh, whether anything exists in that file or not.
- **Opening a file for appending:** You open a file for appending when you want to write into a file, but only at the end of the file. This process differs from opening a file for writing in that appending doesn't wipe out the current contents; it only amends it. You can open a new file for appending, which is the same as opening it for writing because you're adding to the "end" of this new file in both cases.

You cannot read and write to a file at the same time. At first, you may be frustrated by this fact, but a very good reason exists why you can't do both simultaneously. If you write into some part of the file and then attempt to read it near the place where you wrote, Perl isn't sure whether it should read strictly what is on disk (that is, before you just wrote to the file) or whether it should read what is on disk plus what you just wrote. Perl is absolutely sure of what you want to read only if you write out what you want to disk.

You have to tell Perl in the `open` statement which of the three modes (reading, writing, or appending) you want to open the file in. It would be nice if you could tell Perl with something like

```
open(INFILE, 'read', 'sample.txt');
```

but you can't. Instead, Perl looks at the first character or two of the filename you give it and determines the open mode from that. For instance,

- To read a file, precede the name with < or with no special character.
- To write a file, precede the name with >.
- To append to a file, precede the name with >>.

Here are some examples of filenames that determine how a file is opened:

```
open(INFILE, '<sample.txt');  # For reading
open(INFILE, 'sample.txt');  # Also for reading
open(INFILE, '>sample.txt');  # For writing
open(INFILE, '>>sample.txt');  # For appending
$TheFile = '>sample.txt';  # Prepare for writing
open(INFILE, $TheFile);  # This will open for writing
```

Determining if a file really opened

The `open` statement returns a value of true if Perl is successful at opening the file. For reading a file, `open` returns true if the file exists and is readable. For writing or appending a file, `open` returns true if the file can be written to. If the file exists and you are attempting to open it for writing, it must not be set "read only" in the operating system; otherwise, the `open` statement returns false.

A file doesn't have to exist to be written to, but you can't always create a file that you can write to; for example, you may not have permission to write to the directory in which the file is located.

If an `open` statement doesn't work, it returns a false value. This is the catalyst for the "open or die" statements contained in the sample programs in Chapters 3 and 4. This type of statement translates to "quit the program immediately if the open fails."

Using files after they're opened

After you open a file, all the other Perl statements that you use on that file have the file handle as an argument. Specifically, you use the file handle and not the filename in an `open` statement because not every Perl file has a name. Also, file handles are usually much shorter than filenames:

```
open(THEDATA, "C:\EMPLOYEE\DATA\NAMES.DB");
```

You can have multiple files open in a single program. In fact, it's quite common to have two or more files open if your program converts a file into a new file. In this case, your program would have `open` statements near the beginning of the program that look like this:

```
open(ORIG, 'original.txt') or die "Can't open input.\n";
open(NEW, '>new.txt') or die "Can't open output.\n";
```

In this example, the rest of the statements in the program would then use the `ORIG` file handle when reading from the file being converted and the `NEW` file handle when writing into the new file.

Closing Files

When you finish processing a file, you can close it with Perl's `close` statement. If you forget to close a file, it's no big deal: Perl closes all open files when a program ends. The `close` statement takes one argument, the file handle of the file you want to close:

```
close(ORIG);
```

Close a file that you opened for writing or appending as soon as you are done with it because Perl won't necessarily write out the last part of the file to disk until the file is closed. If another program opens the file for reading before you have closed the file, that program may think the file is shorter than you intend it to be because Perl hasn't written out the last part. Always use an explicit `close` for any file that you are writing or appending, just in case your computer crashes before the program finishes.

Specifying Filenames and Directory Paths for the Various Operating Systems

Most of the filenames I use in this book are generic enough to work on every operating system (Windows 95/98, Windows NT, MacOS, and UNIX). Perl allows you to use any name that's valid in the operating system you use. However, each operating system has different rules for naming files. For instance, the following open statement works on a Mac but not on Windows because Windows filenames cannot have a slash (/) character in them:

```
open(EITHER, "This/that");
```

Chapter 10 explains how Perl searches in different directories for files that you include with the require statement. The open statement doesn't search for files, however. You must give an explicit path to the file in the filename; otherwise, Perl looks only in the current directory for that file. For example, if you want to read a file by using the statement

```
open(IN, 'jan97.dat');
```

that file must be in the directory from which you started Perl or Perl won't be able to find the file.

To explicitly state the default directory that you want to be in, use Perl's chdir function. The chdir function takes one argument — a string with the name of the directory you want. For example, on UNIX, you may use

```
chdir('/usr/bin/accounting/data');
```

The chdir function returns false if Perl can't change to a specified directory, so you should always check the value returned. For example, the following statement checks to see whether the chdir was successful:

```
chdir('/usr/bin/accounting/data') or die "Could not " .
    "change to the accounting data directory.\n";
```

If you use the open statement to open a file for writing or appending and don't specify the directory into which you want to write the file, you should make a note of which directory you're in before opening the file. If you're in a directory other than the one you want, you may unintentionally wipe out or alter a file that you didn't mean to touch. At a minimum, you may have a hard time later finding a file you created if you're not sure what directory you were in.

The way that you specify directories in the various operating systems differs. Under Windows 95/98 and Windows NT, you must use the drive letter followed by a colon, and then the directory names separated with a backslash character (\):

```
open(IN, "D:\ORDERS\DATA\JAN97.DAT");
```

On the Mac, you must use the disk name and folder names separated with colons:

```
open(IN, "Main:Order entry:Data files:January 1997 data");
```

On UNIX, you must use the standard path name to a file, with the directory names separated by a slash character (/):

```
open(IN, "/usr/home/orders/data/jan97.dat");
```

Fun with the Mac's Open command

Now it's time for Mac lovers to gloat a bit. You probably know how to specify a file by its name. MacPerl also lets you specify a file's name with the standard file interfaces that you use with the Open and Save commands in every Mac program. (Perl-Win32 should have features for this but doesn't yet.)

To create a filename string using the Mac interface, you must include the library called StandardFile.pl. Therefore, the following statement must appear near the beginning of your program:

```
require 'StandardFile.pl';
```

The StandardFile.pl library contains subroutines called `GetFile` and `PutFile`. You use `GetFile` for the same reason you use the Open command in programs: to select a file. You use `PutFile`, on the other hand, like you would the Save command in programs: to choose a folder and enter a name for the file you want to save.

The arguments for the `GetFile` and `PutFile` subroutines are a bit confusing, but luckily you can safely use these subroutines with no arguments. For example, to get the full filename for a file that already exists, you can use something like the following statements (which have no arguments):

```
$InFile =
    StandardFile::GetFile();
open(INPUT, $InFile);
```

In order to get the name of a file that the user wants to create from that user, you can write something like this:

```
$NewText =
    StandardFile::PutFile();
open(TEXTOUT, ">$NewText");
```

You can use *relative references* rather than absolute filenames. A relative reference refers to a directory relative to the current directory. For instance, under Windows and UNIX, the directory named `..` indicates the directory above the current directory. On the Mac, you specify the folder above the current folder with two colons (`::`). For example, you can specify that you want to open for writing the process.log file in the directory above the current directory with the following:

```
open(PLOG, '>..\process.log');  # for Windows
open(PLOG, '>::process.log');   # for the Mac
open(PLOG, '>../process.log');  # for UNIX
```

Reading from a Text File the Easy Way, with the File Input Operator

Perl offers you an economical way to read text files. The *file input operator* returns a line from a named text file. By "a line," I mean all the text up to and including the next line separator. The first time you use the file input operator on a file handle, Perl returns the first line of text. The next time you use the file input operator on the same file handle, you get the next line, and so on until there is no more text to be read from the file.

The file input operator consists of angle brackets around the name of a file handle. For instance, in the following statement,

```
while(<INFILE>) {
. . .
}
```

the file handle `INFILE` is surrounded by the file input operator.

Imagine that you have a text file that contains the following information:

```
What I Did Over Summer Vacation

I wanted to go to the park and play ball a lot, but my
mother made me read a bunch of boring books instead.
The first one I read was about a dumb programming language
. . .
```

If this file has the handle `IN`, the first thing returned by `<IN>` is the string `What I Did Over Summer Vacation\n` (that's a single linefeed character at the end of the string). The next item returned by <IN> is the single character \n, then I wanted to go to the park and play ball a lot, but my\n, and so on.

Every string returned by the file input operator ends in a line terminator.

You have two ways to get the result of the file input operator. One is to assign a string to the input, such as in the following statement:

```
$ThisLine = <INPUT>;
```

The other is to use Perl's $_ special variable, which gets assigned by the file input operator.

You typically see the file input operator in Perl programs as part of while loops. For instance, here is a little Perl program that prints a file:

```
open(A, "somefile.txt");
while(<A>) { print $_ }
```

Many programmers also assign $_ to a variable in the first statement inside the while loop:

```
while(<INPUT>) {
     $ThisLine = $_;
     chomp($ThisLine);
     . . .
}
```

If you intend to use the line you got from the file input operator in more than one statement, you should immediately assign $_ to a variable and use that variable instead of $_ because another statement may wipe out $_ and put in its own results.

The while(<HANDLE>) syntax is very handy because it accomplishes a few things at once. The file input operator always returns a true value as long as text is left in the file. As such, the while statement gets a true value when text is in the file and a false value as soon as no additional text remains to be read in the file.

For some programs, you want to use both a variable assignment and a loop with the file input operator. For example, if you're not sure that the file you are opening is the right one, check the first line before processing the file by using something like this:

```
open(THEFILE, $FileName);
$FirstLine = <THEFILE>;
unless($FirstLine eq "What I Did Over Summer Vacation\n")
    { die "This is not the right file.\n"}
while(<THEFILE>) {
    $Line = $_;
    . . .
}
```

In scalar context (described in Chapter 7), Perl reads one line and puts it into the variable. In list context, Perl reads the *entire* file into a list in one step. Therefore, avoid using the file input operator in list context in a loop because everything happens in one call (instead of needing the loop).

A simple file printing program, using the list context, would look like

```
open(A, "somefile.txt");
@B = <A>;  # reads the whole file
print @B;
```

You can also use a `while` loop to read each element of the list:

```
open(A, "somefile.txt");
@B = <A>;  # reads the whole file
while($Line = shift(@B)) { print $Line }
```

The previous two programs accomplish the same thing — `@B` is filled with the lines of the file, one line per element. However, you can't use the following statement to fill `@B` because the `shift` function doesn't put the value it got into `$_`;:

```
while(shift(@B)) { print $_ }  # This is WRONG
```

The file input operator is intended for use with text files only, not binary files. The operator actually works just fine with binary files, but the file input operator is slower than the binary file statements described in Chapter 12.

Writing Text to a File the Easy Way, with the `print` *and* `printf` *Statements*

After you know how to read text from a file, you'll probably want to learn how to write it to a file. You may already know how to do that, almost. The `print` and `printf` statements have a format that enables you to put strings into a file instead of on screen:

```
print HANDLE LIST;
printf HANDLE FORMAT LIST;
```

Note: You do not put a comma after the file handle.

For example, the following program creates a file with ten lines in it.

```
open(OUT, '>lineout.txt') or die "Couldn't open the " .
    "lineout.txt file for writing.\n";
for($i = 1; $i <= 10; $i += 1)
    { print OUT "This is line $i\n" }
```

The previous program doesn't display anything: Instead, it creates a file called lineout.txt whose contents are simply

```
This is line 1
This is line 2
```

and so on through `This is line 10`.

The `printf` statement produced similar results in the same context. For example, the following program

```
open(OUT, '>lineout.txt') or die "Couldn't open the " .
    "lineout.txt file for writing.\n";
for($i = 1; $i <= 10; $i += 1)
    { printf OUT "This is line %.2d\n", $i }
```

creates a file with these lines:

```
This is line 01
This is line 02
```

and so on through `This is line 10`.

As a special bonus, you discover in Chapter 12 that you can use `print` and `printf` to write to binary files as well. Not bad, huh?

When used without file handles, the `print` and `printf` statements print to the screen. (Actually, they print to the *standard output*, which is described at the end of this chapter in "Moving File Streams in UNIX: Standard In, Standard Out, and Standard Error.") When you want to print to a file, normally you use that file's handle in the `print` and `printf` statements. However, Perl lets you change where Perl will print when you don't use the file handle.

The `select` statement, which you can see in the following sample program, tells Perl to cause `print` and `printf` to start printing to the specified file handle (but not to the screen):

```
open(OUT, '>lineout.txt') or die "Couldn't open the " .
    "lineout.txt file for writing.\n";
select(OUT);
for($i = 1; $i <= 10; $i += 1)
    { printf "This is line %.2d\n", $i }
```

The `printf` statement writes to the lineout.txt file because of the `select` statement.

The `select` statement returns the file handle that it's replacing. This makes it easy to use the file handle temporarily and then switch back. The following statements show switching between two file handles, `FH1` and `FH2`:

```
select(FH1);
print "This will go to the file with FH1.\n";
$TempHandle = select(FH2);
print "This will go to the file with FH2.\n";
select($TempHandle);
print "This will go to the file with FH1.\n";
```

I tend to avoid using `select` for the following reason: If you use it and later in the program forget that you did, you may wonder why a `print` statement doesn't result in anything being shown on screen. (Of course, that's true for what happens when you forget almost anything in a Perl program!) The only advantage that `select` gives you is that the `print` and `printf` statements are a bit shorter, but that isn't worth the confusion that it may cause.

Running Tests to Get Information on a File

In addition to reading and writing text files, you may also want to get some information on a file before you open it. Perl has a number of test functions that enable you to determine whether a file exists, how long it has been since the file was created or last updated, the file's size, and other characteristics of the file. The file tests are written in this form:

```
-X FILENAME
```

Here, X represents the specific test, and FILENAME is, as you may guess, the name of the file. Note that the file tests take filenames, not file handles. There's a good reason for this: You may want to test a file before opening it. Or, you may want to test a whole slew of files because it takes less time to run simple file tests than to open and close several files.

For example, the -w test is used to find out whether you can write to a file. When used in a program, it appears like this:

```
if(-w 'somefile.txt') { open(CLIST, '>somefile.txt') }
```

The most widely used file tests also happen to be common to all operating systems. Table 11-1 lists the file tests that return true or false. By the way, the stat function (which is covered in Chapter 12) returns values for many of the file characteristics that are tested.

Table 11-1 Common File Tests

Test	*What It Tells You*
-e	File exists
-r	File can be read
-w	File can be written to
-z	File is exactly 0 bytes long
-d	Named item is a directory, not a file
-T	File is a text file (A portion of file is examined and if fewer than approximately 30 percent of the characters are nonprintable, it's a text file.)
-B	File is a binary file (A portion of file is examined and if fewer than approximately 30 percent of the characters are printable, it's a binary file.)

Some file tests make sense only on UNIX because they address aspects of UNIX that have no equivalent on Windows or the Mac. Table 11-2 lists the UNIX-specific tests; they all return true or false values. (Some of these make sense on Windows NT as well, but they aren't yet implemented in Perl-Win32.)

Table 11-2 UNIX-Specific File Tests

Test	What It Tells You
`-x`	File can be executed
`-o`	File is owned by the effective user of the running program
`-R`	File is readable by the real user of the running program
`-W`	File is writeable by the real user of the running program
`-X`	File is executable by the real user of the running program
`-O`	File is owned by the real user of the running program
`-u`	File has its `setuid` bit set
`-g`	File has its `setgid` bit set
`-k`	File has its sticky bit set

Some file tests return numbers. For instance, the `-s` test tells you how large a file is. `-C`, `-A`, and `-M` tell how long it has been (in days) since the file was created, accessed, or updated. The values returned by these three tests are measured from when the program started (see Table 11-3).

Table 11-3 File Tests That Return Numbers

Test	What It Tells You
`-s`	Size of the file in bytes
`-C`	Creation age of file
`-A`	Access age of file
`-M`	Modification age of file

The tests listed in Table 11-3 are useful for programs that are supposed to execute on files that are older than a certain age. For instance, if you write a backup program that checks whether a file has been modified in the past 12 hours, you can write something like the following:

```
if((-C $TheFile) < 0.5) { &BackupThis($TheFile) }
```

File tests used for more advanced levels of programming are listed in Table 11-4 but are rarely used, even by high-powered Perl programmers. I list them here just in case you run across them in Perl programs that other programmers have created.

Table 11-4 Advanced Programming File Tests

Test	What It Tells You
`-f`	Named item is a plain file (not a special file or directory)
`-l`	Named item is a symbolic link
`-p`	Named item is a pipe
`-S`	Named item is a socket
`-b`	Named item is a block special file
`-c`	Named item is a character special file
`-t`	Named item is a file handle that is opened to a terminal

Moving File Streams in UNIX: Standard In, Standard Out, and Standard Error

Perl's roots in UNIX show up at times I wish they wouldn't. A case in point is the UNIX *standard file* descriptors, which are methods for displaying and receiving data. Although most experienced UNIX jockeys are able to use these descriptors effortlessly, lots of other folks have trouble making heads or tails out of them.

The concept of *standard file input/output (I/O)* runs throughout file handling with Perl. Understanding standard file input and output is useful for getting ahead in Perl. UNIX, and Perl by extension, defines a file as an ordered stream of bytes that can be identified by the operating system. The stream can be from any input process (such as keyboard entry or reading from a disk file) to any output process (such as an on-screen display or writing to a disk file).

Distinguishing the big three file streams

Three file streams have special properties in Perl — *standard file in, standard file out,* and *standard file error* (you can also drop the "file" part and call them *standard in*, *standard out,* and *standard error*). They're also often referred to by the abbreviations STDIN, STDOUT, and STDERR. These streams constitute a system's standard file input/output (I/O) because they are universal to all UNIX implementations.

- STDIN is the byte stream associated with a keyboard, which means that when you type something while a Perl program is running, what you type becomes the contents of STDIN.
- STDOUT is the byte stream that is sent to your computer screen. When you write to STDOUT, it's like saying, "Instead of writing to a file, write to the screen."
- STDERR is a bit more complicated. It's a defined file stream, but different operating systems handle it differently. For instance, most versions of UNIX display characters sent to STDERR on screen, just as STDOUT does. However, you can also tell UNIX to send error messages to a file instead of to the screen. This technique comes in handy when you want to keep a log of error messages but not one for the regular text displayed on the screen.

Perl lets you use STDIN, STDOUT, and STDERR as predefined file handles. This means that you don't have to use open to name these file handles. For example, you can say

```
$GetALine = <STDIN>;
```

The previous statement causes Perl to wait for you to type something followed by an end-of-line character on the keyboard; it then assigns what you entered to the $GetALine string.

If you want to print to STDERR instead of STDOUT, you can use something like the following statement:

```
print STDERR "Bad user input.\n";
```

Perl allows you to use the empty file input operator, <>, instead of <STDIN>, if you do not give arguments on the program's command line. In this case, <> means "all of the files listed on the command line." This can be pretty darn confusing, and you may want to avoid using <> because of it.

Piping data in and out of a program

UNIX allows you to use something called *pipes* to give a stream of bytes (that is, a file) to a program, or take a stream of bytes from a program, through the standard file input and output. You can use pipes in Perl's open statement.

Employing pipes in a program is strictly a UNIX activity. Windows 95/98 and Windows NT users can use stream input through some MS-DOS programs in the MS-DOS box that Perl runs in, but doing so may crash their systems. Mac users can't use the features described here unless they have a programming

environment with the ToolServer program. A program that uses STDIN to take in data can also take in data through a pipe. A program that puts out its data on STDOUT can output its data through a pipe. The pipe acts as a conduit for data going from one source to another.

For instance, UNIX's `uptime` program displays how long a system has been up and its load averages. The `uptime` program displays these statistics by sending them to STDOUT, so you can capture this information with a Perl `open` statement that has a pipe from `uptime` to a file handle:

```
open(UPIN, 'uptime |');
```

This `open` statement tells Perl "run the `uptime` command and take its STDOUT output and feed it into the `UPIN` file handle." `uptime` outputs only a single line, and you can read it with something like this:

```
$UptimeInput = <UPIN>;
```

For UNIX programs that output many lines, you can use a `while` loop just as you would for reading from actual files. For instance, the following example program can be used to find out which directories exist under the `/tmp` directory on your system:

```
open(LSIN, 'ls -l /tmp | ');
while(<LSIN>) {
    $TheLine = $_;
    chomp($TheLine);
    if(substr($TheLine, 0, 1) eq 'd') {
        $LastSpace = rindex($TheLine, ' ');
        $DirName = (substr($TheLine, $LastSpace +1));
        print "$DirName is a directory\n";
    }
}
```

You can also use pipes to write to other programs, although this is done infrequently. A few UNIX programs can take input from STDIN; for example, the `mail` program allows you to send mail with the message coming from STDIN. You can create a program like the following, which sends mail that is created in a Perl program:

```
$MTo = 'someone@someplace.com';
$MSubject = 'Data from the accounting program';
open(DOMAIL, "| mail -s $MailSubject $MTo");
print DOMAIL <<"EndOfMessage";
Your department has a balance of $DeptBal.
If you have questions about this, please send mail
to accounting@someplace.com.
EndOfMessage
```

The rule for using pipes in `open` statements is this: When piping *from* a `print` statement, put the pipe to the left of the UNIX command; when piping *to* a file handle, put the pipe to the right of the UNIX command.

Chapter 12

Beyond the File and Directory Basics

In This Chapter

- Managing binary files and databases
- Changing file settings
- Grouping files by matching characters
- Examining some UNIX-only features
- Getting file statistics
- Handling directories

This chapter covers a zillion (give or take a few million) things about files, such as what to do if you want to read or write to a nontext file, how to change file characteristics and statistics, and how to deal with directories. (For more-basic information on dealing with files, see Chapter 11.)

Reading from and Writing to Binary Files

As I note in Chapter 11, to read a text file line by line, you can use the *file input operator* (the name of the file handle enclosed in angle brackets), as shown in the following statement:

```
$TheLine = <ACCTFILE>;
```

In some cases, the file you want to read from may not be a text file: It may be a binary file. In this case, you must use a set of functions that enables you to read from any part of any file so that you can access just the part of the file you want. (Incidentally, you can also use these functions on text files.)

To read from a binary file, open it using the open statement just as you would with a text file, and then use the read function to read from the file. The format of the read statement is

```
read(HANDLE, VARIABLE, LENGTH, POSITION);
```

The first argument, HANDLE, is the handle name (handles are covered in Chapter 11) from which you want to read; the second argument, VARIABLE, is the place that you want to read into; LENGTH is the number of bytes to read; and POSITION is the byte in the file from which you start reading. Perl uses 0 as the position for the first byte in a file.

For example, to read the first seven bytes from a file that's the handle ACCTDATA, you use the following statement:

```
read(ACCTDATA, $Start, 7, 0);
```

The read statement returns the number of bytes actually read. That number comes in handy when you don't know how long a file is, but you want to know whether you've accidentally read beyond the end of the file. For instance, if you tell Perl to read 7 characters with the read function and Perl tells you that it has read only 5 characters, you know that you haven't read off the end of the file. For example, you can detect whether you've read to the end of a file by using something like this:

```
$NumGot = read(ACCTDATA, $Start, 7, 0);
if($NumGot < 7)
    { print "You read off the end of the file.\n" }
```

Keeping track of your position in a file

Perl keeps track of where you've read in a file relative to the beginning of the file. For instance, after the read function in the example in the previous section, Perl sets the file position keeper for the ACCTDATA file handle to 6, which is the position in the file that was last read. You can use the eof function to test whether the next read starts at the end of the file. The eof function returns true if the pointer is at the end of the file. (By the way, "eof" is dweeb-speak for "end of file.")

The following example demonstrates the use of the eof function in an until loop that is reading data:

```
unless(eof(ACCTDATA)) {
    $NumGot = read(ACCTDATA, $Start, 7, 0);
    if($NumGot < 7)
```

```
        { print "You read off the end of the file.\n" }
}
else { print "Already at end of the file.\n" }
```

Note that `eof` won't tell you if you're near the end of a file, only if you're *at* the end of a file. That's why you need to check how many characters you receive with each `read` to be sure that you don't receive fewer characters than you expected.

The `seek` statement enables you to place the file position keeper anywhere you want. Its format is

```
seek(HANDLE, RELATIVEPOSITION, FROMWHERE);
```

The third argument in the previous `seek` statement determines the starting point of the relative position of the second argument: a `FROMWHERE` of `0` means the second argument is relative to the beginning of the file; `1` means the second argument is relative to the current file position; and `2` means the second argument is relative to the end of the file. So to move the position keeper forward 12 positions, you would use

```
seek(ACCTDATA, 12, 1);
```

Or, to move the position keeper to the second byte in the file, you would use

```
seek(ACCTDATA, 1, 0);
```

The file position keeper is useful because you don't always have to remember how far you've progressed if you're reading through a file from start to finish. You can leave the last argument off the `read` function, and Perl uses the file position keeper instead. For instance, to read a file ten bytes at a time until the end of the file, you can use the following:

```
seek(ACCTDATA, 0, 0);  # If it wasn't at the beginning
while(read(ACCTDATA, $Start, 10)) {
    # $Start is now the next ten bytes of the file
    #    If this is the last chunk of the file, it might
    #    be less than ten bytes long, however.
}
```

If you want to know where the file position keeper currently is, use the `tell` function. For example,

```
$FilePos = tell(ACCTDATA);
```

Writing to a binary file

So, you use `read` to read from a binary file: What do you use to *write* to a binary file? If you said `write`, you're wrong. Perl's `write` function has nothing to do with writing to a binary file. Instead, you use `print` with a file handle, as described in Chapter 11.

To write nontext data to a file using the `print` function, you can employ functions such as `chr` and certain special characters (see Chapter 5). For instance, to write the five characters whose values are 23, 97, 192, 12, and 0, you can use something like the following:

```
@PrintThese = (23, 97, 192, 12, 0);
foreach $Item (@PrintThese) { print ACCTDATA chr($Item) }
```

Forcing binary reads

The Windows operating system treats binary files differently than text files. If you're running Perl on Windows and are using the `read` function, you must first use the `binmode` function so that Perl can tell the operating system to do binary reads (yes, this is incredibly annoying, but unfortunately a necessity in some cases). The function is called in this way:

```
binmode(FILEHANDLE);
```

Using `binmode` in the programs in which you employ the `read` function won't cause errors, even on operating systems other than Windows. If you later copy a Perl program to a less-intelligent operating system (that is, a Windows-based system), you don't have to remember to search through your programs for `read` functions because you've already covered yourself by including the `binmode` function.

Reading one character at a time

Another method exists for reading characters from a file, but I have to warn you, it's very slow. The `getc` function returns the next character from a named file; if you're at the end of the file, `getc` returns the null character. For example, the following program reads a character and checks whether you are at the end of the file:

```
$TheChar = getc(ACCTDATA);
if($TheChar eq '') { print "At the end of the file.\n" }
```

Changing File Characteristics

Perl gives you complete access to doing anything with your files within your programs. For instance, you can rename or delete a file from a Perl program while you're working in the program or running a program. Not all programming languages give you this luxury.

Renaming files

The `rename` function takes two arguments: the old name and the new name. It returns true if successful at renaming the file. The following example program renames a file and checks to see whether the rename worked :

```
unless(rename('somedata.txt', 'somedata.old'))
    { print "The rename failed.\n" }
```

The `rename` function comes in handy for changing file extensions. (In Windows, file extensions are significant in defining a file. For instance, double-clicking on a file that has a `.txt` extension causes Windows to do something completely different than double-clicking on a file that has the `.exe` extension.) Assume that you want to change the current extension of a file to `.old`. If the file name is kept in `$FileName`, you can use the following program to accomplish that:

```
$PeriodPos = index($FileName, '.');
if($PeriodPos == -1) { $BareName = $FileName }
else { $BareName = substr($FileName, 0, $PeriodPos) }
$NewName = "$BareName.old";
rename($FileName, $NewName);
```

Changing file access and modification times

To change the times that your computer thinks that a file has been accessed or modified, you can use the `utime` function. The function takes as its argument a list in the following format:

```
(ACCESSTIME, MODIFICATIONTIME, FILE1, FILE2, ...)
```

Hacking off the ends of files

In a slash-and-burn mood? The `truncate` function tells Perl to whack off the end of a file. The `truncate` function takes two arguments: the name or file handle of the file and the abbreviated length of the file. For example, to make the `nowshort.txt` file exactly 100 characters long, and tell Perl to discard whatever is in the file beyond that point, you can use this:

```
truncate('nowshort.txt', 100);
```

For instance, if you want to change the access and modification time of a file to the current time, you can use

```
$Now = time();
utime($Now, $Now, 'somedata.txt');
```

Deleting files

To delete a file, you can use the `unlink` function. This peculiar function name comes from the way that UNIX deletes files from a directory — by unlinking them from the directory structure. The `unlink` function takes a list of the names of the files that you want to delete and returns the number of files deleted. For example, the following statement attempts to delete two files, a.dat and b.dat, and prints a message if either or both files aren't deleted:

```
unless(unlink('a.dat', 'b.dat') == 2)
    { print "One of the files didn't get deleted.\n" }
```

UNIX users beware: The `unlink` function doesn't delete a file if it has multiple links to it. The function simply removes the single link for that file in the named directory or in the current directory. A file isn't really deleted from the system until you remove all links to the file.

Great Globs of Files: Grouping File Names by Matching Characters

Perl 5 introduced a humorously named feature called *file globbing* that enables you to easily create a list of files based on matching characters in file names. With the `glob` function, you can use an asterisk (*) as a wildcard character just as you can in Windows or UNIX file commands.

For you Macintosh users who haven't had the pleasure of working with Windows or UNIX, the asterisk wildcard character is used to match one or more other characters in file names. When you search for files in a directory, you can match one or more files using the asterisk in your test file name to indicate that you want to find any file that has one or more other characters in that place.

For example, imagine that you have a directory with five files whose names are

```
chartabl.pl
counter1.pl
edata.txt
empdata1.pl
hexchart.pl
```

Searching for the file `c*` matches chartab1.pl and counter.pl because both file names start with the letter c and have one or more characters after the c in the file name. Similarly, searching for `*pl` matches chartab1.pl, counter.pl, empdata1.pl, and hexchart.pl because all these files have one or more characters followed by the letters pl.

In a similar fashion, the `glob` function returns a list of files in the current directory that matches the text argument. For example, to get a list of all the files that start with the letter m, you can use

```
@XFiles = glob('m*');
```

The results of the `glob` function can be used to process groups of files that you know have similar names. For instance, imagine that you want to delete all the files in a directory that have .tmp at the ends of their names. The following statement will accomplish that:

```
unlink(glob('*.tmp'));
```

Suppose that you want to create one big file that contains the contents of every file that starts with the letters "flow." You'd enter something like this:

```
open(BIG, ">bigflow");
@AllFlow = glob('flow*');
foreach $FileName (@AllFlow) {
    open(IN, $FileName);
    print "Inserting the file $FileName\n";
    print BIG <IN>;
    close(IN);
}
close(BIG);
```

File Features Strictly for UNIX Users

Perl was originally created for UNIX system administrators, and many aspects of the UNIX system are meaningful to only those folks. Nevertheless, some of Perl's file features are useful to UNIX users who at least know how to navigate the UNIX file system and use UNIX file commands. (If you want to find out more about UNIX, I recommend *UNIX For Dummies, 3rd Edition*, by John R. Levine and Margaret Levine Young [IDG Books Worldwide, Inc.].)

Perl's version of `chown` and `chmod`

You UNIX folks may be familiar with the `chmod` and `chown` commands in UNIX: They change, respectively, file access privileges and the owner of a file. Perl has its own `chmod` and `chown` functions that act like the UNIX commands.

The `chmod` function takes a list as its argument. The first item of the list is the numerical permission you want on the files, and the rest of the list is the files you want changed. For example, to make a file readable and writable by a file owner and group, with no permission granted to others, you can use the following statement:

```
chmod(0660, 'somefile', 'someotherfile');
```

If you're not familiar with numerical permissions under UNIX, avoid using this function, because changing the permissions can make a file unavailable.

Most UNIX systems display the numeric file permissions in octal, and you can use these permissions directly in `chmod`. The octal value `0660` in the previous example looks pretty cryptic, just the way UNIX systems folks like it. Unfortunately, Perl's `chmod` function doesn't enable you to use the alphabetic file permissions such as "rw-rw——". I find that alphabetic file permissions are much more readable than the octal values because you don't have to do an octal conversion in your head.

The `chown` function also takes a list as its argument. The first item in the list is the numeric user ID, the second item is the numeric group ID, and the rest consists of the files you want to change:

```
chown(100, 12, 'somefile', 'someotherfile');
```

Functions for creating links

The UNIX file system enables you to create file names that are nothing more than links to other files on a computer. If you're a UNIX user and familiar with symbolic links, you can use Perl to create both hard links and symbolic links. The `link` and `symlink` functions take two arguments: the existing file and the link you want to create.

The `link` function is like the UNIX command `ln` with no arguments, and `symlink` is like the UNIX command `ln -s`. For instance, to create a new file in the current directory, TheLog, that is a symbolic link to the /var/log/maillog file, you can use

```
symlink('/var/log/maillog', './TheLog');
```

The `readlink` function, whose argument is a file name, returns the value of a symbolic link. The value of the link is the name of the file that the symbolic link connects to. For example, to see the name of the file to which the symbolic link TheLog is linked, you can use

```
print readlink('./TheLog');
```

Getting the Nitty-Gritty Stats on Files

If you turn to Chapter 11, you can find information on file tests that return a true or false value on a number of file characteristics. Perl also makes it possible to get the information you'd obtain through individual file tests all at once in a list.

The `stat` function, which takes either a file handle or a file name as its argument, returns a wealth of information about a file. The `stat` function returns a list whose elements are shown in Table 12-1. Most of the returned elements have no meaning except on UNIX, as you can see.

Table 12-1 Information Returned by the `stat` Function

Element	*Information Returned*
0	Device number (UNIX only)
1	Inode number (UNIX only)
2	Inode protection mode (UNIX only)
3	Number of links to the file (UNIX only)
4	User ID of owner
5	Group ID of owner
6	Device type (UNIX only)

(continued)

Table 12-1 *(continued)*

Element	*Information Returned*
7	File size (in bytes)
8	Time of last access (seconds from OS base time)
9	Time of last modification (seconds from OS base time)
10	Time of last file status change (seconds from OS base time)
11	Optimal block size (UNIX only)
12	Number of blocks allocated for the file (UNIX only)

If you're on UNIX and examining a file that's a symbolic link, the `lstat` function returns the information on the file that the function's argument is linked to, not the link itself. That's useful if you want the real fine information, not just the information about the link (which itself is a file).

The following is an example of how to use the `stat` function to determine the size of a file.

```
@FileStuff = stat(MYFILE);
$TheSize = $FileStuff[7];
```

Directories: Dealing with Gangs of Files

At times you may want to process a whole directory at once, instead of dealing with files one at a time. Perl offers a set of functions that handles directories similar to the way that files are handled. Instead of examining characters in a file, however, they examine the files in a directory.

The directory functions use directory handles as arguments. *Directory handles* are similar to file handles except that you use them for directories (see Chapter 11 for information on file handles). Directory handle names must adhere to the same rules as file handle names and are used in generally the same way.

Opening directories

You tell Perl to start processing a directory by using the `opendir` statement, which functions like the `open` command for files. (Perl also has an equivalent `closedir` function.) An `opendir` statement takes two arguments: the name of the directory handle you want to use and the name of the directory you want to open. For example,

```
opendir(DOCS, 'C:\TREES\DOCS');
```

You can also open directories relative to the current directory. In that case, you use just the directory name, not the full path to the directory. For instance, to open the directory called "Nancy" relative to the current directory, you can use:

```
opendir(TEMP, 'Nancy');
```

To open the current directory, you can use the special directory name "." on UNIX and Windows and ":" on a Mac. To open the directory above the current one, you can use the special directory name ".." (or "::" on a Mac). For example, to open the current directory in UNIX or Windows, you can enter:

```
opendir(TEMP, '.');
```

Returning file names in a directory

The `readdir` function, when used in a scalar context (with strings or numbers), returns the next file name or subdirectory name in the directory. For example,

```
$ThisName = readdir(DOCS);
```

When used in a list context, `readdir` returns all the file names and subdirectory names at once in a list. For example,

```
@AllNames = readdir(DOCS);
```

The `telldir` function returns the value of the directory position keeper.

The `seekdir` changes the position of the directory position keeper.

The three directory functions `readdir`, `telldir`, and `seekdir` are similar to `read`, `tell`, and `seek` for files (which are covered in Chapter 11) except that `readdir` can return only one file name, whereas `read` can read one or more characters.

The `rewinddir` function sets the directory position keeper to the beginning of the directory list.

One catch in using the directory functions is that you can't tell when you get to the end of a directory except by checking to see if `readdir` returns a null string. Unfortunately, no directory equivalent of the `eof` (end of file) function exists. Therefore, using `readdir` in a list context causes `readdir` to return all the file names at once into your list.

Walking through directories

The `readdir` function returns the names of files or subdirectories in a seemingly random order. The order in which files and subdirectories are returned is the order assigned by the operating system, which is usually neither alphabetical nor related to size.

The `readdir` function returns both file names and subdirectory names. On UNIX and Windows systems, it also returns the special directory entries "." and ".." (Mac users don't have to concern themselves with this). So, when you look through the results of a `readdir` statement, don't automatically assume that what you have is a file name.

Assume that you want to find out the total size of every file in the current directory. You can use something like the following program:

```
opendir(HERE, '.');  # Mac users would use ':' instead
@AllFiles = readdir(HERE);
$TotSize = 0;
foreach $Name (@AllFiles) {
    if(-d $Name) { next }  # It's a directory: skip it
    $TotSize += (-s $Name);  # Add its size to the total
}
```

Or, you may want to know the names of the subdirectories of a directory. In which case, you can use a program like this one:

```
opendir(HERE, '.');  # Mac users would use ':' instead
@AllFiles = readdir(HERE);
foreach $Name (@AllFiles) {
    if(-d $Name) { print "$Name\n" }
}
```

Creating and destroying directories

Two directory functions, `mkdir` and `rmdir`, are used, respectively, to make or delete a directory. Neither function uses directory handles; instead, they use directory names. Both functions return true if they're successful, and false if they aren't.

The `mkdir` function takes two arguments: the name of the directory you want to create and a mode. The mode is relevant only on UNIX systems and is ignored on Windows and the Mac. On UNIX, the mode consists of the read and write permissions for the directory (the settings that say whether you can read from or write to that directory). You can see `mkdir` at work in the following statement:

```
mkdir('subdir', 0770);
```

To delete a directory, use `rmdir`, which takes one argument: the name of the directory to delete. For example,

```
rmdir('subdir');
```

Chapter 13

Stringing Along: Pattern Matching and Regular Expressions

In This Chapter

- Examining regular expressions
- Searching for strings within strings
- Changing text selectively
- Modifying matches
- Determining the results of the matches
- Translating strings into other strings

Perl uses a *regular expression* as one consistent means of finding specified text in a program. You can use a regular expression in many ways. For example, you can search through strings for tab characters and turn them into line breaks, or change every instance of two spaces into one, or make sure that every period has a space after it. You can even quickly determine if a string has a particular letter anywhere in it.

With all of these tasks, Perl first searches for text in a string and then does something with the text (such as copy it to a variable). This kind of searching is called *pattern matching* because you give Perl the pattern of characters that you are looking for, and it finds all the text that matches that pattern.

Different programming languages and operating systems have their own methods for enabling you to say, “I want to specify some text that I'm looking for.” Perl uses UNIX's regular expressions for this kind of searching. (You UNIX users may already know how to specify searches, or at least you have been exposed to it.) Because regular expressions come from the murky world of UNIX, many people find them difficult to understand, but this chapter can help you grasp how they're used to simplify text handling in your programs.

In this chapter, I first describe the simple (yet powerful) regular expressions that you can use in your everyday Perl programming. Later on, I describe other regular expression features that you can use in your more advanced programming efforts.

What's So Regular about Regular Expressions?

Regular expressions turn up in a number of Perl programming applications. Consider the split function, for instance (which you can read about in Chapter 7 and later in this chapter in "Using the split Function with More-Advanced Regular Expressions"). The split function takes a regular expression as its first argument. The function searches through a string for a particular substring and then splits the string into smaller strings anywhere the substring is found. You express split arguments with a slash (/), followed by the specific text to be found, and another slash, as shown in the following statement:

```
@TheFields = split(/\t/, $TheRecord);
```

In the preceding example, the regular expression is \t. This line of code returns a list of strings that are found in the $TheRecord variable, where each string is the text between tab characters (\t indicates a tab). Therefore, if $TheRecord contains the word Speakers, followed by a tab character, the numeral 2, another tab character, and the word High, the split function in this example returns

```
('Speakers', '2', 'High')
```

The simplest kind of regular expression consists of the exact character or characters you want to search for, such as the single tab character in the previous example. You can also place more than one character between the slashes in the argument. For example, assume that you have a database in a text file in which you use three pound signs (###) between fields instead of a tab character. In which case, you would change the split statement to the following:

```
@TheFields = split(/###/, $TheRecord);
```

Conducting true-false searches with the m// operator

When you're getting the hang of using regular expressions, the m// operator comes in handy because it allows you to write small programs to test strings. The m// operator returns true or false depending on whether the operator finds what is being tested for. (Because most programmers use a slash [/] character at the beginning and end of their regular expressions, the m operator is written as the m// operator instead.)

The m// operator is followed by the regular expression that you want to test and preceded by the =~ operator (also called the *binding* operator). The binding operator tests the expression against something that is entered to its left. For example, to test whether the string "abc#def" contains the string "#", you can use the following:

```
if("abc#def" =~ m/#/)
    { print "True\n" } else { print "False\n" }
```

Running this statement prints True on your screen.

You can also place variables on the left side of the =~ operator. For example

```
if($Test =~ m/#/)
    { print "True\n" } else { print "False\n" }
```

results in True being printed if the $Test string contains one or more # characters.

You may also want to generate a true value if the pattern you are searching for is not found. To get a positive result if the searched-for pattern is not found, use the !~ operator instead of the =~ operator. For example, to determine whether no # character exists in a string, you can use something like the following:

```
if($Test !~ m/#/)  # If there is no hash character...
    { print "True\n" } else { print "False\n" }
```

You can use variables in your search. In the following line, if $Find contains the string you want to search for, and $Test is the string you want to search within, you can enter

```
if($Test =~ m/$Find/)
```

Watch out for patterns that are equivalent to the *null string* (that is, a string of zero length) in the patterns you search for. If the pattern you give is the null string, Perl uses the value in the special variable $_ as the search pattern, and you may have no idea what's in $_ at the time (see Chapter 12 for more on the special variable $_). If you use a variable as the search pattern, make sure you know what's in that variable first.

Tightening up your statements

Perl has to know where your regular expressions begin and end. More programmers use a slash (/) than any other character to signal the beginning and end of expressions, also known as *delimiting*. (Because almost every Perl program I've seen uses the slash character, that's my choice, too.) But, you can delimit your regular expression with any character, such as a vertical bar (|) for example:

```
if($Test =~ m|#|) . . .
```

Although you can use any character for delimiting, you may want to stick with the slash character because it enables you to use the short form of the m// operator (which most Perl programmers do). If you use the slash character, you don't have to include the m:

```
if($Test =~ /#/) . . .
```

To make your statements even more compact, if you're searching in Perl's special variable $_, you don't need the =~ operator at all. The file input operator <> puts the next line of the file into $_ (see Chapter 12 for more on file input operators). So, you may use something like this:

```
while(<INFILE>) {
    if(/Proprietary/) {  # The line has the keyword
    . . .
```

Accounting for those special metacharacters

Regular expressions frequently use special characters that you may also want to search for. For example, the vertical bar (|) has a special meaning in a regular expression. If you want to search for a vertical bar and ignore its special meaning, you have to precede the vertical bar with a backslash (\). So, to search for a vertical bar character, you have to construct something like this:

```
if($Test =~ /\|/) . . .
```

Sure, this statement looks kind of goofy, but it's the only way to tell Perl not to treat the vertical bar as anything special. Now you may be asking, "How do I search for a backslash?" Good question, same answer: Precede it with a backslash:

```
if($Test =~ /\\/) . . .
```

Characters that have special meaning to Perl are called *metacharacters*. The following metacharacters require the backslash treatment I just described when you want Perl to disregard their special significance:

```
^ $ + * ? . | ( ) { } \ [ ]
```

Add slash (/) to this group of metacharacters if you use it as a delimiter for your regular expressions.

How about some cruel and unusual punishment? Determine if a string has the pattern "slash, backslash, vertical bar, slash, vertical bar, backslash, caret" in it. Give up? Try this:

```
if($Test =~ /\/\\\|\/\|\\\^/) . . .
```

If you're not sure whether a string has metacharacters in it, you can use the *quotemeta* function available in Perl 5 and later versions. The quotemeta function takes a string and returns a string with backslashes in front of its metacharacters. For example,

```
print quotemeta('ab/cd|ef');
```

displays

```
ab\/cd\|ef
```

Making Inexact Matches in Regular Expressions

At times, you may not know the exact characters you're searching for when you're writing your program. For example, you may be searching for "the letter x or the letter X," or "one or more hash characters," or even "a hash character followed by any other character followed by a hash character." Regular expressions make these imprecise character matches fairly easy to do.

Alternating matches

To indicate that you want to match either one character or another, insert a vertical bar (|) between the characters you want to match. This technique is called *alternating* because you give Perl a list of alternate choices to look for. For example, to search for either "x" or "X," you can use the following statement

```
if($Test =~ /(x|X)/) . . .
```

which matches exactly one "x" or "X" in the `$Test` variable.

Enclosing like items in parentheses

Just as you would with a numeric equation (which I cover in Chapter 6), you can enclose a group of related items in your regular expression with parentheses in order to group them together. You can have more than one kind of item in a regular expression, such as a fixed expression and an alternating list. For example, to search for the words "candle," "candy," and "candid," you can use

```
if($Test =~ /can(dle|dy|did)/) . . .
```

Matching characters using a wildcard

If you don't know which character you want to match, you can use a period (`.`) as a wildcard character. For example, if you want to match "the letter N followed by any character followed by the letter T," you can use the following statement:

```
if($Test =~ /N.T/) . . .
```

In this example, the statement returns true for NET and N3T and N+T, but returns false for NEST (because NEST has two characters between the N and the T). Note that this statement returns false for "net" because regular expressions are case-sensitive and therefore distinguish between uppercase and lowercase characters.

The period wildcard matches any character, printable or not, other than `\n`. Therefore, the wildcard won't match across a line break but does match anywhere else.

Matching character classes

Regular expressions can also match *character classes,* which are lists of individual characters to be matched. To specify a character class, you enclose the characters in square brackets (instead of parentheses) and list the characters. For example, to match "x" or "X" with a character class, you can use this statement:

```
if($Test =~ /[xX]/) . . .
```

To indicate that you want to match any character *not* in a particular range, insert a caret character (^) in front of a list of characters in that range. For example, to match any character that's not one of the first five capital letters, you can use

```
if($Test =~ /[^ABCDE]/) . . .
```

Character classes are structured more compactly and are easier to read than an alternating list when you're searching for many single characters, such as "any digit." For example, the following statement is the *alternation* version (that is, the list of alternates) of a search for the numerals 0 through 9:

```
if($Test =~ /(0|1|2|3|4|5|6|7|8|9)/) . . .
```

Using a character class, the previous statement looks like this:

```
if($Test =~ /[0123456789]/) . . .
```

Character classes can be specified as ranges by using a hyphen (-). So, the "any digit" example I just provided can be simplified even more:

```
if($Test =~ /[0-9]/) . . .
```

If you want to test for "any uppercase or lowercase letter," you can use the following:

```
if($Test =~ /[A-Za-z]/) . . .
```

Note that a range indicated with a hyphen is different than a range indicated with the *range operator* (..) described in Chapter 7, which is used to create a list of numbers.

Because ranges are frequently used in Perl, you should make use of a couple of shortcuts so that you don't have to specify the actual range. These shortcuts (see Table 13-1) are somewhat like the backslash codes used for special characters (such as \t for the tab character) that are described in Chapter 5, except that they indicate a range to be matched.

Table 13-1 Shortcuts for Character Ranges

Code	*Replaces*	*Description*
\d	[0–9]	Any digit
\w	[a–zA–Z_0-–]	Any alphanumeric character
\s	[\t\n\r\f]	A whitespace character
\D	[^0–9]	Any nondigit
\W	[^a–zA–Z_0–9]	Any nonalphanumeric character
\S	[^\t\n\r\f]	A nonwhitespace character

Given the shortcuts listed in Table 13-1, you can reduce your "any digit" search statement to the following:

```
if($Test =~ /\d/) . . .
```

You can test for "A capital letter followed by two digits" by using this:

```
if($Test =~ /[A-Z]\d\d/) . . .
```

To find "a word that has three letters," meaning "three alphanumeric characters that are preceded by and followed by a whitespace character," you use

```
if($Test =~ /\s\w\w\w\s/) . . .
```

Location, Location, Location: Searching in That Special Spot

At times, what you want to match in a string is at the very beginning or end of a string. In this case, you use a carat (^) to indicate the beginning of the string and a dollar sign ($) to indicate the end. For example, to see if a string starts with Beg, use the following statement:

```
if($Test =~ /^Beg/) . . .
```

This statement wouldn't find the string "I Beg Your Pardon" because it doesn't start with Beg.

To match in a string that ends with don, for example, use

```
if($Test =~ /don$/) . . .
```

Using the $ character to indicate the end of a string may result in a big surprise if you don't know about newline characters. If the last character in the string is the newline character, $ forces the search to occur only at the end of the line. Therefore, if the variable `$Test` is either "I Beg Your Pardon" or "I Beg Your Pardon\n" (without or with a newline character), searching for `don$` returns true.

Perl enables you to specify that a search should start at a *word boundary* (the point between an alphanumeric and a non-alphanumeric character, for example) by using the `\b` character combination. The `\b` code is useful for finding text at the beginning of a word. For example, to determine if a word in a string starts with the letter Y, you can use

```
if($Test =~ /\bY/) . . .
```

Or, to find the letter J at the end of a word, you can use

```
if($Test =~ /J\b/) . . .
```

The `\B` code indicates the opposite of the `\b` code: a location that's not within a word boundary (that is, in the middle of a word).

You Can Count on It: Using Quantifiers for Numerical Matches

What happens when you want to match on an unknown number of repetitions of a string? For example, assume you want to find "one or more hash characters (pound signs)" in the string `abc#def`. You can use the following statement:

```
if("abc#def" =~ /#|##|###|####/) . . .
```

Using exact strings like the one in the previous example isn't a general enough usage for many applications you want to write. Instead, you can use other special characters outside of the slashes to indicate how many copies of what's inside the slashes to match on. Characters used for this sort of counting are called *quantifiers* because they enable you to tell Perl the number of times that a string can exist before it is matched. (See Table 13-2 for a list of the quantifiers.)

For example, to search for "one or more hash characters," you use

```
if($Test =~ /#+/) . . .
```

Or, to search for “exactly three digits,” you use

```
if($Test =~ /\d{3}/) . . .
```

Table 13-2 Pattern-Matching Quantifiers

Symbol	*Meaning*
+	Match 1 or more times
*	Match 0 or more times
?	Match 0 or 1 time
{n}	Match exactly *n* times
{n,}	Match at least *n* times
{n,m}	Match at least *n* but not more than *m* times (these values must be less than 65,536)

You can combine quantifiers with character classes to do some pretty fancy stuff (see “Matching character classes” earlier in this chapter for information on character classes). For example, to search for a word that ends in a digit, you can use

```
if($Test =~ /\w+\d/) . . .
```

This statement translates to “search for one or more alphanumeric characters followed by one digit.”

The most frequently used quantifier in regular expressions is the + quantifier. You can also put the * quantifier to good use. Consider the following line of code:

```
if($Test =~ /N.T/) . . .
```

The previous line matches NET but doesn’t match NEST because NEST contains one too many characters. This line doesn’t match NT either because NT has one too few characters. (The single “.” character must match a single character.)

If you want to match “N followed by *one or more* arbitrary characters, followed by T,” you can use

```
if($Test =~ /N.+T/) . . .
```

The previous line matches NET and NEST and NEATEST, but not NT.

If you want to match “N followed by zero or more arbitrary characters, followed by T,” you would instead use

```
if($Test =~ /N.*T/) . . .
```

This line matches NT, NET, NEST, and so on.

Getting the Match Results

With open-ended matches, it would be nice to find out precisely *what* is in fact matched. For example, if the following statement

```
if($Test =~ /N.*T/) . . .
```

returned true, it may be useful to know which string or strings actually matched.

To get the results of a test, use *grouping parentheses* in the regular expression and then check Perl's special variables `$1`, `$2`, `$3`, and so on. Grouping parentheses indicate the exact point in a regular expression where the matching should be done. Consider the following program:

```
$Test = 'NESTING';
if($Test =~ /(N.*T)/)
    { print "True\n" } else { print "False\n" }
print "$1\n";
```

When you run this program, Perl displays

```
True
NEST
```

`$1` matches the result of the first set of parentheses, `$2` matches the result of the second set, and so on. For example, when you run the following program

```
$Test = 'NESTING';
if($Test =~ /(N.)S(.I)/)
    { print "True\n" } else { print "False\n" }
print "$1\n$2\n";
```

Perl displays

```
True
NE
TI
```

Perl's greedy matching

Some of you are probably asking, What is in the string that Perl returns when you have more than one match? For example, what can you expect Perl to print when you run the following program?

```
$Test = 'NITWITS';
if($Test =~ /(N.*T)/)
{ print "True\n" } else { print "False\n" }
print "$1\n";
```

The answer is this:

```
True
NITWIT
```

By default, Perl always uses a method that is affectionately called *greedy matching.* It's greedy because it matches as much as possible on the first try. Perl sees quantifiers as an open invitation to get greedy.

You can suppress Perl's greedy ways by following a quantifier with a question mark (?). Perl then matches the shortest possible string instead of the longest string. For example, note the following small change to the second line of the previous program:

```
$Test = 'NITWITS';
if($Test =~ /(N.*?T)/)
{ print "True\n" } else { print "False\n" }
print "$1\n";
```

The slight change results in different output:

```
True
NIT
```

If for some odd reason you want to suppress $1 or $2 to prevent them from getting assigned, add a ?: after the left parenthesis (this only works with Perl 5 and later versions):

```
$Test = 'NESTING';
if($Test =~ /(?:N.)S(.I)/)
    { print "True\n" } else { print "False\n" }
print "$1\n";
```

When you run this program, Perl displays

```
True
TI
```

More Programming Magic with the m// Operator

Many functions and operators, including the m// operator (which returns true or false depending on whether the operator finds what it's looking for) work hand-in-hand with regular expressions. In the following sections of this chapter, I show you how the m// operator can be employed with regular expressions.

The m// operator when used in a *scalar context* returns true or false depending on whether a string is matched. In *list context,* however, the m// operator returns a list of the strings matched in the parentheses. Using m// in list context is essentially like creating a list that contains the special variables $1, $2, and so on. For instance, the following program demonstrates how to create the list @Birds as a result of m// search:

```
$Test = 'NESTING';
@Birds = ($Test =~ /(N.)S(.I)/);
print join("\n", @Birds);
```

When you run this program, Perl displays

```
NE
TI
```

If no grouping parentheses are used in the regular expression, Perl returns the list (1) — a list with a single true value in it.

Using m// operator modifiers

The m// operator uses modifiers that change the way m// searches in some respects (see Table 13-3). The modifiers follow the closing slash character, such as the i modifier that follows the / in the following:

```
if($Test =~ /(N.*T)/i) . . .
```

Table 13-3 Modifiers for m//

Modifier	Description
g	Returns each occurrence (global search)
i	Ignores case
m	Allows multiple lines in the string
o	Compiles the pattern once
s	Treats the pattern as a single line
x	Allows whitespace for comments

The `m`, `s`, and `x` modifiers are available in Perl 5 or later versions.

The `i` modifier forces Perl to ignore case when searching. For example, if `$Test` is "nest" then the statement

```
if($Test =~ /(N.*T)/i) . . .
```

would be true.

The `o` modifier prevents Perl from using variable substitution in the pattern you are searching when the value of the variable changes. Using the `o` modifier allows your program to run slightly faster but prevents you from using variable substitution in the pattern. Generally, the speed increase gained by using the `o` modifier is slight, relative to the speed of the whole program.

The `x` modifier enables you to add spaces, line breaks, and text comments in your regular expressions as a way of making them more readable. You usually need to add spaces and breaks to complex regular expressions only. For example, instead of saying

```
if($Test =~ /(N.)S(.I)/) . . .
```

you can write the following, which is clearer:

```
if($Test =~ /
    (N.)  (?# Start with N and any letter)
    S  (?# ...followed by the letter S)
    (.I)  (?# ...followed by another letter, then I)
    /x) . . .
```

On the other hand, I don't think that these kind of comments make most regular expressions more readable than a regular Perl comment on the line before them. So, it's up to you if you want comments to precede the regular expression or if you want to place your comments in the regular expression.

Doing global searches in the `m//` operator

The `g` modifier causes Perl to do a global search on a string. This may sound odd because Perl is supposedly already searching the whole string. The term *global* as it's used here, however, refers to the way that Perl returns different results based on the `g` modifier.

In a list context, Perl returns a list of the strings matched using parentheses. But, if the regular expression (which is `N` in the following example) contains no parentheses, Perl creates a list of each matched item as you can see here:

```
$Test = 'NESTING';
@Birds = ($Test =~ /N./g);
print join("\n", @Birds);
```

When you run this program, Perl displays

```
NE
NG
```

Getting a list is a handy way to find all the matching strings if you don't know how many you'll have.

In scalar context, Perl returns true and false for each match in the string. Perl remembers where in the string it found the last match and starts from there for the next search. Performing `m//` searches in a scalar context is a good method for determining how many matches exist without looking at the matches. The following example shows how you can examine the number of matches without looking at the matches themselves:

```
$Test = 'NESTING';
$i = 0;
while($Test =~ /N./g) { $i += 1 }
print "There were $i matches.\n";
```

You can use the `pos` function to determine where Perl is going to start the next global search in scalar context. The argument to `pos` is the string you are searching in. For example,

```
$Test = 'NESTING';
$i = 0;
while($Test =~ /N./g) {
    $i += 1;
    print "Now at " . pos($Test) . ".\n";
}
print "There were $i matches.\n";
```

When you run this program, Perl displays

```
Now at 2.
Now at 7.
There were 2 matches.
```

If you want to change the point at which Perl starts searching the string, you can set the starting position in the string to any number you wish. For example, to start searching two characters farther ahead than the current position, you can say

```
pos($Test) += 2;
```

Searching for multiple lines in a string

The `^` and `$` characters match the beginning and end of a string. But, you may want `^` to match the beginning of lines and `$` to match the end of lines in a string that has more than one line in it.

In Perl 4, to get `^` and `$` to match the beginning and end of each line in a string, set the `$*` special variable to `1` before the test. By default, `$*` is set to `0`, so `^` and `$` match the beginning and end of the string, and not lines in the string.

In Perl 5 and later versions, you can use the `m` modifier in a regular expression in order to get `^` and `$` to match the beginning and end of each line in a string. For example, this statement finds a tab character at the beginning of any line in the string.

```
if($Test =~ /^\t/m) . . .
```

The special characters `\A` and `\Z` can be used in a regular expression to indicate the beginning and end of a string whether or not the `m` modifier is used. That is, these characters always mean "the string" and not "the line."

The UNIX User's Favorite Function

If you want to do a search for the same regular expression within every element in a list, the `grep` function is what you need. This function takes two arguments: a regular expression or a block, and a list. It then evaluates the regular expression or block on each element of the list and looks for true and false results.

The name of the grep function comes from a handy UNIX utility of the same name. The UNIX command's name was derived from the acronym for "global regular expression and print." Perl's grep function doesn't print, but because it checks the regular expression globally on each item in the list, it's good enough to be called grep.

In a list context, grep returns the elements from the list for which the regular expression or block returns true; in scalar context, it returns the number of elements that return true. For example, assume that you want to look through the list @LastNames for every name that starts with the letter S. To get the actual names, you can use the following statement:

```
@JustSNames = grep(/^S/, @LastNames);
```

To merely find out how many names start with S, you can use

```
$TotSNames =  grep(/^S/, @LastNames);
```

The grep function also enables you to use a block instead of a regular expression as the first argument to the function. In this case, the special variable $_ is set to the value of the list element being tested. (This is similar to the map function described in Chapter 8.) For example,

```
$TotSNames =  grep({/^S/}, @LastNames);
```

As you become more comfortable with regular expressions, you can find many uses for grep. For example, if you've read all the lines of a file into a list by using a statement such as the following,

```
@TheFile = <INFILE>;
```

you can then create other lists that contain certain kinds of lines. With the following statement you can create a list of all the lines that have a whitespace character at the end of the line:

```
@RealLines = grep(/\s$/, @TheFile);
```

Doing Simple Substitutions with the s/// Operator

The s/// operator acts much like the m// operator except that you specify the replacement for the found string. You put the replacement between the second and third slashes. The s/// operator returns the number of times it substituted the second string for the first string. It takes the same modifiers as the m// operator.

Suppose that you want to change all the lowercase e characters in a string to uppercase E:

```
$Count = ($Test =~ s/e/E/g);
```

A slightly more complex exercise involves changing all the vowels in a string to the letter V:

```
$Count = ($Test =~ s/[aeiouAEIOU]/V/g);
```

As with the m// operator, if you don't use the =~ operator before the s/// operator, Perl assumes that it's working on the special variable $_. The following is an example of using $_ as input to the s/// test:

```
while(<INFILE>) {
    s/\t/|/g;  # Change the tabs to vertical bars
    . . .
}
```

You can use variables in either part of the s/// operator. For example, you can search for a group of digits at the beginning of a string and change it to the value of $NewLabel by using the following statement:

```
s/^\d+/$NewLabel/;
```

Using match results in your substitutions

In the section "Getting the Match Results" earlier in this chapter, I show you how to use the $1 and $2 special variables in your Perl programs to find out what was matched by the m// operator. With the s/// operator, these variables prove useful because you may want to replace what you found with something else related to it.

For example, if you want to find all the lines in a program that begin with a number and substitute each number with the word "Line" followed by that number, you can use the following statement:

```
$Test =~ s/^(\d+)/Line $1/;
```

The more-complex example that follows changes strings that are formatted as Lastname, Firstname to Firstname Lastname:

```
$Test =~ s/([^,]+), (.+)/$2 $1/;
```

This test statement first finds all the characters up to the comma and puts those characters into $1. (The regular expression [^,]+ means "find all characters other than a comma.") The expression matches the comma and the space, and then it matches the rest of the characters and puts them into $2. The substituted text is $2, followed by a space, followed by $1.

Using expressions in the replacement text of s///

The s/// operator has one modifier that the m// operator doesn't: the e modifier. The e modifier causes Perl to evaluate the second part of the s///, that is, the string that is the replacement, as an expression rather than a string.

Using an expression for what is replaced can be useful if you want to base the replacement on $1, $2, and so on, but need to change the results. For example, assume that you have a string that begins with a number, and you want to find the first number in the string and increase the number by one. You can use the following statement to do that:

```
$Test =~ s/(\d+)/$1 + 1/e;
```

In this case, if Test is Line 23: go, it's changed to Line 24: go.

Using the split Function with More-Advanced Regular Expressions

The first argument in the split function is a regular expression, not just a string (see Chapter 7 for more on split). The split function can be used with simple regular expressions, but it also has some other advanced and complex uses.

For example, assume that someone at your firm is using a text editor to create a database for you. You told him to insert a tab character and nothing else between fields, but you suspect that he may have accidentally entered one or more spaces before or after the tab in some records. Instead of the following simple split statement

```
@TheFields = split(/\t/, $TheRecord);
```

you may use

```
@TheFields = split(/ *\t */, $TheRecord);
```

The previous regular expression says "look for zero or more spaces, followed by exactly one tab, followed by zero or more spaces."

You can get around the text entry problem noted in the previous example in another way — you can preprocess the record with an s/// operator to get rid of the typos before using the split function. In the following example, the first statement substitutes a single tab for any tabs that were entered incorrectly (that is, with spaces before or after the tab), and the second statement then splits the result:

```
$TheRecord =~ s/ *\t */\t/g;
@TheFields = split(/\t/, $TheRecord);
```

Quoting words, briefly

If you use the split function to split on whitespace (as described earlier in the chapter in "Matching character classes"), Perl 5 and later versions feature a quoting function, qw, that makes statements easier to read. For example, instead of the following statement

```
@TheFields = split(/\s+/, $TheRecord);
```

you can use the qw function:

```
@TheFields = qw($TheRecord);
```

The characters qw stand for "quote words," which is exactly what this function does. (Quoting is described in more detail in Chapter 5.)

Returning delimiters in split

The split function does not normally return the delimiters in list items. You can, nevertheless, use parentheses in your regular expression and split returns whatever is in the parentheses as items in the list. For example, when you run the following program

```
$TheRecord = "Serling|Rod|Twilight Zone|";
@TheFields = split(/\|/, $TheRecord);
```

Perl returns

```
('Serling', 'Rod', 'Twilight Zone')
```

By comparison, when you run the following program, in which the | delimiter is enclosed in parentheses,

```
$TheRecord = "Serling|Rod|Twilight Zone|";
@TheFields = split(/(\|)/, $TheRecord);
```

Perl returns

```
('Serling', '|', 'Rod', '|', 'Twilight Zone','|')
```

You can suppress your desire to have the delimiters returned by using the `(?:` extension to regular expressions. For example, given the following statements

```
$TheRecord = "Serling|Rod|Twilight Zone|";
@TheFields = split(/(?:\|)/, $TheRecord);
```

Perl returns

```
('Serling', 'Rod', 'Twilight Zone')
```

Mass Translations: Using the `tr///` Operator

Although the `s///` operator works fine for simple one-on-one changes, such as changing one word to another, at times you may want to change multiple elements simultaneously, such as translating uppercase letters to lowercase letters. For this sort of task, you need the `tr///` operator.

The `tr///` operator enables you to specify individual letters, or ranges of letters, with a hyphen (`-`). For example, you can use the following to change the case of the uppercase letters to lowercase in `$Test`:

```
$Test =~ tr/A-Z/a-z/;
```

For historical reasons, the y/// operator exists, even though it does exactly the same thing as the tr/// operator. The y/// operator is rarely used because most people switched when the tr/// operator was introduced.

The `tr///` operator returns the number of changes that it makes. It also has some modifiers that are different than those for the `m//` and `s///` operators (see Table 13-4). ***Note:*** The `tr///` operator does *not* use regular expressions for its pattern matching, only actual characters and character ranges.

Table 13-4 Modifiers for `tr///`

Modifier	*Description*
c	Uses all characters other than what are listed in the first part of the operator
d	Deletes matching characters that are not replaced
s	Removes duplicates in the characters that are replaced

The `c` modifier is useful for shortening the list of characters between the first and second slash. For example, if you want to change all characters other than digits into linefeed characters, you can use

```
$Test =~ tr/0-9/\n/c;  # Note that "c" to invert range
```

The d modifier enables you to delete, rather than replace, certain characters. For example, if you want to delete all nondigits in a program, you can use

```
$Test =~ tr/0-9//cd;  # Change non-digits into nothing
```

The `s` modifier is useful for collapsing duplicate characters into a single character. This modifier causes Perl to treat all the found characters as one before doing the translation. For example, you may want to change every instance of two or more adjacent commas into just one comma. To accomplish that, you can enter

```
$Test =~ tr/,/,/s;
```

Chapter 14

Looking Like a Pro: Subroutines, Imported Code, and Graceful Exits

In This Chapter

- Creating subroutines to save time
- Using parts from other programs
- Leaving your programs with `die` or `exit` statements

Perl is a great language for creating useful programs quite simply. In fact, a surprising number of widely used Perl programs running on the Internet are fewer than five lines long. And, unlike other languages, you don't have to bang out lengthy instructions at the beginning of your Perl programs in order to set up the language first before you can use it.

Perl also has plenty of features that can make the average program run faster and more efficiently. This chapter covers a number of those structural techniques you can employ in order to save yourself some time and create a smoother-running program.

Saving Yourself Some Steps with Subroutines

By and large, *subroutines* are used to consolidate repeated sets of statements into a single block. For instance, assume you're writing a program that uses the same set of statements in several different places. Instead of repeating the lines every place they're needed, you can use a *subroutine* to define the set of lines and have *calls* to (that is, functions that execute) that subroutine. This method has a number of advantages:

- If you need to make changes to a set of lines, you can enter those changes just once in the block, instead of having to search the program for every instance of those lines.

- Your program is shorter and therefore runs faster.
- In lengthy programs, subroutines can act like named "subprograms" in order to help you organize the program.

Having everything in a single place so that updates are easier to enter is essential to efficient programming. I can't tell you how many times I've gotten lazy when writing a program and didn't use subroutines, only to be bitten later when I wanted to change numerous repeated lines.

Structuring a subroutine

Creating a subroutine using the `sub` statement is fairly easy. The statement has the following format:

```
sub NAME { BLOCK }
```

The rules for creating subroutine names are the same as those for variable names: Don't use spaces, the only punctuation you can use is the underscore (_), and subroutine names are case-sensitive.

To call a subroutine, you use the ampersand (&) character followed by the subroutine name. If the subroutine takes arguments, you include the arguments in parentheses just as you do for Perl's built-in functions. (In Perl 5, you don't have to use the `&` character if an argument is in parentheses. But doing so lets everyone reading your program know that you are referring to a subroutine, not one of Perl's built-in functions, such as `if` or `print`.)

Inside the block, you can do whatever you please, just as you can in any other Perl block.

Because most subroutines contain arguments, you need a way to use those arguments in the block of code you are writing in the subroutine. Perl makes the argument called available in the special list `@_`, which is a variable built into Perl. In the preceding example, the argument was a list, so `@_` is the entire list.

Subroutines that contain one or two arguments that are *scalars* (that is, either strings or numbers) are commonplace. If you have scalar arguments, you can use the `shift` function to get the arguments out of the `@_` list in the same order in which they went in. For example:

```
sub JustAdd {
    $First = shift(@_);
    $Second = shift(@_);
    return($First + $Second);
}
```

Perl creates the variable $First to hold the first argument and $Second to hold the second argument. You can then treat these variables as you would treat any other variable in your Perl program.

Most subroutines return a value, just as most Perl functions do. The return function, described in "Returning a value from a subroutine" later in this chapter, is the most common method used to return a value. Some subroutines also change the values of variables in the main program, but most subroutines don't. Instead, most subroutines allow the program to make the changes to the variables by using the value that is returned from the subroutine.

Incidentally, if you want a smaller, cleaner program, you can replace the first two lines of the preceding subroutine (called JustAdd) with

```
($First, $Second) = @_;
```

You don't have to create new variables in your subroutines. You can just use slices of @_, although that can get cumbersome if you have numerous arguments or if your subroutine is lengthy. For instance, the JustAdd subroutine that appears in the four-line block of code earlier in this section can be written more compactly (although the longer form may be easier to read):

```
sub ShorterJustAdd { return(@_[0] + @_[1]) }
```

Saving on labor and avoiding errors with subroutines

Imagine a program that contains a dozen or so lists, and at different points in the program, you want to print just the last item in each list and put a copy of that item into a list variable called @Big. Without subroutines, this program would look like the following:

```
. . .
printf("Price: \$%.2f\n", $ListPrice[$#ListPrice]);
push(@Big, $ListPrice[$#ListPrice]);
. . .
printf("Price: \$%.2f\n", $CustPrice[$#CustPrice]);
push(@Big, $CustPrice[$#CustPrice]);
. . .
printf("Price: \$%.2f\n", $NewPrice[$#NewPrice]);
push(@Big, $NewPrice[$#NewPrice]);
. . .
```

Now imagine that you want to change the way that @Big is constructed and push the last two items, instead of just the last item, in each list onto the end of @Big. You have to search for each push function, make sure that the function you find is one that is pushing onto @Big, and change the item that's currently in that function to a *slice* (a portion of a list):

```
push(@Big, @ListPrice[$#ListPrice-1..$#ListPrice]);
```

As you can imagine, the task I just described can be really tedious. In addition, you're also prone to error because of the number of replacements you have to do by hand. Subroutines can eliminate this problem.

By adding a subroutine and changing the pairs of printf and push statements to a single subroutine call in the six-line program that appears earlier in this section, that program now looks like this:

```
# Print the price and push it on @Big
sub PrintPushBig {
    @TheList = @_;
    printf("Price: \$%.2f\n", $TheList[$#TheList]);
    push(@Big, $TheList[$#TheList]);
}
. . .
&PrintPushBig(@ListPrice);
. . .
&PrintPushBig(@CustPrice);
. . .
&PrintPushBig(@NewPrice);
. . .
```

Instead of repeating the lines that have the push function, they're contained in the subroutine. To make the previously described change (to push a slice instead of a single item) to the subroutine, you simply change the push statement to

```
push(@Big, @TheList[$#TheList-1..$TheList]);
```

After you change this statement, the change is reflected each time the subroutine is called.

My, what a local variable you have: Using the my and local functions

You're not going to like hearing this, but the subroutines I show in the previous sections of this chapter have a major flaw in them. The examples

work, but they could cause harm to other variables in the program that calls them. In order to make these first examples easier to read, I didn't do one thing that's very important.

In those subroutines, the first assignments assign values from @_ to variables. But what if those variables are already being used in the program? For instance, in the JustAdd subroutine shown in the section "Structuring a subroutine," you may already have a variable called $First that you're using to keep track of who's on first. (I hear an Abbott and Costello routine coming on. . . .) In this case, when you call JustAdd, that subroutine wipes out the previous value of $First, which is probably not what you want to do.

You may be asking, "Why not just use variables in your subroutine that aren't used in the main program?" That would certainly avoid the problem, if you are sure to do that every time. Without carefully reading each line in the program, you won't know which variable names are safe for you to use in your subroutine. For example, you may think that the variable $First hasn't been used in the program yet, but you may have simply missed it. Fear not: Perl has a simple solution to this problem.

The my and local functions cause Perl to create a local copy of the variable for the block that makes up the function. A *local copy* is a variable that can only be seen inside that block, so the outer program that called the function won't be affected by changes made to the local variables. Generally, the my and local functions accomplish the same thing, but my runs faster. (***Note:*** my was introduced in Perl 5, so Perl 4 users must use local instead.)

You should use my and local when you first use a variable (using a variable the first time is called *declaring* the variable). You can declare a variable at any time in a block. However, most programmers prefer to declare a variable at the very beginning of a block so that they know where to look for their variable declarations. This programming convention is probably a holdover from other programming languages that require you to declare all your variables before you use them. Perl is accommodating enough not to require predeclaration. You just create a new variable when you feel like it. Nevertheless, if you're going to use my or local to safely declare a variable, you have to do so before using that variable.

The my and local functions can be used as statements by themselves or placed to the left of an assignment. For example, if you just want to declare that a particular variable is a local one, you can simply say

```
my($AirCondNum);
```

In this example, if you want to also set the variable's value when you first declare it, you can say

```
my($AirCondNum) = 3;
```

Given the JustAdd subroutine presented in "Structuring a subroutine" earlier in this chapter, if the subroutines declare their variables as local, the JustAdd subroutine would then look like this:

```
sub JustAdd {
    my($First) = shift(@_);
    my($Second) = shift(@_);
    return($First + $Second);
}
```

The first two lines cause Perl to create new copies of the variables $First and $Second that are used only inside the subroutine. If $First and $Second exist somewhere else in the program, they're unaffected by a call to the subroutine.

The my and local functions in essence enable Perl to remember other variables that have the same name and store them off to the side. After a subroutine finishes, Perl throws away any new instances of variables and restores the old variables that it momentarily stashed off to the side. That's why these functions are said to create "local" variables: The variables exist only when the subroutine is being run.

You can declare variables with my and local in any block, not just the block of a subroutine, although those functions are found mostly in subroutines. Perl acts the same way given any kind of block: It preserves any variable with the same name as the argument to my and local, creates a local version of the variable with the desired name, and then destroys the local version at the end of the block.

You can declare as many variables as you desire in my or local. For example, if you know that you're going to use $i, $j, and $k as loop variables in a block, you can define them all at once with a statement such as the following:

```
my($i, $j, $k);
```

It's good to get into the habit of using the my function when you write subroutines. Even if you're certain that you haven't repeated any variable name in a program when you create a subroutine, you may forget and end up using that name later on. Furthermore, a handy way of creating subroutines that you can use in other programs is to include code from other existing Perl programs. In that case, you definitely want to use my for every variable in those pre-existing subroutines.

You may at times want a subroutine to modify something outside of the subroutine. For example, take a look at the following PrintPushBig subroutine:

```
sub PrintPushBig {
    my($TheList) = @_;
    printf("Price: \$%.2f\n", $TheList[$#TheList]);
    push(@Big, $TheList[$#TheList]);
}
```

The purpose of the previous subroutine is to both print something and to change the value of a list (@Big) that's in the main program. Therefore, this subroutine produces a change outside the subroutine, namely the addition of an element to @Big.

If you write subroutines that will change the variables in your program, remember to insert an explanatory comment at the top of those subroutines. Then later on, you won't be puzzled as to why the variables in your program keep changing.

Some programmers are adamant about subroutines never changing anything in a program. They believe that making such changes leads to mysterious results in the future after you've forgotten what was changed and why. If you subscribe to this theory, you can return one or more values and force the calling program to change values based on the returned values. (Return values are described in the next section.)

Using the my function essentially "hides" a variable from all other blocks in a program — both the blocks that call the block with my and subroutines called from the subroutine with my. Using local, on the other hand, hides the variable only from the enclosing block, leaving the variable visible to subroutines that are called from the block with local in it. The following example points out some differences between the local and my functions in action:

```
# Simple subroutine to print the value of $J at the moment
sub PrintJ { print "The value of \$J is $J\n" }
# Simple subroutine to print the value of $K at the moment
sub PrintK { print "The value of \$K is $K\n" }
# Here's the test
my($J) = 5;
local($K) = 10;
&PrintJ;
&PrintK;
```

Because $J is undefined in the PrintJ subroutine and $K is passed through to the PrintJ, you get the following result:

```
The value of $J is
The value of $K is 10
```

Returning a value from a subroutine

Every Perl function returns a value to the program that called the function. At times, you don't need to bother with what's returned, such as when you call a function solely for another aspect of the function. For instance, the `chomp` function described in Chapter 5 returns a value (the character or characters it chomped), but most of the time, you just want to use the function to hack off characters at the end of strings. (Subroutines also return values, which you can pay attention to or ignore.)

The most efficient way to return a value is with the `return` statement. This statement causes the subroutine to end and returns the list that you give as its argument. Thus, in the `JustAdd` subroutine that follows, the `return` statement is used to return the value of the two arguments that are added together:

```
sub JustAdd {
    my($First) = shift(@_);
    my($Second) = shift(@_);
    return($First + $Second);
}
```

You can also use `return` with no argument, in which case Perl returns the value 0.

You don't have to use a `return` statement in your subroutines, although it does make subroutines easier to read. If you don't have a `return` statement waiting when Perl hits the end of a subroutine's block, the subroutine ends and Perl returns the value of the last statement. Therefore, you can write a subroutine like the following one:

```
sub JustAdd {
    my($First) = shift(@_);
    my($Second) = shift(@_);
    $First + $Second;
}
```

Using `return` makes things a little clearer because the last line of the previous subroutine doesn't look like it's *doing* anything, even though it is returning the value of the expression. My preference is to show functions that suggest action, such as `return`, rather than just having a plain value dangling at the end.

The `return` function also comes in handy if you want to stop a subroutine before you get to the end. You can use `return` somewhat like the `last` statement (covered in Chapter 8) in loops, and your subroutine can have many `return` functions in it. Here is an example of a subroutine with more than one `return` statement:

```
# Subroutine that returns the string "long" if the
#    argument is longer than 10 characters
sub IsLong {
    my($TheStr) = pop(@_);
    if(length($TheStr) > 10) { return('long') }
    else { return('short') }
}
```

The `return` function can return either a scalar or a list. For example, you can write a subroutine that returns a number raised to the second, third, and fourth power that looks like the following:

```
# Returns the argument raised to 2, 3, and 4
sub Raised {
    my($Sq, $Cub, $Quad);
            my($Val) = pop(@_);
    $Sq = $Val ** 2; $Cub = $Val ** 3; $Quad = $Val ** 4;
    return($Sq, $Cub, $Quad);
}
```

You may call this subroutine using a statement such as

```
@Powers = &Raised(12.3);
```

or

```
($TheSq, $TheCube, $TheFourth) = &Raised(12.3);
```

Who's calling?

If you're in a subroutine and want to know the name of the program that called you, you can use the `caller` function to find out. This function may not be all that important, but it can provide you with a nice little diversion. In a list context, the caller function format looks like this:

```
($PackageName, $FileName,
   $LineNum) = caller;
```

In a scalar context, `caller` simply returns true if it is called in a subroutine, or inside an `eval` function (described in Chapter 18) or `require` function (see the section "Importing Prewritten Perl Code into Your Programs").

Importing Prewritten Perl Code into Your Programs

After you write a number of Perl programs, you may to want to reuse some old Perl programs in order to save yourself some time when writing new ones. For instance, imagine that you wrote a really handy subroutine that reads a file and creates a list of all the capitalized words in the file. You wrote this subroutine in a program six months ago. Now you find yourself wanting that same subroutine in a program you're writing today.

Using your text editor, you can simply copy the subroutine from the old program to the new one. Keep in mind, though, if you want to use 10 or 20 old subroutines, your new program can get pretty hefty before you have even begun writing the new code. Instead, you can put the subroutines in one or more separate files and simply call those files into your new program.

Each time you create a new, useful subroutine, you can put it in a file. You can put many subroutines in a single file, or put each one in its own file. Then you can draw upon your library of subroutines whenever you need it.

You may not need to write many of your own subroutines. The CD-ROM that comes with this book has gazillions of well-written programs that you can use. Almost all of them use Perl's object-oriented features described in Chapter 19. You can also include existing programs in your new programs by employing the `require` function that you use for including your own collection of subroutines.

The `require` function takes one argument — the name of the file that you want to include in your program. For instance, if a subroutine you want to use resides in the numsubs.pl file, you can include that subroutine (and all the other subroutines in the file) in your current program by using this simple statement:

```
require('numsubs.pl');
```

It's not unusual to see the `require` function without parentheses around the argument:

```
require 'numsubs.pl';
```

Adding a required statement for included files

Stashing away your subroutines in files has one little complication: The `require` function demands that whatever it reads in a file must return a true value. As it turns out, simply having a subroutine in a file doesn't cause Perl to return a true value. So, you must have at least one statement in the subroutine file apart from a subroutine, and that statement must return true. A common trick is to insert this little statement:

```
1;
```

You insert `1;` somewhere in the file, usually at the end. This statement returns the value 1 (a value for true). For this reason, you usually see such a line, or a line with just a string, at the end of every file that is intended to be included with `require`.

Helping Perl search your libraries for included files

The `require` statement (covered in "Adding a required statement for included files" earlier in this chapter) needs a filename in order to know which file to open. The trick is, a file can reside in any one of countless places on your computer. To solve this problem, your `require` statement can specify exactly where a file should be, or you can put the file in one of the directories in Perl's search path.

You want to provide a complete description of where a particular file is located, but that can involve a fair amount of key stroking. For instance, the following three `require` statements may appear in Perl programs under Windows, Mac OS, or UNIX:

```
require('C:\LANGS\PERL5\LIBS\NUMSUBS.PL');
require('Felicity:Perl 5:My Libraries:numsubs.pl');
require('/usr/home/phoffman/libraries/numsubs.pl');
```

Requiring a particular version of Perl

The `require` function can be used to specify which version of Perl is needed in order to run a particular program. When you use a number as the argument to `require` (instead of a file name), Perl stops the program if the version of Perl isn't that number or higher. For example, the statement `require 5.005;` indicates that Perl must be version 5.005 or higher. If it isn't, Perl stops and you get an error message that tells you what version is required and which is running. For example, the previous version of Perl-Win32 is only 5.001, so this `require` function would cause the program to stop.

When you use full path names to your libraries, you have an added disadvantage of not being able to move your libraries without rewriting all your Perl programs to point to each new library location. A much better method involves storing your libraries somewhere that Perl would look for libraries and then letting Perl search through those places.

The `@INC` special variable holds the list of directories that Perl searches in order to find your library files. For example, `@INC` in Perl for Windows may contain the following path names:

```
('C:\PERL\5.005\lib', 'C:\PERL\site\lib')
```

In MacPerl, the default value of `@INC` is a single value of the `lib` folder where MacPerl was installed, for example

```
('Felicity:Perl 5:lib')
```

On UNIX, `@INC` usually lists a few different places for the lib folder, such as

```
('/usr/local/lib/perl5/5.005/i386-bsdos',
  '/usr/local/lib/perl5/5.005',
  '/usr/local/lib/perl5/site')
```

If you stash your libraries in one of the directories listed in `@INC`, you need to use just the specific filename in the `require` function:

```
require('numsubs.pl');
```

Every implementation of Perl I've ever seen has a sensible definition for `@INC`, but even if it doesn't, you can change this variable yourself. For instance, assume you're a Windows user and you want to store all your libraries in the C:\PROGR\PERL5\MYSUBS directory. You can add this directory to the `@INC` list before you make use of any `require` statements by using the following `push` statement:

```
push(@INC, "C:\PROGR\PERL5\MYSUBS");
```

You can use a similar `push` statement for other operating systems.

Wrapping your programs in packages

One method Perl has to keep variables local to a set of subroutines involves the use of packages. A *package* is a set of things for which you need a set of local variables. An included file is one example of something that may have its own set of variables (see the previous section in this chapter for more on included files).

The `package` declaration tells Perl to start a new package. Until you use `package` for the first time, Perl keeps all your variables in a default package called `main`. To name a package, simply use the declaration followed by the package name:

```
package NetworkStuff;
```

If you use `include` to pull in files that have different packages, when you go to use the subroutines, you must refer to the subroutines in those packages by their package names. You can have two subroutines with the same names in different packages and you must be able to differentiate them. (Because the subroutines in the programs shown earlier in this chapter are all in the same package [`main`], you wouldn't have to specify a package name.)

When you want to call a subroutine that's in a different package than the one you're programming in, you must list that package name, followed by a double colon (::). (In Perl 4, use a single quotation mark ['] instead of the double colon.) For instance, if you have a package called "NetworkStuff" and a package called "MySubs," you can invoke your subroutines with the following statements:

```
&MySubs::Router;          # Perl 5
&NetworkStuff::Router;    # Perl 5
&MySubs'Router;           # Perl 4
&NetworkStuff'Router;     # Perl 4
```

You can also refer to variables in other packages using the double colon. For example, to refer to the variable `$i` in the package called MySubs, you use `$MySubs::i`.

Including code other than subroutines

A file you include using the `require` function may contain any sort of Perl code. For example, you can include statements that set variables or print text. However, this inclusion can be a bad idea because you may not always remember what every included file does when you use `require`.

Limiting the files that you use with `require` solely to subroutines is always a good idea. The programs in the subroutines should also be designed to change any variable carefully and should declare every variable they use (other than Perl's special variables) with `my` and `local`.

Running programs in eval

Yet another way exists for you to run imported programs in Perl: the `eval` function. As its name implies, `eval` causes Perl to evaluate its argument. After Perl evaluates the argument, Perl runs it. You use `eval` to include parts of a program when you don't know what they'll be until the program runs. For example, you may want to enable the user to see the value of any desired variable while the Perl program is running. In which case, you can fashion something like the following statements:

```
print "Name of the variable do you want to see: ";
$Resp = <STDIN>;
print eval($Resp);
```

If you find that a particular task in your program can't be performed without some information that you won't have until the program is running, you can use `eval` to create a "mini-program" to use that run-time information. Advanced programmers typically use `eval`, so you don't need to worry about it too much for now.

Ending Perl Programs Gracefully

You may notice that the Perl programs you see in this book don't end with a statement that says something to the effect of "Hey, this is the end of the program." That's because Perl programs end when Perl runs out of statements to execute. When Perl gets to the last line of the program, it's smart enough to know that you intended that line to be the end.

You also have the option of actually telling Perl that you want to end a program. I tell you about those options in the sections coming up.

The die function

The `die` function causes Perl to print a message and then stop the program immediately. The `die` function is somewhat like the `print` function. It displays its argument (which can be a list) so you're not restricted to displaying a single string. If the last value in the list doesn't end with a *newline character* (which is usually entered in strings as `"\n"`), Perl also prints the name of the program and the line number, followed by a newline character. If you're in an *input loop* (in which you are awaiting input from the keyboard), Perl also prints the number of times you've gone through the loop.

Warning without exiting

Perl's warn function acts like the die function except that warn doesn't cause the program to quit. Instead, it just prints out a warning string that you supply, but the program continues on. For most people, this process means that warn does just the same thing as print. The difference between warn and print is that warn displays its message on the *output stream* called STDERR (see Chapter 10 for information on output streams) instead of in the STDOUT output stream. Because most operating systems make whatever appears on STDERR also appear on the standard output stream, warn and print are indistinguishable for most people. Like warn, die actually puts its argument on STDERR.

The exit *function*

The exit function is a more conventional way to end a Perl program than the die function. Instead of displaying a list, exit takes a numeric argument and returns that argument to the program from which you ran your Perl program. However, the exit function doesn't allow you to create a message for the end user. You can run a Perl program from your operating system (such as from the command line in Windows); in this case, Perl returns the value in exit to the operating system.

Most operating systems ignore the number returned from the Perl program (called the *return code*), or at least don't do anything interesting with it. However, if your operating system does do something significant with this number, such as display the return code of programs when they exit, you may find the exit function useful. If you don't supply an argument to exit, Perl uses 0 for the return code.

Structuring die *and* exit *statements*

The die and exit functions typically appear to the right of the or operator in logical expressions (more on or can be found in Chapter 8). If a conditional test in your program absolutely has to result in a true value, you can then exit the program immediately if it's false. Many programmers use the die and exit functions with if and unless statements to end a program if a test doesn't return a true value. For instance, the following two examples both check to see if $Now is greater than $StartTime+3, and if so, will exit the program with a message to the user.

```
unless($Now > ($StartTime + 3)) { die "It's too soon.\n" }
```

```
($Now > ($StartTime + 3)) or die "It's too soon.\n";
```

Include the \n string at the end of the final string you use in a die statement; otherwise, Perl adds the program name and the line number to the end of whatever it prints. If you do not include /n at the end of the string, such as in the following statement

```
($Now > ($StartTime + 3)) or die "It's too soon.";
```

Perl displays the following:

```
It's too soon. at LabMonitor.pl line 12.
```

As you can see from the examples in this book, I prefer die to exit. It's always courteous to give users an explanatory message when a program ends so they're not left staring at the screen and wondering what happened. You can create plenty of useful messages with die, such as

```
Program ended because the file 'input.txt' was not found.
All done. Thank you!
Finished at 08:27:52 in .03 seconds.
Unable to find the specified file; exiting.
```

Try to provide the kind of error messages that you'd need to see if you were running a program for the first time. Make your end-user messages friendly, or even humorous if you have the knack for it. We've all been stymied by incomprehensible error messages, and the best way to remind others to write understandable error messages is by doing so yourself.

Part IV
Advanced Perl Demystified

The 5th Wave
By Rich Tennant
The Perls of Pauline
©RICHTENNANT
Help! I'm losing depth recursion!
My subroutines are confusing!!
My hash tables are degrading–
heeeeellp!!

In this part . . .

Although this book is largely designed for novices and intermediate users, I also recognize the irresistible allure of some really heady stuff like associative arrays, XML, and object-oriented programming. The chapters in this part of the book cover subjects that are useful for more advanced programmers, yet still accessible to most beginners.

Chapter 15

Perl Gets Cozy with the Web, E-Mail, and XML

In This Chapter

- Using Perl's library of modules for grabbing stuff off the Web
- Creating your own Internet clients
- Checking POP mailboxes

Internet users are now well used to working with fancy point-and-click interfaces to the Web thanks to browsers like Netscape's Navigator and Microsoft's Internet Explorer. Many Internet users also make use of graphical interfaces to read and send mail through programs like Qualcomm's Eudora, the mail program in Netscape's Navigator, or one of the mail programs from Microsoft.

These Internet programs are easy to use, but they don't provide the flexibility that all users want. For one, they are difficult or downright impossible to program. For example, suppose that you have a list of 100 domain names that host Web sites and you want to download the home pages of each site for later viewing. Navigator and Internet Explorer do not have point-and-click interfaces for doing this sort of thing. Naturally, this sounds like a job for Perl.

Lots of good Internet tools are already written in Perl, so you don't have to reinvent the wheel. In fact, the tools are fairly easy to use, and you can write programs with just a few lines of code that do things like get FTP files. The result is not a graphical program. Instead, it's a very character-oriented one, but that may be just what you want.

This chapter covers how to use a few of the Internet tools from the Comprehensive Perl Archive Network (CPAN) library. These tools are all on this book's companion CD-ROM, so they're easy to load and run. (See Appendix B for more information.)

Working the Web by Using the libwww-perl Library

To many people, the Internet is the Web, and the way to get to the Internet is through their Web browsers. By the time you read this, more people may think that e-mail is more interesting than the Web, but (sadly) I doubt it.

You may have many reasons for wanting to create a Perl program that knows how to go out and snag pages from the Web. For example, you may want to create a robot to get all the available Web pages from one site or from many sites. Or you may want to send out a Web request every hour to see if the information on a particular Web page has changed since the previous hour. Or you may want to check a list of Web links to make sure that they're still valid. All these tasks require some amount of programming and can't be done easily with a standard *Web client* (a program that requests information from a Web server), such as Netscape.

The best means for accessing the Web is through a library of utility functions called libwww-perl. The library's name comes from the fact that the Perl library is based on the earlier libwww library written in C. (We don't want those C programmers mistaking our library for theirs, do we?) Perl-Win32 and MacPerl come with libwww-perl built in, but UNIX users must install it from the CPAN library on the Web if they want to use it.

The libwww-perl library can be used for more than just accessing the Web: It contains modules for accessing FTP, Usenet news, Gopher, files on your computer, and even sending mail. In technical terms, this means that libwww-perl can handle all the following types of URLs:

- http:
- ftp:
- news:
- gopher:
- file:
- mailto:

Installing libwww-perl on UNIX

Readers who do not already have libwww-perl (namely those on UNIX systems) can find the libwww-perl library in its compressed form on the CPAN library on the Web. (CPAN is described in more detail in Chapter 23.) When you download the latest version of libwww-perl from CPAN, it comes with detailed instructions on how to install it. Instead of repeating those instructions here, you can read them from the copy you download because different versions of libwww-perl have different installation instructions.

Getting documents from the Web and FTP

libwww-perl is a set of Perl 5 modules, so you normally use Perl's object-oriented syntax (described in Chapter 19) when interacting with it. Luckily, libwww-perl includes a simple interface so that folks who aren't geared to object-oriented programming can easily use the library's basic parts. The interface is the `LWP::Simple` module. (LWP is an abbreviation for libwww-perl.) At the beginning of a program, you can tell Perl that you want to use the `Simple` package in LWP with the following statement:

```
use LWP::Simple;
```

Table 15-1 contains the four functions in the `LWP::Simple` module that get the contents of a document based on its URL.

Table 15-1 `LWP::Simple` Functions

Function	*Description*
`get($URL)`	Gets the document at the URL and returns it
`getstore($URL, $Filename)`	Same as `get` except that it writes the document on disk into the named file
`getprint($URL)`	Same as `get` except that it prints the information returned to the function to standard file output
`mirror($URL, $Filename)`	Same as `getstore` except that it gets the document only if it is newer or of a different size than the file on disk

The `get` function returns the document into a string, `getstore` puts it in a file, `getprint` puts it out on standard file output, and `mirror` gets the file only if it needs to. For example, if you just want to print the contents of a Web page, you can use this little program:

```
use LWP::Simple;
getprint('http://www.dummies.com');
```

If you want to download a file from an FTP site, you can use this program:

```
use LWP::Simple;
getstore('ftp://ftp.internic.net/rfc/rfc822.txt',
'rfc822');
```

The preceding program gets the file from the FTP site and stores it on your hard disk with the name rfc822.

If you give an invalid URL to `get` or `getstore`, such as the name of a Web site that does not exist or a filename that's spelled wrong, `LWP::Simple` returns an empty string; `getprint`, on the other hand, fills the string with an error message.

Checking out a Perl program that tests Web links

You're probably going to use Perl to get a whole group of Web pages instead of just one at a time. This section shows you how to get a group of pages or how to check multiple links in one fell swoop.

An extremely handy program is one that can check whether all the links from one Web page actually work. Listing 15-1 shows a program called linkchck.pl that reads a Web page, picks out all the links from the page, and then goes out on the Web and tests whether those links are valid. If you don't feel like typing in the program, it can be found on this book's CD-ROM.

Listing 15-1: Program for checking the links from a Web page.

```
$TheURL = $ARGV[0];  # Get the URL from the command line
# Section A
use LWP::Simple;
$TheMain = get($TheURL);  # Get the main page
if($TheMain eq '')
    { die "The starting URL was not valid.\n" }
# Section B
$TheMain =~ tr/A-Z/a-z/;  # Lowercase everything
$TheMain =~ s/\"/'/g;     # Double quotes to single
$TheMain =~ s/\n/ /g;     # Get rid of the linefeeds
$TheMain =~ s/\s+/ /g;    # Compress spaces/tabs

# Section C
# First find any "base href='URL'" for relative URLs.
$BasePos = index($TheMain, '<base href');
if($BasePos > -1) {
    $OpenQuote = index($TheMain, "'", $BasePos);
    $BaseStart = $OpenQuote + 1;
    $CloseQuote = index($TheMain, "'", $BaseStart);
    $BaseLen = $CloseQuote - $OpenQuote - 1;
    $URLBase = substr($TheMain, $BaseStart, $BaseLen);
}
```

```
else { $URLBase = '' }
# Section D
# Keep a list of the URLs we find
@URLList = ();
while(1) {  # Loop forever, rely on "last"
    $TheA = index($TheMain, '<a href');  # The next link
    if($TheA == -1) { last };
    # Find the URL in the quotes
    $OpenQuote = index($TheMain, "'", $TheA);
    $URLStart = $OpenQuote + 1;
    $CloseQuote = index($TheMain, "'", $URLStart);
    $URLLen = $CloseQuote - $OpenQuote - 1;
    $TheURL = substr($TheMain, $URLStart, $URLLen);
    # Put the URL into @URLList
    push(@URLList, $TheURL);
    # Chop off beginning of $TheMain to our position
    $TheMain = substr($TheMain, $CloseQuote);
}

# Section E
@CheckURLs = ();
foreach $TheURL (@URLList) {
    # Determine which URLs are relative. Absolute URLs
    #   start with 'http:' or 'ftp:' or 'mailto:';
    #   others are relative to the base. Relative URLs have
    #   $URLBase added to the beginning.
    unless($TheURL =~ /^(http:|ftp:|mailto:)/)
        { $TheURL = $URLBase . $TheURL }
    # Don't check URLs starting with 'mailto:'
    unless($TheURL =~ /^mailto:/)
        { push(@CheckURLs, $TheURL) }
}

# Section F
# Now check each URL in the list for error messages
foreach $TheURL (@CheckURLs) {
    $TheCheck = get($TheURL);
    if($TheCheck ne "") { print "OK:   $TheURL\n" }
    else { print "Fail: $TheURL\n" }
}
```

The first line of the program in Listing 15-1 tells Perl to get the URL for the page you want to check from the command line. For example, you can run the program with

```
linkchck.pl http://www.mycompany.com/accts/main.html
```

The set of statements labeled "Section A" in Listing 15-1 loads the `LWP::Simple` package, gets the document, and loads it into the string `$TheMain`. The program then checks whether the `$TheMain` variable has anything in it and ends if the string doesn't.

The four lines labeled "Section B" employ techniques described in Chapter 14. These lines

- Convert the document to all lowercase characters at once so that you don't have to for each string you're looking for.
- Change all the quotation marks to apostrophes. URLs can be in either single- or double-quotation marks, so this conversion makes them easier to find.
- Change all linefeeds to spaces to prevent any HTML tags being split over a line break.
- Change all multiple spaces and tab characters into a single space. This prevents the program from missing some tags if they have multiple spaces or tabs within them.

The program's next task, which is covered in the statements in "Section C" of Listing 15-1, is its search for an HTML `base` tag. If the page you get has a `base` tag, some of the URLs on the page may be *relative* URLs, meaning that they don't have the full URL, just the last characters of the URL. At the end of that set of lines, `$URLBase` is set to either the base URL or the null string if no base URL exists.

The statements in "Section D" then go through the `$TheMain` string and look for HTML `a` tags that are links. The loop is exited when no additional HTML `a` tags exist. This set of statements finds the beginning of the tag and then the quoted URL inside the tag. Each URL is added to the end of the `@URLList`. The `$TheMain` string is then shortened up to the point where the tag was found, and the loop begins again.

The next statements in "Section E" go through all the URLs that were found to determine whether they are *absolute URLs* (that is, ones with the full URL syntax) or relative URLs. In the latter case, the program tacks on the base URL to the beginning of the URL. The program also checks to see if the URL is a `mailto:` URL. If it is a `mailto:` URL, the program ignores it because `mailto:` URLs are never relative URLs, so they don't need to be checked.

The statements in "Section F" go out and check each remaining URL. If the `get` function is successful, the program prints `OK:` and the URL; otherwise, the program prints `Fail:` and the URL. You can quickly see which of the URLs that came back without documents so you can investigate them.

Using libwww-perl with objects

I want to emphasize that libwww-perl does *much* more than what I showed you with the `LWP::Simple` package covered in the preceding two sections. The `LWP::Simple` package is a great example of what's inside libwww-perl because it allows those who aren't familiar with the object-oriented features in Perl 5 to use Perl to get documents from Web servers and FTP servers.

Even if you've read Chapter 19, which describes object-oriented Perl and shows you a bit about how to use the libwww-perl objects, I strongly recommend that you take a look at the other parts of the libwww-perl package. The package contains many useful features that allow you to

- Make Web robots that can download all the documents linked from a particular Web page.
- React to different HTTP headers that are returned on Web requests.
- Convert HTML to a more readable format for humans.
- Traverse directory trees on FTP servers so that you can get every file found in a particular directory and in its subdirectories.
- Get and send Usenet news.
- Send electronic mail.

Getting Your Mail

Much of the information on the Internet is available only through e-mail and not through the Web or FTP. For example, many mailing lists contain valuable information resources that are not accessible by any other means. And, of course, e-mail provides quick and efficient person-to-person communication over the Internet.

Many versatile, graphically based Web clients exist for viewing pages on the World Wide Web. Also, there are many versatile, graphically based e-mail clients for reading and sending e-mail messages exist. But, like their Web client brethren, few e-mail clients can be programmed to do what you want.

Assume that you're on ten active mailing lists — wouldn't it be nice to have a program filter the messages into a number of different files so that you can find the particular items you are interested in? You may also want to have a program act as an interface for e-mail if you use e-mail to receive regular reports from other computers; you can use the program to look for the reports, pull out the needed information, add it to previous reports, and so on. If you get your e-mail from a Post Office Protocol (POP) server, all these tasks can be performed easily with the `Mail::POP3Client` module, which I describe in the following sections.

Accessing the `Mail::POP3Client` *module*

The `Mail::POP3Client` module, which Windows users can download from the ActiveState Web site and UNIX users can download from CPAN, provides a simple interface to POP servers. A *POP server* is a server that enables your mail client to get e-mail from the server's hard disk. You can use the module to check your mail or grab particular messages, for example.

The module has to be installed before you can use it. You UNIX users can (hopefully) get your system administrator to install it. Perl-Win32 users can install the module with the following steps:

1. **Launch your Internet connection.**

   Because the PPM (the Perl-Win32 Perl Package Manager described in Appendix B) downloads the latest version of the module from the ActiveState Web site, you have to be connected to the Web before you use the PPM.

2. **Run the PPM by issuing the following command:**

   ```
   C:\perl\5.00502\bin\perl ppm.pl
   ```

3. **Download the `Mail::POP3Client` module by issuing the following command:**

   ```
   install Mail-POP3Client
   ```

   Note the hyphen in place of the "::" seen elsewhere in this section.

4. **Quit from the PPM by issuing this command:**

   ```
   quit
   ```

Unlike the libwww-perl module, `Mail::POP3Client` has only an object interface (that is, it doesn't have a simple function-based interface). But you can still do a few neat things with the `Mail::POP3Client`. You can create useful mail-collecting programs even without knowing anything about object-oriented programming.

With any mail program, you need to know three things in order to talk to a POP server:

- The mail account name
- The mail account password
- The domain name of the mail server

Given these three things, your program may begin with a few variables, such as the following:

```
$Name = 'larry';
$Pass = 'AouerGyvvt';
$Serv = 'mail.yourisp.com';
```

Creating a simple client object

To use the `Mail::POP3Client`, you must first include it in your program and create a *client object.* The client object is the thing that communicates with the POP server. When you create a new client, you supply the user name, password, and server name as arguments. Therefore, you can start your program off with the following statements:

```
use Mail::POP3Client;
$Client = new Mail::POP3Client($Name, $Pass, $Serv);
```

At this point, your Perl program has logged into the POP server. The POP server is waiting for you to send it POP commands. You should know the following things about POP before writing your programs:

- After you have logged into a POP server, you can send it commands that give you information about either the entire mailbox or about individual messages. For example, you can ask for a count of all the messages or for the contents of a particular message.
- Each message in a POP mailbox has a message number. Message numbers start at 1, and not at 0, as you may expect by having worked with other Perl programs.

You use `Mail::POP3Client` methods to send POP commands to the POP server and to examine the results. Many of the `Mail::POP3Client` methods take one argument, namely the message number on which you want the methods to act. Table 15-2 contains a few of the more-interesting `Mail::POP3Client` methods.

Table 15-2 Methods for the `Mail::POP3Client` Module

Method	*What It Does*
`Count`	Tells how many messages are on the server
`Head(num)`	Gets the header lines of the message
`Body(num)`	Gets the body of the message
`HeadAndBody(num)`	Gets the entire message
`Delete(num)`	Marks the message for deletion
`List`	Lists all the messages and their sizes
`Close`	Closes the connection, deleting any marked messages
`State`	Tells whether or not the connection is alive

Examining a program for processing reports in your mailbox

Assume that you have a program that mails you a report every day. You want to process your mailbox to find out whether the report was sent and, if so, to save the report on disk and delete that message from your mailbox. That way, you can use your graphical client to read the rest of the messages but still process the report automatically. Listing 15-2 shows you how such a program is built. (The program is also on the CD-ROM under the name popcheck.pl.)

Listing 15-2: A sample program that checks for a report in a POP mailbox.

```
$Name = 'larry';
$Pass = 'AouerGyvvt';
$Serv = 'mail.yourisp.com';
$Subj = 'Subject: Daily logging report';

use Mail::POP3Client;
$Client = new Mail::POP3Client($Name, $Pass, $Serv);
$TheState = $Client->State;
if($TheState eq 'AUTHORIZATION')
    { die "Bad user name or password.\n" }
elsif($TheState eq 'DEAD')
    { die "Mail server unreachable or unavailable.\n" }
# Find out how many messages there are
$NumMsg = $Client->Count;
#Loop through the messages (starting at 1)
```

```
for($i = 1; $i<=$NumMsg; $i +=1) {
     $Headers = $Client->Head($i);
     @HeadList = split(/\n/, $Headers);
     foreach $Line (@HeadList) {
          if($Line =~ /^$Subj/) {
               # Found the message; get the body, then delete
               $Body = $Client->Body($i);
               $Client->Delete($i);
               # Process the report and leave
               &ProcessReport($Body);
               last;
          }
     }
}
# Close the connection so the delete happens
$Client->Close;
sub ProcessReport {
     my($Report) = pop(@_);
     # Do something here that is processing the report
     return;
}
```

The first few lines of the program in Listing 15-2 set up variables for use later on in the program. The following statement uses the `State` method on the client:

```
$TheState = $Client->State;
```

The three possible results of the `State` method are: `TRANSACTION`, meaning things are fine; `AUTHORIZATION`, meaning that the POP server is trying to authorize the client; and `DEAD`, meaning that the POP server wasn't found. If you end up in `AUTHORIZATION` after giving a user name and password, that means that the combination didn't work. The program then gets the number of messages and loops through each one. The following statement gets the headers for the current message:

```
     $Headers = $Client->Head($i);
```

The headers are then split into an array and checked for the subject header that identifies the message you want. If that subject header is found, `$Body` gets the body of the message, the message is deleted, the report is processed, and the loop terminates.

A Glimpse into the Future of Web Programming: Perl and XML

Most of the text documents on the World Wide Web are formatted with HTML, the language that allows you to specify how your Web page text will be styled. HTML has served the Web very well since the Web's inception in the early 1990s, but many people (including me) believe that HTML needs to be replaced with something better in order for the Web to reach its full potential. (HTML is covered in more detail in Chapter 11.)

In 1996, the World Wide Web Consortium started doing serious work on the follow-up to HTML. XML (which stands for *eXtensible Markup Language*) has capabilities well beyond those of HTML, which is why so many people are interested in it. HTML is really only good at determining how text will look when it's displayed; XML, by comparison, describes each part of a text document so that the displaying program can decide on its own how to display the document.

Defining XML

Don't think of XML as just another Web-related technology that gets hyped in the media but then never amounts to much. Although XML is still very young, I have no doubt that it will be of special importance to programmers for a number of reasons. XML is useful for many things other than displaying text on the Web: It can be used as a mechanism for exchanging databases, such as medical records, or for conducting commercial transactions between individuals who have never met face to face, among many other applications.

XML is a method for adding text to a document that makes the document richer. The XML *tags* that you add to a document allow a program that is processing that document to understand more about the content, such as what part is the title of the document, what part is a table, what parts are footnotes, and so forth. Although a human can read an XML document and absorb some of this information, XML is designed so that its documents are processed by programs.

XML is complex and powerful, and the subject could fill a whole book, which in fact it has — *XML For Dummies* by Ed Tittel, Norbert Mikula, and Ramesh Chandak (IDG Books Worldwide, Inc.). Because I think that XML is so important for the future of the Web, I strongly suggest that anyone who is developing Web sites should try to find out more about XML.

Seeing how XML looks

Most elements in XML have a start tag and an end tag. For example, you may see the following in an XML document:

```
I want that cake <yell>now</yell>!
```

`<yell>` is the start tag and `</yell>` is its matching end tag.

Some tags have attributes in them. For example, note the difference between the tags in the following example from those in the previous one:

```
I want that cake <yell volume="loud">now</yell>!
```

In the second example, `volume` is the name of the attribute and `loud` is the value of that attribute. A tag can have many attributes.

One note of caution: XML isn't found on the Web yet. At the time of this writing, none of the popular Web browsers are able to display XML; therefore, very few Web pages have been created in XML. In addition, the Perl tools for handling XML are still in the early stages of development. By the time you read this, those tools will likely have changed for the better. Nevertheless, getting some information on those tools now can help you better understand this important emerging technology.

Combining XML and Perl

Perl is a particularly good language for processing XML documents. One of Perl's biggest strengths is its ability to process text, and XML documents are all text. Another of Perl's strengths lies in its list handling, and programs that process XML documents need to keep many lists as they work, particularly when checking if the XML markup in the document is valid (that is, no XML language mistakes are in the document).

Because of the good match between the demands of XML and the features of Perl, the Perl programmer community is busy creating Perl modules that work with XML. Larry Wall, Perl's creator, has been involved since the early days of XML, and many other Perl programmers have contributed to the effort. Some folks in the XML industry (notably Tim Bray, one of the inventors of XML) have also been involved in creating Perl modules for processing XML.

Almost all of the work being done with Perl and XML is in the area of processing existing XML documents rather than in creating new XML documents. If you have created HTML documents, you know that it's easier to use an HTML editor to create the documents than it is to enter the HTML tags by hand by using a text editor. The same is true for creating XML documents. Because Perl is rarely used to create something like a text editor, it hasn't been used to create XML documents. (Of course, this may change in the future.)

Processing XML with Perl

People who talk about XML see it being used primarily for text processing and data interchange. Although text processing is the area that gets the most attention, I think that using XML in data interchange is the much more exciting Web application, particularly in the area of commercial transactions.

The following example involves processing a data file in XML format. Assume that you have a Web server that receives data files from Web users, and the data files consist of customer orders for houseplants. Further assume that the data files are in an XML format that you define. A data file such as I just described may look like this:

```
<order>
<purchaser name="Chris Chambers" id="CC230"/>
<shipping method="ground"/>
<item>
<itemid quantity="20" color="sapphire">13572</itemid>
</item>
<item>
<itemid quantity="3" size="3 feet">72400</itemid>
</item>
</order>
```

I recommend entering this XML document into a file called theorder.txt, or you can save some time by copying it off this book's companion CD-ROM.

XML defines two types of documents, *well-formed* and *valid*. A valid document has to conform to more-stringent rules than well-formed documents. The previous example is well-formed but not valid, but that's not a problem in this scenario because you can use XML documents that conform to the XML structure you've already defined for your orders.

On your Web server, you want a program that can take documents in the XML format you have specified and pick out the various items. In the preceding example, you would want it to pick out parts of a customer order. For example, you want to know who ordered an item, what the item is, how much it cost, and so on. You could then use these selected parts for filling an order.

Processing with XML::Parser

A few different modules for parsing XML documents have been written for Perl. In this section, I show you how to use the most popular module as of this writing, the `XML::Parser` module. Windows users can download this module from the ActiveState Web site, and UNIX users can download it from CPAN.

So much activity with Perl and XML is going on that the `XML::Parser` module is changing almost every week. It's likely that all future versions of the module will work with programs written for earlier versions of the module, but no guarantee exists that the program coming up will work with future versions of `XML::Parser`.

Perl-Win32 users can install the `XML::Parser` module by using the following steps (which are similar to the steps in "Accessing the `Mail::POP3Client` module" earlier in this chapter).

1. **Launch your Internet connection.**
2. **Run the PPM by issuing the following command:**

   ```
   C:\perl\5.00502\bin\perl ppm.pl
   ```

3. **Download the `XML::Parser` module by issuing the following command:**

   ```
   install XML-Parser
   ```

4. **Quit from the PPM by issuing the following command:**

   ```
   quit
   ```

Parsing an XML document

Listing 15-3 presents a program that parses an XML document that consists of customer orders. The program assumes that the document has the same XML format as shown in "Processing XML with Perl," earlier in this chapter. The following program prints out information from the order. If you don't feel like typing in the program, you can find it on this book's CD-ROM under the filename orderpar.pl.

Listing 15-3: A sample program that reads an XML document.

```
# Section A
use XML::Parser;

$ItemCount = 0;
@ItemList = ();
# Section B
$parser = new XML::Parser(Style => 'Stream');
$parser->parsefile('theorder.txt');
# Section C
print "The total number of items ordered was $ItemCount\n";
for($i = 1; $i <= $ItemCount; $i+=1) {
    print "Item $i is $ItemList[$i][3]\n",
        "Quantity: $ItemList[$i][0]\n",
        "Color: $ItemList[$i][1]\n",
        "Size: $ItemList[$i][2]\n\n";
}
exit;
# Section D
sub StartTag {
    my $Handler = shift(@_);
    my $Name = shift(@_);
    my %Attr = %_;

    # Section D1
    if($Name eq 'order') { }  # Nothing to do
    # Section D2
    elsif($Name eq 'purchaser') {
        $PurchName = $Attr{'name'};
        $PurchID = $Attr{'id'};
        if($PurchID eq '')
            { die "There was no purchaser ID\n" }
    }
# Section D3
    elsif($Name eq 'shipping') {
        $ShipMethod = $Attr{'method'};
    }

    # Section D4
    elsif($Name eq 'item') {
        # Add 1 to the count of items ordered
        $ItemCount += 1;
    }
```

```
    # Section D5
    elsif($Name eq 'itemid') {
        $ItemList[$ItemCount][0] = $Attr{'quantity'};
        $ItemList[$ItemCount][1] = $Attr{'color'};
        $ItemList[$ItemCount][2] = $Attr{'size'};
    }

    # Section D6
    else {  # Here if there was an unknown start tag
        die "Found an unknown start tag:\n$_\n";
    }
}

# Section E
sub Text { $TheText = $_ };
# Section F
sub EndTag {
    my $Handler = shift(@_);
    my $Name = shift(@_);

    if($Name eq 'itemid') {
        $ItemList[$ItemCount][3] = $TheText;
    }
};
```

The first line in "Section A" of Listing 15-3 loads the `XML::Parser` module. The following two lines in the section initialize the `$ItemCount` variable, which keeps track of how many items are in this order, and the `@ItemList` variable, which holds a multidimensional list that has the information about a particular item in the order. (Multidimensional lists are covered in Chapter 16.)

The two lines in "Section B" do almost all the work of the program. The first of these two lines initializes the XML parser by creating a new parser object. (Objects are described in Chapter 19, but you don't need to know about them to follow along here.) The second line uses the parser object that was just created to parse the file that contains the XML document. After this line has been executed, the file is completely parsed.

"Section C" contains the statements that tell Perl what to do after it has parsed the XML document. These lines display information about the order, including the number of items ordered and a description of each item. If you were using this program in a real order-entry system, you would probably add statements for printing out a mailing label or telling the warehouse what had been ordered. After this section is run, the program exits.

You may be thinking, "Hey, how does the parser know how to handle each of those XML tags?" That's where the rest of the program sections come into play. In the "stream" style of `XML::Parser`, which was specified on the first line of "Section B" of Listing 15-3, your program is expected to have subroutines that tell the parser what to do when it comes to a start tag, an end tag, and the text in between. The `StartTag` subroutine gets called each time the parser comes across a start tag, the `EndTag` subroutine gets called each time the parser comes across an end tag, and the `Text` subroutine gets called each time the parser comes across text that is between a start and end tag.

"Section D" and its subsections describe what the parser should do when it comes to a start tag. The first three lines of the subroutine define the variables that are passed to the subroutine from the parser. (Subroutines and their variables are described in Chapter 10.) The two variables of note are `$Name`, which holds the name of the tag, and `%Attr`, which is an associative list of the attributes of the tag.

The six subsections of "Section D" in Listing 15-3 describe the five kinds of start tags that can be found in the XML format in this scenario.

- "Section D1" shows the `order` tag. There's nothing for the program to do at this point because you don't need any special processing at the beginning of the order.
- "Section D2" contains the `purchaser` tag. This tag sets the two variables `$PurchName` and `$PurchID` based on the attributes of the tag. The `if` function checks to see a purchaser identifier exists and, if not, aborts the program.
- "Section D3" contains the `shipping` tag. This tag sets the `$ShipMethod` variable.
- "Section D4" contains the `item` tag. This tag increments the `$ItemCount` variable so that you know how many items are in the order.
- "Section D5" contains the `itemid` tag. This tag fills in the slots in the `@ItemList` multidimensional list.
- "Section D6" gets run if the tag isn't any of the ones in this list. It causes the program to abort with a message.

"Section E" contains the subroutine that tells the parser what to do with any text it comes across. Because the end tags deal with any text that precedes them in the program, this subroutine simply stuffs the text into the `$TheText` variable, which will be used by the end tag processor.

Speaking of the end tag processor, it appears in "Section F." The only tag that has text that needs to be processed by the end tag is the `itemid`. In this subroutine, the value of the text that appears before the end tag for the `itemid` is put into the multidimensional list for the current item.

When you run the program, it produces the following output:

```
The total number of items ordered was 2
Item 1 is 13572
Quantity: 20
Color: sapphire
Size:
Item 2 is 72400
Quantity: 3
Color:
Size: 3 feet
```

Chapter 16

Associative Arrays and Multidimensional Lists

In This Chapter

- Locating items and examining records by using keys
- Writing associative data to a file
- Creating multidimensional lists
- Writing the files for lists within lists

Perl has many strengths, and one of its greatest is its ability to handle lists. Perl lists, which are basically an ordered collection of items, are useful for myriad applications. You can use them to hold names, addresses, phone numbers, and loads of other kinds of data that appear in your programs.

In this chapter, I cover some advanced aspects of working with lists in Perl, including creating and managing a special kind of list called an associative array and the multidimensional lists within lists. (Information on standard list structures in Perl can be found in Chapter 7.)

Some Basics on Associative Arrays

Items in a list are usually accessed by using the item's numerical position (for example, `$Names[4]` is the fifth item in the `@Names` list). Or, for example, assume that you're searching through a list for "an item whose value is 82"; that item is actually defined by its position in the list and not its value.

Imagine that you're working with a printout containing two columns of information: employee numbers and names. Exactly one employee exists for each employee number, and the numbers are not sequential. For example,

ID	*Name*
742	Kathi Stennis
5280	Roberta Wallace
3279	Daniel Exon

You can use this printed list to look up an employee by his or her ID number or to look up an ID number by using an employee's name. To create such a list in Perl, you would write the following statement:

```
(742, 'Kathi Stennis', 5280, 'Roberta Wallace',
     3279, 'Daniel Exon')
```

But this Perl list isn't as easy to read as a printed list because the even-numbered items are ID numbers, and the odd-numbered elements are names. To search for a particular ID number, you have to look at every other item in the list, instead of every item.

Locating items by their keys

Lists in which the elements have two parts, an index and an associated value, are commonplace in programming. So, Perl offers a second kind of list, called an *associative array,* which acknowledges that sometimes you don't want to find an item by its position, but instead by its index. (In Perl, the terms *list* and *array* mean the same thing.) Instead of looking up an item by its position in a list, you look it up by its *key.* An associative array is a list of *key-value* pairs, and each key-value pair is called a *record.*

In the employee ID example given earlier, the associative array has three records. One record has the key `742` and the value `Kathi Stennis`, another record has the key `5280` and the value `Roberta Wallace`, and another record has the key `3279` and the value `Daniel Exon`. In an associative array, the order of the records is unimportant and, in fact, the order is usually randomized by Perl.

You use keys to get to the records instead of record numbers as you do with normal lists. Therefore, using the previous example, "the record associated with key 5280" is the one that has "the value Roberta Wallace."

Identifying records solely by their keys leads to an important attribute of associative arrays: Only one record can be associated with a particular key. You're guaranteed that when you say "the record with key 5280," either zero or one record will be associated with that key. This also means that associative arrays aren't good for some tasks. For example, if you have a list of telephone numbers and names, you don't want to use an associative array because two people may have the same phone number and one person may have more than one phone number.

Some Perl programmers call associative arrays *hashes* because technically that's how they're stored in your computer's memory; Perl uses a *hash function* (a mathematical way of storing and retrieving values quickly) to determine how to best store the keys and values. However, I prefer "associative array" to "hash" because these arrays are used to hold associations.

You don't need to use associative arrays (except in the few cases when they're handed to you by Perl as the return value of an operation). However, they have a couple of major advantages over simple lists for many applications.

For lists of name-value pairs, associative arrays are useful because you have a handful of built-in Perl functions for them that save you the trouble of having to create your own functions to do certain things, such as finding a value based on a name or deleting a name-value pair from the middle of the list.

Searching through an associative array is much faster than searching through a simple list, particularly if the list contains lots of data. Finding a particular record in a hash is much faster than looking through every other item in a list. The average search through a list of key-value pairs requires Perl to look at half the pairs before finding the one you want. Hashes, on the other hand, require much less processing power to find the same record.

Comparing associative arrays with standard lists

Associative arrays use different notations than regular lists. (See Chapter 7 for more information on lists.)

- You name an associative array with a percent sign (`%`) instead of the `@` used in regular lists (for example, `%IDList`).
- You refer to an element in an associative array by its key.
- You put the key in curly braces (`{` and `}`) instead of the parentheses used in regular lists.

Given this, the following assigns the value of a record whose key is `5280` to the variable `$NextPerson`:

```
$NextPerson = $IDList{"5280"};
```

Creating an associative array

You assign a record to an associative array as a pair of items. For example, to create the associative array `%IDList`, you can use

```
%IDList = (742, 'Kathi Stennis', 5280, 'Roberta Wallace',
    3279, 'Daniel Exon');
```

The preceding statement may be a bit difficult to read, given that you have to view the assignment in pairs. Perl 5 and later versions enable you to use the => operator instead of the comma operator to separate the values in a list. Many programmers use the => operator between the key and the value (indicating "this key is associated with this value") and commas between records, as you can see in the following statement:

```
%IDList = (742 => 'Kathi Stennis',
    5280 => 'Roberta Wallace',
    3279 => 'Daniel Exon');
```

If the key is more than a single word, it must be in quotation marks. For example, if you have an associative array whose keys are street names and whose values are zip codes, you use

```
%Streets = ("Pine" => "92484", "North Elm" => "92481",
    "River" => "92484");
```

If you want to start an empty associative array before adding records, you can use the following simple statement:

```
%Streets = ();
```

Adding records to an associative array

To add a record to an associative array, you must assign a value to a key. For example, to add another record to the array `%Streets`, you can use

```
$Streets{"South Elm"} = "92481";
```

When Perl sees an assignment statement, such as the one in the previous example, it looks to see if the key `South Elm` already exists. If so, Perl replaces the corresponding value with `92481`; if not, Perl creates a key and gives it that value. Assigning values in associative arrays is just like assigning values in regular lists, except that you use keys instead of locations in the list.

Removing records

To remove an existing record, use the `delete` function. This function takes as its argument the key you want to remove. For example

```
delete($Streets{"North Elm"});
```

The `delete` function returns the value of the key it just deleted.

Examining records with the `keys` function

You saw earlier in this chapter, in "Comparing associative arrays with standard lists," how to examine the value of a record by placing its key within curly braces. The format for this is

```
$ARRAYNAME{"KEY"}
```

You may want a list of all the keys in an associative array so that you can look at each record in the array. The (appropriately named) `keys` function accomplishes this for you. The argument to `keys` is the name of the associative array. For example, the following program prints the records from an associative array:

```
@AllKeys = keys(%Streets);
foreach $TheKey (@AllKeys)
    { print "$TheKey is the key for $Streets{$TheKey}\n" }
```

The order in which the keys are returned is fairly random. Because `keys` returns a simple list, you can sort the returned list before using it with a statement, such as the following one:

```
@AllKeys = sort(keys(%Streets));
```

Returning values with the `values` function

The `values` function returns a list of the values in an associative array. This is useful when you just need to know the values in the array but not which key each value is associated with. When you use the `values` function, remember that you may have duplicate values (but never duplicate keys).

For example, to create an array `@AllVals` that contains all the values in the associative array `%Streets`, you can use the following:

```
@AllVals = sort(values(%Streets));
print join("\n", @AllVals), "\n";
```

Do not assume order

Perl stores records in a seemingly random order. By "seemingly random," that means the order makes no sense if you just look at the keys or the values in the list. As soon as you assign a record to an array, Perl determines where in the hash the record should go and puts it there, disregarding the order you put the records in. However, Perl knows the order based on the hash function it uses to store the records.

The following program demonstrates that associative arrays are not necessarily kept in the order in which you enter them. The result of running the program may surprise you.

```
%IDList = (742 => 'Kathi Stennis',
    5280 => 'Roberta Wallace',
    3279 => 'Daniel Exon');
print join("\n", %IDList);
```

When you run this program, Perl displays

```
3279
Daniel Exon
742
Kathi Stennis
5280
Roberta Wallace
```

Note that the records come out in a different order than they went in; that's because Perl outputs them in the order they are stored internally in Perl.

Stepping with the `each` *function*

If you have a very large associative array, you may not want to create lengthy lists with the `keys` and `values` functions. Instead, you can use the `each` function to step through the records one at a time. The `each` function returns a two-element list: the key and the value. When you reach the end of the associative array, `each` returns a false value.

For example, the following program prints out the key and the value for every record in `%BigList`. It does this by using the `each` function to get each record one at a time:

```
while(($TheKey, $TheVal) = each(%BigList))
    { print "$TheKey is the key for$TheVal\n" }
```

The counter used by `each` is reset when you use either a `keys` or `values` function, so don't not use either of those functions in your loop. The `each` function works correctly if you delete records, but not if you add them.

If you just want to check to see that a particular key is in an associative array, use the exists function:

```
unless(exists($Streets{"Main"}))
    { print "Main Street has disappeared.\n" }
```

Checking for any existing records

You can find out whether any records at all exist in an associative array by evaluating the array in a scalar context. This process returns true only if any records exist. For example, the following shows the %IDList associative array used as the argument of the unless function, which forces the array into a scalar context:

```
unless(%IDList) { print "The assoc. array is empty.\n" }
```

Writing Associative Array Data to a File

Rarely do you keep all the data that a Perl program uses. Instead, you probably keep the data in a file on your hard disk and read it into your program. You may also use Perl to change the data in your database and then write the file to disk. You can use files that contain data with associative arrays pretty much the same way you use files with simple lists. (See Chapter 11 for more information.)

For example, you may keep the program data as a tab-delimited text file and read it into the program when the program first starts up. You can write the data to the file by using something like the following program, which writes out each key and value pair. Each pair is separated by a tab character, and each record is written on a separate line.

```
open(STREETOUT, ">streets.txt") or
    die "Couldn't write to streets.txt file.\n";
foreach $Key (sort(keys(%Streets)))
    { print STREETOUT "$Key\t$Streets{$Key}\n" }
close(STREETOUT);
```

You can read the file that the previous program creates with a program like this one:

```
%Streets = ();
open(STREETIN, "streets.txt") or
    die "Couldn't read from streets.txt file.\n";
```

(continued)

(continued)

```
while(<STREETIN>) {
    $TheRec = $_; chomp($TheRec);
    ($Key, $Val) = split(/\t/, $TheRec, 2);
    $Streets{$Key} = $Val;
}
```

Chapter 17 describes how to use database files with much faster access than the files I just described.

Multidimensional Lists

Until Perl 5 arrived, Perl programmers were limited to creating lists that consisted solely of scalar items (either strings or numbers). For my money, multidimensional lists are among the greatest features introduced.

A *multidimensional list* is essentially a "list of lists." For example, assume that you want to create a list of company employees, and within each item you want to list each employee's name, ID number, and telephone number. Or you may want to create an inventory list in which each item consists of a list of the item's inventory location, part number, name, and the quantity in stock. Perl 5 introduced an easy way to handle lists that have items consisting of other lists. You can even have associative arrays whose values are lists.

In the following sections, I show you how to use lists of lists, but not what the individual symbols and operators that are used with multidimensional arrays mean. If you want to find out more about these symbols and operators, you can look up "references" in the Perl documentation. Otherwise, you can still use lists of lists just fine without knowing every detail of how and why they work. (Lists of lists are based on Perl *references* and *pointers* — familiar to most advanced programmers, and included in most modern programming languages.)

Creating two-dimensional lists

In this section, you have an example program to assemble and use a list that has lists as its items. Assume that you have an inventory database, `@AllInv`, composed of various items. Each item has four parts:

- Warehouse location
- Part number
- Part name
- Quantity in stock

An item in the database may be represented by the following Perl statement:

```
('Shelf 17B', '35J912', 'Tool chest, black', 11)
```

Another item may be represented as

```
('Shelf 19A', '20N14', 'Allen wrench set', 47)
```

Lists composed of items like those in the previous examples are called *two-dimensional lists.* In this case, one dimension consists of rows, and the other dimension consists of columns. Each row contains the specific item in stock, and each column is a category, such as the item's location or part number. Suppose that you want to create a list that contains the preceding two lists. You may assume that the following statements can accomplish the task (but you'd be wrong):

```
#  WRONG, BUT CLOSE
@AllInv = (
    ('Shelf 17B', '35J912', 'Tool chest, black', 11),
    ('Shelf 19A', '20N14', 'Crescent wrench set', 47)
);
#  WRONG, BUT CLOSE
```

In lists of lists, you need to enclose the lists within lists in square brackets ([and]), not parentheses. Therefore, the following is the correct way to enter the previous example:

```
#  THE RIGHT WAY
@AllInv = (
    ['Shelf 17B', '35J912', 'Tool chest, black', 11],
    ['Shelf 19A', '20N14', 'Crescent wrench set', 47]
);
#  THE RIGHT WAY
```

Always mark the outermost list with parentheses, just as you would with simple lists, and the inner lists with square brackets.

Accessing list elements one piece at a time

In a simple list, you access a list element by using a *subscript* (the value to be offset from the beginning of an array) in square brackets. For example, the sixth element of `@MyList` is identified with `$MyList[5]`. (The first element in a list is always at offset 0.)

In two-dimensional lists, you need to use two subscripts to access a list element — first the row, and then the column. For instance, in the example in the preceding section, the fourth column in the second row of `@AllInv` is accessed with `$AllInv[1][3]`. Therefore, the following statement

```
print $AllInv[1][3];
```

displays

```
47
```

You can set values in lists of lists exactly as you do in simple lists. For instance, using the example in the preceding section, if you want to decrease the number of crescent wrenches in stock to 35, you use

```
$AllInv[1][3] = 35;
```

You can also use variables in the subscripts. For instance, to double the number of all the items in this example, you can use the following statements:

```
$NumItems = @AllInv;
for($i = 0; $i < $NumItems; $i += 1)
    { $AllInv[$i][3] *= 2 }
```

You may want to get a whole row as a list instead of each of its pieces. This task seems easy, but the syntax to accomplish it is a tad bizarre-looking due to the way that Perl handles references. The format looks like this:

```
@{@ARRAYNAME[ROW]}
```

For example, you may have something in your program that fills in an array called `@TopRow` with the first record of your database. It may look like this:

```
@TopRow = @{@AllInv[0]};
```

You have no direct way to refer to an entire column in a similar fashion, so you always have to take multiple steps if you want to fill an array with the values from a column.

Adding rows and columns to two-dimensional lists

You may want to add items to a list one full row at a time (for example, when new items are added to a list of in-stock inventory). You can use the venerable `push` function (described in Chapter 7) for this. For example, if you have a list called `@NewItem` that you want to add to the end of the list `@AllInv`, you can use

```
@NewItem = ('Floor 2J', '82B297', 'Keyhole saw', 18);
push(@AllInv, [ @NewItem ]);
```

If you don't want to use a temporary variable, such as `@NewItem`, you can say

```
push(@AllInv, [ 'Floor 2J', '82B297', 'Keyhole saw', 18 ]);
```

Adding a column takes a little more work than adding a row, but the process is still fairly easy. It requires your adding an item to the end of each list in the main list. For example, if you want to add a column at the end of each list that shows the date you last examined the item, you can write something like the following:

```
# Start by using today's date
($Second, $Minute, $Hour, $DayOfMonth, $Month, $Year,
    $WeekDay, $DayOfYear, $IsDST) = localtime(time);
$RealMonth = $Month + 1;
$Today = sprintf('%02d/%02d/%02d', $RealMonth,
    $DayOfMonth, $Year);
$NumItems = @AllInv;
for($i = 0; $i < $NumItems; $i += 1)
    { $AllInv[$i][4] = $Today }
```

Perl automatically extends a list as you add columns to the end of it, just as it does for simple lists.

Creating Associative Arrays Consisting of Lists

The more you work with Perl, the more uses you find for associative arrays that have lists as values. Instead of searching record by record in order to find information on an item in a list, an associative array enables you to find the record quickly by using its *key.* (See the section "Locating items by their keys" earlier in this chapter.)

You can create associative arrays with list values by using statements like these (here, the part numbers `'35J912'` and `'20N14'` are the keys):

```
%AllInvByNum = (
    '35J912' => ['Shelf 17B', 'Tool chest, black', 11],
    '20N14'=> ['Shelf 19A', 'Crescent wrench set', 47]
);
```

You can look at an individual item with the following statement:

```
$WrenchCount = $AllInvByNum{'20N14'}[2];
```

You can add records to an associative array with an assignment. For example, you can add a record whose key is `'82B297'` with the following statement:

```
$AllInvByNum{'82B297'} = [ 'Floor 2J', 'Keyhole saw', 18 ];
```

Beyond two dimensions

In Perl, it's possible to have lists of lists of lists of . . . well, you get the picture. Perl doesn't restrict you to two-dimensional lists. In fact, many programs have multidimensional lists with three or more dimensions. For example, imagine that the parts inventory database `@AllInv` is meant to inventory *all* the locations in your company, not just one. The location and amount fields would then have more than one entry in them.

You can specify lists within lists within lists just as easily as you can specify just lists within lists. For example, a multilocation inventory list may be written in Perl to look like this:

```
@AllInv = (
    [['New York Shelf 17B', 'Ohio Slot 135'] ,
'35J912',
        'Tool chest, black', [11, 13]],
    [['New York Shelf 19A', 'Ohio Slot 142'],
'20N14',
        'Crescent wrench set', [47, 12]]
);
```

This example program indicates that 11 tool chests are in stock at "New York Shelf 17B" and 13 tool chests are in stock at "Ohio Slot 135," and so on. To access this information directly, you need to use a third subscript, such as the following:

```
$OhioQuant = $AllInv[0][3][1];
```

You can find a particular record in a multidimensional associative array with a statement like this:

```
@Tools = @{$AllInvByNum{'35J912'}};
```

When using the associative array functions (`keys`, `values`, `each`, and `exists`), you have to be careful how you handle anything that's a value. (Remember that the value is a list, not a scalar.) For example, in order to print a list of inventory locations sorted by part number, you can use

```
foreach $Part (sort(keys(%AllInvByNum))) {
   print "Key $Part is found at location " .
      "$AllInvByNum{$Part}[0]\n";
}
```

If you want to print out the records, you can use

```
foreach $Part (sort(keys(%AllInvByNum))) {
    print "Key $Part:  ",
        join("--", @{$AllInvByNum{$Part}}), "\n";
}
```

Writing the Files for Lists within Lists

If you want to keep your data that's handled in lists of lists in a file on disk, be careful how you read it and write the data. Actually, the reading part isn't so difficult, but writing data that's in a multidimensional list isn't as straightforward a process than if it were in a simple list.

I generally use tab-delimited files for all my data storage. Each line in the text file is an element of the top-level list. This sort of file structure simplifies reading and writing data, and I can always examine the files with a text editor if I need to troubleshoot any problems with a file.

Text files for two-dimensional lists of lists

For a two-dimensional list, you can use something like the following program to write your data to a text file:

```
# Format is location, part number, description, quantity
open(INVOUT, ">inventory.txt") or
    die "Couldn't write to inventory.txt.\n";
$NumItems = @AllInv;
for($i = 0; $i < $NumItems; $i += 1)
    { print INVOUT "$AllInv[$i][0]\t$AllInv[$i][1]\t" .
        "$AllInv[$i][2]\t$AllInv[$i][3]\n" }
```

To read the preceding database file, you can use something like this:

```
# Format is location, part number, description, quantity
@AllInv = ();
open(INVIN, "inventory.txt") or
    die "Couldn't read from inventory.txt.\n";
while(<INVIN>) {
    $TheRec = $_; chomp($TheRec);
    @NewItem = split(/\t/, $TheRec, 4);
    push(@AllInv, [ @NewItem ]);
}
```

Text files for more-complicated lists of lists

If your list of lists has more than two dimensions, you have to be especially careful when you write and read the text file on which your list is based. Otherwise, you may accidentally fail to write out the data, but instead write out a Perl structure that doesn't include the data. When writing to a text file, remember to get the data for every item in the lists within the main list. For example, in the program that was presented in the preceding section, you'd use the following lines because of the additional dimensions in the list:

```
# Format is New York location, Ohio location, part number,
#    description, New York quantity, Ohio quantity
open(INVOUT, ">inventory.txt") or
    die "Couldn't write to inventory.txt.\n";
$NumItems = @AllInv;
for($i = 0; $i < $NumItems; $i += 1) {
    print INVOUT "$AllInv[$i][0][0]\t$AllInv[$i][0][1]\t" .
        "$AllInv[$i][1]\t$AllInv[$i][2]\t" .
        "$AllInv[$i][3][0]\t$AllInv[$i][3][0]\n";
}
```

To read the preceding database file, you can use the following:

```
# Format is New York location, Ohio location, part number,
#    description, New York quantity, Ohio quantity
@AllInv = ();
open(INVIN, "inventory.txt") or
    die "Couldn't read from inventory.txt.\n";
while(<INVIN>) {
    $TheRec = $_; chomp($TheRec);
    @NewItem = split(/\t/, $TheRec, 6);
    push(@AllInv, [ [ $NewItem[0], $NewItem[1] ],
        $NewItem[2], $NewItem[3],
        [ $NewItem[4], $NewItem[5] ] ] );
}
```

Chapter 17

Dancing with Databases

In This Chapter

- Storing data on disk
- Gaining quick access to keyed data
- Closing databases when you're done with them

I've used probably a dozen different database-management software packages in my life. Among them, I've seen the good, the bad, and the just plain ugly. How Perl accesses databases is so amazingly simple that at first I couldn't believe it would even work. But, I can assure you that Perl does an admirable job of managing databases, as this chapter shows you.

Database Management: It's Done with Associative Arrays

In order to use Perl with database files, you first need to understand how associative arrays work (I cover that topic in Chapter 16). In fact, that's about all the basic information you need, besides a couple of Perl functions for opening and closing databases — `dbmopen` and `dbmclose`.

How does Perl dispense with the dozens of different commands that are common to most database-management programs? Perl binds an associative array to the database file so that any changes you make to the associative array are also made to the database. When you look up a key in the associative array, Perl actually gets the value from the database. (Associative arrays and keys are described in Chapter 16.)

Perl uses *DBM files* for its databases stored on disk. DBM is a UNIX standard (that is, a traditional way of doing things on UNIX systems) for simple *key-value databases* (databases in which every record has a key that is usually used for getting at the record). Many varieties of DBM files exist, and Perl can handle most of them. At the time this book was written, the flavors of DBM files that Perl comprehends include GDBM, BSD-DB, SDBM, NDBM, and ODBM. The bottom line is this: Perl saves you from having to program DBM.

Opening Databases

The dbmopen function takes three arguments: the name of the associative array, the name of the database on disk, and a mode, as you can see in the following line:

```
dbmopen(%AllInv, "/usr/general/inventory", 0600);
```

The *mode* is the numeric UNIX file mode in which you want to open the file. If you aren't a UNIX grunt, or you are and you tend to get the file modes mixed up, the two modes you're most likely to use are 0600 if you want to read and write to the database and 0400 if you just want to read it.

When you use the dbmopen function, every time you access the associative array in the function, you actually access the database on disk.

Closing Databases

After you're done working with a database, use the dbmclose function, whose argument is the name of the associative array. This closes the file on your hard disk. For example,

```
dbmclose(%AllInv);
```

Tips on Opening and Closing Databases

Opening and closing a DBM database takes time (although not as much time as reading through a long text file), so you don't want to open and close the database for each record you are examining or updating. However, if you are accessing a database that others are also using, you should close the database as soon as you are finished.

The dbmopen and dbmclose functions are special instances of the Perl tie and untie functions. Although I don't get into the specifics of tie and untie in this book, it's worth knowing that these functions provide useful ways to associate Perl variables with an action. In the case of dbmopen and dbmclose, they allow access to an associative array to be associated with a set of calls that reads and sets values in DBM databases.

Built for speed

The biggest advantage of using the Perl database functions, as opposed to reading a text file from disk into an associative array, is sheer speed. Imagine if you had an inventory database that was a text file 10,000 lines long. Reading the entire file and parsing it into an associative array takes a significant amount of time. If you want to look at just one item, the whole process eats up work hours and computer resources.

Instead, you can use Perl database functions to open a DBM file on disk. For example, a program designed to look up the record for a key that is given in `$ReqKey` may look like this:

```
# Open database for read-only
dbmopen(%AllInv, "/usr/general/inventory", 0400);
. . .
$TheRec = $AllInv{$ReqKey};
($Loc, $PartName, $Quant) = split(/\t/, $TheRec, 3);
. . .
dbmclose(%AllInv);
```

If you want to add a record to the database or change the value associated with a key that's already in the database, you can use something like the following statement:

```
$AllInv{$MyKey} = join("\t", ($Loc, $PartName,
$Quant));
```

Chapter 18

Controlling Your Computer from Perl

In This Chapter

- Understanding Perl's system-level functions
- Using Perl to control PCs and Macs
- Digging into Perl's UNIX roots

Perl interacts with you and your computer in a number of ways. This chapter covers some of the system-level tasks you can perform with Perl. For example, you can use Perl to run other programs or to monitor programs that are running on your computer. This chapter also discusses the functions that can help you gain control over your Windows or Mac systems.

Getting with the System (Functions)

Perl makes it easy to run commands on your computer as if you had entered them on the command line. Perl's `system` function is designed to execute a command. On a UNIX system, for example, you can use the function to execute the `ls` command (which is UNIX's command to list the files in a directory):

```
system('ls');
```

The program you name in the `ls` statement argument can contain command-line arguments, such as

```
system('ls -la /var/spool');
```

Under Windows 95 or Windows 98, you can use the `system` function to give DOS commands, such as the DOS DIR command:

```
system('DIR');
```

The `system` function causes Perl to run the named program and wait for that program to exit. That sounds logical, doesn't it? However, Perl has another function, `exec`, which doesn't wait for the program to exit. The `exec` function acts like the `system` function except that it causes Perl to immediately stop and run the named program, never to return to run the statements after the `exec` statement. The only way any lines after the `exec` statement will ever be run is if the named program isn't found. Therefore, the second line of the following program won't be seen unless an error occurs while Perl looks for the program you name:

```
exec('myprogram');
print "Hmmm, my program didn't seem to run.\n";
```

Getting output from a program

At times you may want to capture the output of a program within a variable and use that information later in the program. In this case, you should use Perl's ' operator, which is know as the *backtick operator.* (Note that this operator is a left-slanting single quote, usually found to the left of the 1 on a keyboard.) Enclosing a program name with the backtick operator causes the output to be returned. Here's an example of how it's used:

```
$TheOutput = 'myprogram';
```

If you use the backtick operator in a scalar context, all output is written into the string variable. If you use the backtick operator in a list context, each line of the output is stored in a list item.

Using backticks takes the standard file output (described in Chapter 12) of the program and passes it into the variable. It does *not* cause the standard error output from the program to go into the variable, only the standard file output. This means that error messages may not appear in the variable.

Perl 5 introduced the `qx//` operator, which acts just like the backtick operator. The `qx//` operator works like Perl's other quoting operators in that you put a string between the two slash characters, as described in Chapter 5. An example of using `qx//` looks like this:

```
$TheOutput = qx/myprogram/;
```

Or, like this:

```
$TheOutput = qx(myprogram);
```

Using the `open` function

The `open` function can also work somewhat like the backtick operator described in the previous section, except that instead of sending the output to a variable, it sends it to a file handle (file handles are described in Chapter 12). To use `open` in this fashion, the command is followed by a vertical bar (|) character (which is sometimes called a *pipe* character) as the second argument to the `open` function. For example:

```
open(THEOUT, "myprogram |");
```

In the previous statement, you can then treat `THEOUT` like any other file handle that has input you want to read from. You do not need to use the `close` function to close programs that send output to Perl.

You can also use `open` in the opposite fashion: to pass data to the standard file input of the program. In this case, you place the | (pipe character) in front of the name of the program in the second argument. You can then treat the file handle of the `open` function like any file that you're writing to. For example, if your program takes data from the standard file input, you can enter something like this:

```
open(THEPROG, "| myprog");
print THEPROG $a1, $a2, "\n";
close(THEPROG);
```

After the `close` function is executed, the program then has all of its input and runs with it.

Using the `open` function to pass data to the standard file input of a program is done much more frequently on UNIX systems than on Windows, because few DOS programs are written to take input from standard file input.

Running programs in MacPerl

Programs running on a Macintosh work differently than programs running on UNIX or Windows. Because of these differences, backticks and the `system` and `exec` functions normally don't work in MacPerl. But, if you have a Mac program called ToolServer, available from Apple, you can use these functions. ToolServer comes as part of Apple's MPW (Macintosh Programmer's Workshop) development software and a few other programming packages.

I should point out that a few backtick commands *do* work on a Mac (see Table 18-1). They make converting some UNIX-based Perl programs easier to do because you don't have to change statements with these backtick commands.

Table 18-1 Backtick Commands that Work on the Mac

Backtick Statement	*Value Returned*
`'pwd'`	The current folder, followed by a newline (you can also use `'Directory'` as well).
`'hostname'`	Name of the Macintosh.
`'glob <argument>'`	List of all files matching the argument. You can use * and ? (for example, `*.c`).

Controlling a Windows or Mac Computer with Perl

Although the user interface for Perl-Win32 is meager (to say the least), it offers a fair number of Windows-specific functions and features. They enable you to monitor system activity, change system parameters, and perform other system-management chores. Most of the functions and features are geared more toward Windows NT than Windows 95/98, but some features work fine on both platforms.

Every extension that comes with Perl-Win32 has the prefix `Win32::`. By the time you read this, there may be more extensions in the most recent version of Perl-Win32. The extensions fall into three categories: variables, functions, and modules. The following sections contain brief introductions to these features (the documentation that comes with Perl-Win32 goes into much greater detail).

Perl-Win32 was originally developed for Windows NT (although it also works well on Windows 95 and Windows 98). Because of this NT orientation, many of the extensions in Perl-Win32 are used for system administration that only works under NT, not under Windows 95/98. For example, NT is a multi-user system, so there are many Perl-Win32 extensions for adding, removing, and controlling user accounts; none of these have any relevance if you are running Perl-Win32 on Windows 95/98.

Mac users need not fear that they have been left behind: the MacPerl package comes with many useful modules for controlling your Macintosh. Some are for advanced users only (such as those that control the network interfaces), but others are for all Perl programmers and give access to Macintosh user interface features.

Using UNIX-Only System Functions

UNIX, quite naturally, has its own set of system control functions. These functions are the ones that interest system administrators the most because the functions are used primarily to examine information on users and user groups.

For user databases

The `getpwent` function reads the user database. On UNIX systems, this database is usually the file /etc/passwd. The `getpwent` function starts at the beginning of the database and keeps track of which record in the database it last read. When you include this function in a program, the function returns a list that contains the following items:

- User name
- Encrypted password (or asterisk)
- User number
- Group number
- Quota field
- Comment field
- gcos field (an obscure UNIX feature that is almost never used)
- Home directory
- Default shell

Because the `getpwent` function gets the next record, it is common to use `getpwent` in a loop, such as in the following `while` statement:

```
while(@PWList = getpwent) { print "$PWList[0]\n" }
```

You can reset `getpwent` to start reading from the top of the user database with the `setpwent` function and close the database with the `endpwent` function (although you don't have to).

Another pair of functions, `getpwuid` and `getpwnam`, returns a list that has the same format as the list `getpwent` returns. However, these functions take a single argument (a userid or a username, respectively) and return the list for that argument. For example, to get the list for user phoffman, you can enter the following statement:

```
@PWList = getpwnam('phoffman');
```

The `getlogin` function returns the login name of the user running the program. You can obtain this name from the /usr/utmp file.

For group databases

The `getgrent` function acts like the `getpwent` function, except that it walks through the *group* database instead of the user database. The `getgrent` function returns

- Group name
- Encrypted password (or asterisk)
- Group number
- String of member names

As you may have guessed, Perl also has `setgrent` and `endgrent` functions, which set the location from which to read the next record in the group database. And, as you may also have guessed, you can use the `getgrgid` and `getgrnam` functions, both of which take a groupid as an argument and return a list that has the same format as the list returned by `getgrent`.

Chapter 19

Object-Oriented Perl

In This Chapter

- Covering some object-oriented programming basics
- Checking out the Perl objects library
- Creating a new Perl object
- Using prewritten Perl objects to access the Web

The programming industry is much less prone to flash-in-the-pan fads than the rest of the computer world. Programming languages stick around forever, long after they probably should have died a quiet death. The one major fad to hit the programming world in the last decade is *object-oriented programming.* Clearly, object-oriented programming is here to stay and Perl has embraced it in a very Perl-like fashion. That is to say, you can use objects if you want to, but Perl doesn't make it a requirement.

In this chapter, I cover Perl's object-oriented programming features so that you can read and use object-oriented programs written by other Perl programmers. Most Perl programmers who write programs for others to use incorporate the object-oriented parts of Perl. In fact, much of the CPAN library on this book's companion CD-ROM uses object-oriented Perl. If you know how to use objects, you can tap into the wealth of prewritten Perl programs, which can save you loads of time.

The Object of OOP: Faster and More Consistent Programming

When people started talking seriously about object-oriented programming in the mid-1980s, many programmers were openly skeptical of it. Its acronym (OOP) didn't help matters, making it the butt of jokes. Nevertheless, over time, more and more programmers became enthralled with the promises that object-oriented programming holds, even though it involves learning some new programming concepts and ultimately requires more work. All in all, OOP has a number of benefits:

- The most important benefit of object-oriented programming is that it allows programmers to reuse prewritten programs for their own applications, which saves them the time and trouble of starting from scratch. (Of course, you still need to obtain legal permission from the original author before reusing his or her work.) For example, you can write a program designed to do a particular task on the Internet, and others can easily include what you've written as part of their programs. Without object-oriented programming, using prewritten programs is still possible, but requires so much work that it's impractical.
- Another significant benefit is that team programming projects are much easier to coordinate when the programmers are all using object-oriented programming. It forces programmers to use a consistent interface on the code that they write, and each piece of the larger project can be more easily integrated with the rest.
- Object-oriented programming also simplifies hierarchical program development in which a program is built from general concept to detailed specifications. If your customer has an idea of what the program is supposed to do in general, but is fuzzy on the specifics, you can start with the basics and then fill in the details at the various levels of the program as the customer provides more information or as the customer's needs change.
- Object-oriented programming helps you to manage complex projects. For example, some projects may not be well-defined and therefore require some trial and error; or turnover in your company's programming staff may mean that too many chefs have been seasoning the program "soup." In addition, programs tend to evolve as they're written and large programs are inherently complex, just because they're designed to do a bunch of stuff. Because the goal of object-oriented programming is to make the programming process *modular* (meaning that it's broken into smaller chunks), performing one task at a time becomes easier to do.

In my opinion, object-oriented programming techniques are great for large programs, and even for some medium-sized ones, but not for the kinds of small programs Perl is often used for. The fact that many Perl programmers employ object-oriented programming is a boon for everyone because their programs can be more easily recycled. But, for most one-person projects, object-oriented programming is not necessary (unless those projects develop into a team effort).

Defining Objects, Methods, and Arguments

In Perl programs, most of the action takes place within variables. You set a numeric variable here, you add items to a list variable there, you split a string variable into other string variables, and so forth. *Variables,* in essence, hold the information in a Perl program.

In an object-oriented program, you do have variables, of a sort. The things used to hold information are called objects and objects are much more than just a variable. An *object* is a collection of variables combined with a collection of actions (called *methods*) that the object is capable of performing. You don't examine or change the variables in an object using the standard Perl commands. Instead, you use an object's methods to handle its variables.

You can think of an object as a black box that's attached to a microphone through which you give the object directions. The box also has a list of instructions you can paste on it and a slot through which various items may emerge (somewhat like a restaurant drive-up window). You don't know exactly what's inside the box or how its innards work, and you don't even know if the instructions are complete. You know only that you give instructions to the object and that you expect a certain result, but you don't necessarily know all the choices available to you.

For example, imagine you have a black box that functions as a "bicycle object." The instructions on the side of the box provide a list of *methods,* including TellColor, GoForward, FallOver, and so on, that you apply to the object. You announce "TellColor" into the microphone, and out comes a slip of paper saying "blue." You say "GoForward 7" into the microphone, and the box jumps forward seven inches. Some methods have *arguments,* which are additional instructions to the object, and some don't; some methods return a value, while other methods just tell the object what to do.

The concept of objects may seem a bit confusing at first because they're so dissimilar to variables. But it's the difference between an object and a variable that enables object-oriented programs to manage complexity. If you could change the innards of an object's variables at whim, writing object-oriented programs with predictable results would be almost impossible. Objects force program developers to use only those methods associated with a particular object, which assures consistent results.

Objects also give you a degree of flexibility. You can change how a method works in an object without changing all the programs that use that object. Take the bicycle object I describe earlier, for example. Assume that some of your colleagues are using this object in their programs. You later discover a much faster way to implement the GoForward method. You can change that method without forcing everyone who is already using your object to change anything they're already doing with their programs.

Objects don't just appear out of nowhere. They're created from *classes.* You can think of a class as a cookie cutter that stamps out many identical objects from one mold. The cookie cutter (the class) and the cookie (the object) are two very different things. (To say that objects are "created from" classes isn't absolutely correct. Technically, an object is *instantiated* from a class, meaning that it has the same features as the class.)

Perl's Objects Made Easy

At this point, you're probably asking, "So, how do I use Perl's object-oriented features to build a Perl program?" Fortunately, the answer is, "Very easily." But first, you need to keep in mind three important things about object-oriented programs: classes, methods, and objects. In Perl 5 and later versions, a class is a called a *package.* Located inside each package are definitions of the various methods of that class. These methods are, in fact, *subroutines* (which are also described in Chapter 10).

One tricky aspect of using Perl's object-oriented features is a part of Perl called *references* that are used to create the objects themselves. The topic of references is beyond the scope of this book, but fortunately, you can use objects without knowing exactly how references work.

The remainder of this chapter refers to the object-oriented interface of the libwww-perl library, which is covered in Chapter 15. You can use the library while following along with the discussion (assuming that the library has been installed on your system as covered in Chapter 15), or you can follow along without it.

Opening a Perl module with the `use` function

Before you create objects, you have to open the latest version of the Perl module that contains the classes you want. To open a Perl module, you need the `use` function. The `use` function normally takes only one argument, the module name. Module names are not placed in quotation marks, and if a module's name ends with ".pm," you may leave off the .pm part of the file name. For example, you can use the following statement to open a Perl module:

```
use(LWP::UserAgent);
```

More frequently, the use function appears without the parentheses. For example,

```
use LWP::UserAgent;
```

You can also include additional arguments in the use statement if you want particular variables from the module. Don't worry about this; it's rarely used.

Making new objects with the new subroutine

After you specify one or more modules for Perl to open, you're ready to create objects. Remember that each object comes with its own methods, therefore you have to create an object before you can use its methods. In Perl, you almost always use the new subroutine of a package to create a new object, as you can see in the following statement:

```
$TheAgent = new LWP::UserAgent;
```

The new statement creates a new object from the LWP::UserAgent class and makes $TheAgent a reference to the new object.

Think of $TheAgent not as "the object," but as "something that points to the object." For example, someone may say to me, "You are Paul Hoffman," when what they mean is, "You are the person who is named Paul Hoffman." I'm the person, not the name, but it's simpler to just think of me by my name.

The new subroutine of a package sometimes requires arguments. The arguments are listed after the name of the module, as the following statement shows you:

```
$Req = new HTTP::Request 'GET', 'http://www.scruz.net/';
```

Most Perl object libraries enable you to invoke the new subroutine with no arguments and use methods instead of arguments to supply what would have been the arguments. Here is an example of a new subroutine with no arguments:

```
$Req = new HTTP::Request;
```

Invoking an object's methods

After you create an object, you can use its methods. You invoke Perl methods with the following format:

```
$OBJECTREF->METHODNAME(ARGUMENTS);
```

For example, in the preceding section of this chapter, you can see an `HTTP::Request` object set to the name `$Req`. All `HTTP::Request` objects have a method called `url` that tells the object the URL to use. You can invoke this method with a statement like the following:

```
$Req->url('http://www.scruz.net/');
```

Note that to the left of the `->` operator is the reference to the object whose method you want to invoke, and to the right of the `->` operator is the method name. Some methods take arguments (in parentheses, of course), and others just appear on their own, as in the following example:

```
$Req->url;
```

A Real-World Object Example

The libwww-perl set of modules is a good example of an object-oriented Perl program that does real work (some modules perform only small tasks). As described in Chapter 15, libwww-perl enables you to create Perl programs that act like Web clients.

This section of the chapter gives you an idea of what you can do with the `LWP::UserAgent` object that acts like parts of a Web browser. (See the Perl documentation that comes with the `LWP::UserAgent` module for a complete list of methods.)

Three types of objects are used in simple `LWP::UserAgent` programs:

- **HTTP user agents:** created with a `new LWP::UserAgent` statement
- **HTTP requests:** created with a `new HTTP::Request` statement
- **Responses from requests:** returned from calls to the `request` method used on HTTP user agents

Each of the three different objects has its own methods, some of which are listed in Table 19-1. The table lists some example-specific methods used in a simple `LWP::UserAgent` program.

Table 19-1 Examples of Methods Used in a Simple `LWP::UserAgent` Program

Object	*Sample Methods*
`LWP::UserAgent`	request, time-out, proxy
`HTTP::Request`	method, url
`HTTP::Response`	content, is_success, is_error, code

To start a libwww-perl program that acts as a Web client, you must create an agent object and a request object. For example, the following statements open the `LWP::UserAgent` object, create a new agent, and create a new request:

```
use LWP::UserAgent;
$TheAgent = new LWP::UserAgent;
$Req = new HTTP::Request;
```

In this example, `$TheAgent` points to the agent object and `$Req` points to the request object.

The request object has a method that specifies the HTTP request method and a method that allows you to specify the URL to which you want to make the method. These methods are called `method` and `url`, respectively. If you just want to get the contents of a Web page, you use the `HTTP "GET"` method. For example, the following two lines,

```
$Req->method('GET');
$Req->url('http://www.scruz.net/');
```

assign the kind of method and URL that you want to use.

You're now ready to make the request over the Web. To do so, you need to tell your agent the request to use with the `request` method. Perl returns the Web page as a response object:

```
$TheResp = $TheAgent->request($Req);
```

With the previous statement, you create a response object that is pointed to by the `$TheResp` variable.

Naturally, after you put together a Web page, you want to look at it. Remember that `$TheResp` points to a response object, not to the content itself. Response objects have a method, namely `content`, that enables you to examine the page's content. For example, the following statement assigns the value of the content to a variable:

```
$TheRespContent = $TheResp->content;
```

`$TheRespContent` is now a string that contains the content.

Response objects have other interesting methods that can give you more information about the response you get from a Web server. For example, `is_success` and `is_error` tell you whether your Web request was successful. Instead of assuming that any content exists, you may want to check first by using the following:

```
if($TheResp->is_success)
    { $TheRespContent = $TheResp->content }
```

If you get an error, the response object can format the error message for you as an HTML document using the `error_as_HTML` method. For example,

```
if($TheResp->is_success)
    { $TheRespContent = $TheResp->content }
else { $TheRespContent = $TheResp->error_as_HTML }
```

Many different methods for these objects exist, and the best way to find out more is by reading their documentation. The documentation for modules can usually be found using the "perldoc" command that comes as part of Perl.

Programming with pragmas

Some built-in Perl modules, called *pragmas*, affect the way that Perl compiles your program before executing it. These modules can be of use in debugging your code or can force you to program more effectively (you can make the Perl compiler alert you more often about possibly unsound programming practices).

You can turn on Perl's pragmas by using the `use` function, just as you do with other modules. Pragmas usually apply only to the current block in which they're set. Therefore, you can turn on a pragma within a block; then, when it reaches the end of the block, Perl returns to its normal mode of operation. For example, to start using the `diagnostics` pragma, you can enter the following line in your program:

```
use diagnostics;
```

After you turn on a pragma, you can turn it off with the `no` function. It is essentially the opposite of `use`. For example,

```
no diagnostics;
```

The most useful built-in pragmas include:

- `Diagnostics` — Causes Perl to produce lengthier and more descriptive error messages
- `English` — Enables you to use easier-to-read names for built-in variables (names such as `$ARG` and `$MATCH` instead of cryptic variable names such as `$_` and `$&`)
- `integer` — Forces integer arithmetic on calculations
- `strict` — Causes compile errors for some possibly unsafe programming practices; this prevents the program from running until you change it

The `strict` pragma checks for symbolic references, and variables that weren't declared with the `my` function (covered in Chapter 10). It helps find some other subtle programming mistakes.

Part V
The Part of Tens

The 5th Wave
By Rich Tennant
...AND THESE ARE OUR OBJECT-ORIENTED PROGRAMMING SPECIALISTS.

In this part . . .

Because I bet you love lists as much as I do, the chapters in this part are presented as lists of top-ten items worth knowing about Perl. A lot of good, quick information is yours for the reading in these chapters, so take a break in your Perl programming to spend a bit of time with them.

Chapter 20

Ten Guidelines for Programming with Style

In This Chapter

- Making your programs easier to read and use
- Taking advantage of mnemonic variable names
- Inserting comments and blank lines as needed

Every programming language has its own hard-and-fast rules for how you must structure a program, as well as many optional guidelines you should follow. Perl certainly has plenty of both. For example, one Perl absolute is: "You must use correct capitalization for function names." (For example, the statement `Print $SomeVariable;` generates a Perl error because of the capital `P` in `Print`.)

If you violate the "should" guidelines for Perl program writing, you probably won't get an error message, and your program likely will work just fine. However, when you follow the "should" rules, your programs are easier to read by you and others, and maintaining your programs is much easier.

Examining the Perl Creator's Style Preferences

Larry Wall, Perl's originator, laid down some of his style preferences early on in Perl's life. A few other early and active Perl users have added to Larry's list. Many programmers take these preferences as gospel, while others more or less follow them by making changes to suit their own tastes. (I'm part of the latter group.)

The Perl documentation offers a useful list of style guidelines, some of which I mention here:

- Indents should consist of a group of four spaces.
- The opening curly brace should be on the same line as the keyword, if possible; otherwise, it should line up with the indentation.
- A space should be inserted before the opening curly brace of a multiline block.
- A one-line block may be put on one line, including its curly braces.
- Do not put a space before the semicolon at the end of a statement.
- You can omit the semicolon in a short, one-line block.
- Insert a space on either side of most operators.
- Insert blank lines between the chunks of your program that have different uses.
- No space should exist between a function name and its opening parenthesis
- Insert a space after every comma.
- Break long lines after an operator (except `and` and `or`, which should be followed immediately by the rest of the statement).
- Insert a space after the last parenthesis on the current line.
- Line up corresponding items vertically.

An example of your being able to choose your own style is the placement of curly brackets in one-line blocks. The guidelines I just listed would have you write something like

```
if($Num < 10) {
    print "$Num is too small.\n"; exit;
}
```

or the following, which makes more sense to me because the `print` and `exit` statements are small:

```
if($Num < 10)
    { print "$Num is too small.\n"; exit }
```

In cases like the preceding example, I'll even use the following construction just because it looks good to me:

```
if($Num < 10) { print "$Num is too small.\n"; exit }
```

Choosing Your Operator

Because Perl has a wealth of operators, you often have a choice between two equivalent operators for the same task. I always recommend that you choose the operator that will make the most sense when you read the program later.

For example, should you use the `++` or `+= 1` operator after a variable? Compare the following two statements:

```
if($Done) { $Count++ }
```

```
if($Done) { $Count += 1 }
```

In my mind, the second construction looks more like "add 1 to `$Count`" than the first one does. Nevertheless, most Perl programmers use `$Count++` instead. Both formats do the same thing, and I can certainly recognize that `$Count++` means "add 1 to `$Count`", however, I prefer to see the numeral `1` in the program.

The preceding example brings up another interesting stylistic preference: Should you use assignment operators, such as `+=` and `.=`, or specify the actual assignment? Compare the following:

```
if($Done) { $Count += 1 }
```

```
if($Done) { $Count = $Count + 1 }
```

To me, the latter statement is clearer, but using `$Count` twice on the same line seems redundant. I almost always prefer using the assignment operator `+=`, but some folks prefer to be more explicit by spelling everything out.

Parentheses Are Your Friends

In many cases, parentheses are optional in Perl programs. In mathematical equations, you can omit the parentheses if you are sure that you understand the order in which the operators will be evaluated. However, it is safer to include them so that you or some other person reading the program can understand what's going on.

You can also omit the parentheses around functions, but doing so makes many Perl statements difficult to read. For example, the following two statements essentially say the same thing:

```
mkdir("/usr/home/paul/Temp", 0700);
```

```
mkdir "/usr/home/paul/Temp", 0700;
```

To me, the first is much more readable than the second because you can see the arguments grouped together in the parentheses. Another Perl programmer may tell you that the parentheses just get in the way and don't add anything to the program.

Sometimes I don't even use parentheses, namely with the `print` function. For example, throughout this book I use statements like

```
print "The name is $Name\n";
```

instead of

```
print("The name is $Name\n");
```

I don't know why I started using `print` without the parentheses, but once I started, I kept it up. Every Perl programmer I know uses `print` without parentheses, so I guess I'm in good company.

Flexible Ordering for Conditionals

In this book, you can see conditional statements (`if` and `unless`) written with the condition appearing first:

```
if($Done) { $Count += 1 }
```

If the block that follows the conditional has exactly one statement in it, such as in the preceding line of code, you can place the statement first, followed by the conditional. You can even pull the expression outside of the parentheses if you wish. Therefore, you can replace the preceding example with either of the following statements:

```
$Count += 1 if($Done);
```

```
$Count += 1 if $Done;
```

To some people, the preceding statements sound a bit more like English: "Do this if that is true." However, I find this setup confusing because it violates the left-to-right reading patterns that we're all accustomed to. The left part is executed only if the right part is true, so you have to read from right to left on lines like the preceding ones. Also, having the conditional test outside of the parentheses just plain bugs me because you can't construct the statement that way if the conditional comes first.

You can use the "statement first" form for `while` and `until` as long as you have only a single statement. For example, the following statement is perfectly legal:

```
&MySub while $Count < 0;
```

The previous statement causes the `&MySub` subroutine to be executed repeatedly until `$Count` is greater than or equal to 0. This statement is equivalent to the following statement:

```
while($Count < 0) { &MySub }
```

Just because I always put the conditional first doesn't mean you have to. In fact, you can find lots of examples of Perl programs (written by very good programmers) that have the conditional second. Because that treatment always makes me stop and stare when I come across it, I choose not to use it.

Commenting about Comments

Programming style is all well and good, but a program without comments is essentially worthless. Yes, that's a strong statement. Yes, I really mean it. And, yes, I sometimes violate this rule myself.

Unless a program has five lines or fewer, you should always start it with at least one line of comments. Even on a little three-line program, adding one line of comments may take you all of 15 seconds and will make the program much more useful in the future.

For multiline comments, I usually indent the second line a few extra spaces to make it clear that it is a continuation of the previous line:

```
# empdata1.pl: a very simple employee database application.
#    This program reads a text file that is an employee
#    database and lets you query it by ID number.
```

Then again, other programmers don't indent run-over lines:

```
# empdata1.pl: a very simple employee database application.
# This program reads a text file that is an employee
# database and lets you query it by ID number.
```

Standout Line Treatments

Some folks like to embellish the comments at the beginning of their programs (and sometimes at the beginning of their subroutines) with long lines of characters to make them more noticeable:

```
##########################################################
# empdata1.pl: a very simple employee database application.
##########################################################
```

As long as a line starts with a # character, it's a comment. Some people, however, get a bit carried away:

```
#--*--*--*--*--*--*--*--*--*--*--*--*--*--*--*--*--*--*--*--#
# empdata1.pl: a very simple employee database application.
#--*--*--*--*--*--*--*--*--*--*--*--*--*--*--*--*--*--*--*--#
```

Some time ago, I came across the following lines written for another language. I think they demonstrate an art deco influence coupled with a Southwestern motif (all of which are completely useless):

```
#_____.___...----~~~~****\/\/||||\/\/****~~~~----....______
# empdata1.pl: a very simple employee database application.
#________....----~~~~****\/\/||||\/\/****~~~~----....______
```

But if this kind of artistry helps you to write clear comments, then by all means use it.

Comments Cohabitating with Code

As if we didn't have enough to argue about, you'll also hear some disagreement about which of the following constructions is better:

```
if($Signature ne 'Dave') { next }  # Wasn't what we wanted
```

or

```
# Check if signature is correct
if($Signature ne 'Dave') { next }
```

I'll admit that I can go either way on this. Sometimes I put the short comment on the same line as the test, and sometimes I insert it before the test. Other folks insist that you should never put a comment on the same line as Perl code because it's harder to read. My suggestion: Try both and see which suits you best.

Naming Your Variables Descriptively

Another common way to "comment" a program is to use descriptive names for your variables. Throughout this book, the variable names (even in the short snippets) often suggest their actual usage — for example, `$Count` and `$TheLine`.

The longer the program, the more variables you generally have. The more variables you have, the more important it is for you to know what each variable does. In short, the variable names become extremely important.

A long history exists of programmers using short, non-mnemonic names for variables, such as `$i`, `$j`, `$x`, and the venerable `$foo` and `$bar`. This practice is fine if you never have to look at the program again after you write it and you're able to remember what each of those arbitrarily named variables stands for.

By the way, you may notice that I use `$i` and `$j` in this book. It's okay to use short names like these in places where the variable is used for one only or two lines, such as in a short `for` statement. In fact, I think it is a good practice because it gives you a visual reminder that "this is a short-lived variable." However, if the variable will be "alive" for more than four or five lines, I recommend giving it a more-memorable name.

Capital Offense, or Not?

Another area of controversy among programmers is in the capitalization of variable names. In Perl, capitalization counts — the variable `$OldFileHandle` is different than `$OldfileHandle` (note the `f`). Some folks like to use mixed case in a variable name because it helps to decipher a jumble of characters; others don't like using mixed case because it can introduce typing errors. Those in the latter group usually use all lowercase characters (such as `$oldfilehandle`) or just an initial capital (such as `$Oldfilehandle`).

I personally like using internal capital letters in variable names (the dweeb-speak term for those letters is *intercaps*). However, I have to agree with the people who say that intercaps can result in increased typos. That type of error is often difficult to find in Perl programs because you don't have to predeclare your variables.

Seek and ye shall find errors: The -w switch

This is a good place to remind you about Perl's `-w` command-line switch. Running Perl from the command line with the `-w` switch causes Perl to scan your program and print warnings about simple errors you may have made before it runs the program. If you are using UNIX, you can also put the `-w` switch on the first line of your program, after the `#!/usr/bin/perl` invocation.

Inserting the `-w` switch on the Perl command line is a good way to avoid many common errors, but it's not foolproof. It is often good at finding mistyped variable names. For example, if you enter the same typo twice, it will probably miss both errors because it thinks that the mistaken variable is one that you really want.

Some programmers avoid intercaps by using all lowercase letters and inserting underscore (_) characters between the parts of the variable name. These folks may have a variable called `$old_file_handle`, for example. I have a hard time with this treatment because you have to use the Shift key to get the underscore, and you may as well make a capital letter out of a lowercase one. Also, underscores just don't look "right" to me, whereas intercaps do. Clearly, you can make your own choice on this.

The Beauty of Blank Lines

The lowly blank line is one of the most neglected types of comment. It doesn't have anything in it, so why bother with it? To me, a blank line is extremely helpful, particularly when I'm reading a program by an author who rarely uses descriptive comments.

A blank line tells you where one operation stops and another begins. You may be able to figure out what's going on by reading the statements in the program, but it helps to be able to scroll down a long program and see where the programmer intended the "sections" to be.

Having said that, I rarely use two blank lines together. One is enough to break the visual flow of a program; two lines can look like a chasm.

Chapter 21

Ten Really Short, Really Useful Perl Programs

In This Chapter

- Seeing just how short a really good Perl program can be
- Printing, sorting, and listing files and directories
- Working with passwords and calculators

Some people believe that short programs aren't good for very much, but that's not so with Perl. Just a couple lines of Perl code can go a long way. This chapter lists some of my favorite teeny, tiny Perl programs.

Collecting Unique Lines

If your text file has a lot of lines that are duplicates and you only want to see the unique lines, you can collect them into an array (in this case, it's called `@Unique`) with the following program:

```
open(IN, "somefile.txt"); @Unique=();
while(<IN>) { unless($i{$_}++) { push(@Unique, $_) } }
```

The trick here is that `$i{$_}++` returns 0 the first time you create a key-value pair with `$_` as the key, and some nonzero value after that.

Getting Rid of Multiple Blank Lines

Some text files have multiple, consecutive blank lines, which make them hard to read, particularly on smaller screens. The following program prints a text file, compressing all instances of two or more blank lines into a single blank line. Note that a "blank line" can have whitespace characters in it, such as spaces and tabs, but no displayable characters.

```
open(IN, "somefile.txt"); $PrevBlank = 0;
while(<IN>) {
    if(/\S/ or !$PrevBlank) { print $_ }
    $PrevBlank = /^\s*$/;
}
```

The `if` statement in this example is true if there are nonblank characters on the line or if the previous line was not blank. The `$PrevBlank` assignment tells you whether the current line is blank, meaning that it has zero or more whitespace characters and nothing else.

Printing Lines from a File in Sorted Order

It's easy to forget how useful Perl's `sort` function is. The following program reads the entire file into an array, sorts the array, and prints the result. Short and sweet, and pretty efficient to boot.

```
open(IN, "somefile.txt");
print sort(<IN>);
```

Printing a Range of Lines from a File

Have you ever wanted to read just a few lines from a file, and not the whole thing? The following program prints just a range of lines. You run the program with two arguments: the range you want and the filename. For example, if you name your program "showline" and you want to see Lines 10 through 20 of the somefile.txt file, you use this command line:

```
showline 10-20 somefile.txt
```

The following program prints a range of lines:

```
open(IN, $ARGV[1]) or die "Could not read $File.\n";
($Start, $Stop) = split(/-/, $ARGV[0]);
for($i=1; $i<=$Stop; $i += 1)
    { $Line = <IN>; if($i>=$Start) { print $Line } }
```

Listing Just the Files in a Directory

At times, you may want to ignore the subdirectories in a directory and just focus on the files. You can use the following -f file test to list all the files in a directory.

```
foreach $f (<*>) { if(-f $f) { print "$f\n" } }
```

Listing a Directory by Size

In order to sort a directory listing by anything other than its filenames, your program has to keep a list of records consisting of the names and other items in the listing. Associative arrays are great to use for this kind of list that has records with a key (the filename) and a value (the other directory information). The following program creates an associative array that lists the size of each file in the directory and then sorts the items for output. (You can easily modify this program to sort by date instead of by size.)

```
foreach $f (<*>) { $i{$f} = -s $f };
foreach $k (sort{ $i{$b} <=> $i{$a} } keys %i)
    { printf "%8d %s\n", $i{$k}, $k }
```

Sorting Directories by Extension

Sorting by a portion of a filename is a slightly more difficult process than sorting by file size or by the date the file was modified. The following program breaks the filename into two and sorts by the second part. If you are running Perl on a UNIX or Macintosh system, this program works predictably only if the filenames have no period or one period.

```
foreach $FullName (<*>) {
    ($Name, $Ext) = split(/\./, $FullName, 2);
    push(@Temp, "$Ext\t$FullName");
}
foreach $Val (sort(@Temp)) {
    ($Ext, $FullName) = split(/\t/, $Val);
    print "$FullName\n";
}
```

A Very Simple Calculator

Ever needed a simple-to-use calculator to knock off some quick-and-dirty math? The following program uses Perl's `eval` function to print out the answers to any equation you enter. To end the program, enter a blank line. Here's that program for creating your own calculator:

```
while(<STDIN>) {
    $i = $_; chomp($i); unless($i) { last }
    $o = eval($i); print "Answer = $o\n";
}
```

When you run the program, you can enter something like the following

```
((2**8) + (3**8))
```

and you get this result:

```
Answer = 6817
```

Randomizing a List

It's easy enough in Perl to generate random numbers, but randomizing the order of an array isn't as simple. Nevertheless, you can use the `splice` function to pull a random element from an array and then place the element in another array. The following program randomizes the list `@MyList`.

```
my @TempList = ();
while(@MyList)
    { push(@TempList, splice(@MyList, rand(@MyList), 1)) }
@MyList = @TempList;
```

The trick here is that `rand(@MyList)` picks a number between 0 and the number of elements in `@MyList`, and `splice` changes this random number to an integer.

Generating Random Mnemonic Passwords

Trying to convince computer users to come up with passwords that aren't easily guessed is one of the most challenging jobs for a system administrator. People always seem to insist on using their birthdates or pets' names for passwords — breaching security then becomes child's play.

The following program generates random passwords. Instead of a jumble of hard-to-remember letters, however, the passwords are somewhat mnemonic because they appear in pairs of consonants and vowels that are pronounceable. By stringing together a few goofy-sounding syllables, you can generate easy-to-remember nonsense phrases.

Each syllable of the password can represent any one of 100 numbers; therefore, a single four-syllable password, such as "votahubo," is one of 100 million (100 to the fourth power) possible passwords generated by the program. Having a system administrator assign these passwords provides much more security than letting users pick their own (easily guessed) passwords.

```
print "Enter a seed number: "; $s=<STDIN>;
srand($s ^ time);
@c=split(/ */, "bcdfghjklmnprstvwxyz");
@v=split(/ */, "aeiou");
for($i = 1; $i <=4; $i += 1)
    { print $c[int(rand(20))], $v[int(rand(5))] }
```

The first two lines of this program initialize the seed for the random numbers (see Chapter 9 for a description of seeds), and the next two lines create lists containing the 20 consonants (minus "q") and 5 vowels of the alphabet. The `for` loop simply prints the four syllables.

Chapter 22

Ten Advanced Perl Topics, In a Nutshell

In This Chapter

- Compiling, debugging, data packing, and other lofty stuff
- Recognizing Perl functions that go beyond the basics

I thought that you may want a glimpse into the sort of stuff advanced Perl programmers lie awake at night thinking about. A number of the functions mentioned in this chapter may be completely foreign to you now, but just give it a while. You, too, may one day dream of that perfect code compiler and debugging routine.

Note: Many of the Perl features listed in this chapter are not yet supported in non-UNIX implementations of Perl.

Compiled Perl

Perl is an *interpreter.* This means that each time you run a program, Perl interprets the source code of a program and turns it into instructions your computer can use. Although this process is done quickly, it's not as speedy as compiling a program once, saving the instructions for your computer to disk, and then running those instructions directly without your having to go through the interpretation process all over again.

Until recently, no method existed to compile Perl. In Perl 5.005, there exists a set of Perl modules that constitute a step toward "compilable Perl." Some of the modules enable you to take a Perl program and output Perl *bytecode,* which causes Perl to execute faster because Perl doesn't have to interpret a Perl program; it just executes the bytecode directly. Interestingly, the new compiler can generate a C program that can then be compiled with a C compiler. That means you can run the program without having to run Perl and without someone else being able to look at your C program.

The Perl compilers are still experimental and will probably change significantly in the future. But they should stabilize within a year or two, making them popular additions to the Perl universe.

Page Formats

Creating reports that are destined for a printer tends to be the bane of a programmer's existence. If you're writing text files to be printed out, you can drive yourself crazy trying to keep track of the number of lines you've entered on a page. But you need to track your lines so you know when you've filled up one page and you need to skip to the top of the next. This is made more difficult if you like to put headings at the top of each page and want to keep field widths constant, because the headings may change in size or the fields may affect other output.

Perl's `format` function enables you to describe the layout of your pages, which are then written out with the `write` function. The `format` function has many ways of letting you determine which page elements you want where, what to do when you have filled up a page, what to do when you need to keep a bunch of lines together when there's no room left at the bottom of the current page, and so on. Using the `format` and `write` functions frees you from having to keep track of line numbers because the functions do all the tracking for you.

Data Packing

If you work with binary data, you know how difficult it is to convert regular numbers to binary encodings and vice versa. The process of converting to binary data is typically called *data packing* because you're basically packing data into smaller units.

Perl can help with the conversion process through its `pack` and `unpack` functions, which feature templates (much like `printf`) that describe how to convert between regular numbers and their binary equivalents. A related function, `vec`, lets you create a binary array quickly and pick values out of it.

Debugging

After you write a program, you test it. And it always works fine the first time you run it. No? Join the club. Rarely do I write a program of more than 25 lines that works exactly as I expect the first time out.

When your program doesn't work as planned, you have to examine your program carefully to try to figure out what went wrong. That may mean adding lots of `print` statements to the program to see what's happening. This incremental test-fix-test-fix-test process is called *debugging*.

Perl also has a built-in debugging mode that lets you look inside your program by using debugging commands. To start Perl in debugging mode, add the character combination `-d` to the command line. Perl lets you *step* through your program, one line at a time, to see what each variable contains. Looking in the variables usually tells you what the values are at each step in the program, and then you know which of the steps changed things in an unexpected way.

System Processes

Perl programs can create their own *processes* (the low-level tasks that your computer executes), which then allow Perl programs to run continually as *daemons* in the system's background. You yourself can examine and alter processes. For example, you can change the priority of a process relative to other processes that are running.

Configuring and examining processes require a deep understanding of the innards of your operating system and are well beyond the scope of this book, but if you're curious, the following functions deal with system processes:

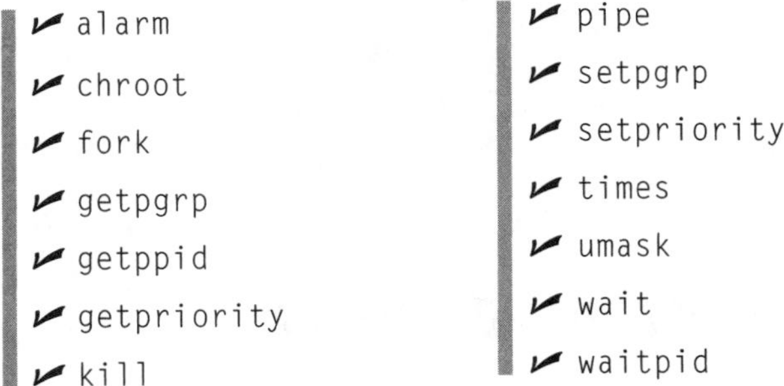

- `alarm`
- `chroot`
- `fork`
- `getpgrp`
- `getppid`
- `getpriority`
- `kill`
- `pipe`
- `setpgrp`
- `setpriority`
- `times`
- `umask`
- `wait`
- `waitpid`

File Handling

Perl has many functions for reading and writing directly to disk, bypassing the normal operating system methods, which do a lot of checking and processing before writing to disk. These functions are convenient if you know what you are doing and are *very* dangerous if you don't. The functions I list here by and large match what's available to UNIX system programmers.

The following functions are used in Perl programs that deal with advanced file handling:

- fcntl
- fileno
- flock
- ioctl
- select
- sysopen
- sysread
- syswrite

Internet Functions

Perl has many advanced Internet-related functions for Internet names and addresses. These functions are used in Perl programs that deal with advanced Internet applications, and are useful only on hosts connected to the Internet:

- endhostent
- endnetent
- endprotoent
- endservent
- gethostbyaddr
- gethostbyname
- gethostent
- getnetbyaddr
- getnetbyname
- getnetent
- getprotobyname
- getprotobynumber
- getprotoent
- getservbyname
- getservbyport
- getservent
- sethostent
- setnetent
- setprotoent
- setservent

Advanced Programmer Aids

Perl features a wide variety of advanced programming functions, such as working with object-oriented programs and looking inside Perl variables. One operator, \, also falls into this category because it is used with references (which are covered briefly in Chapter 16).

The following functions are used as advanced programming aids:

- `bless`
- `dump`
- `import`
- `ref`
- `study`
- `tie`
- `tied`
- `undef`
- `untie`
- `wantarray`

Sockets and Other Forms of Communication

All UNIX networking is based on the concept of *sockets,* electronic data pipes between two computers. Sockets have nothing to do with hardware; they're software metaphors for physical sockets.

If you are creating programs involving network communications, you probably use sockets. Fortunately, the Internet-related functions covered in this book hide all the socket-related functions so you don't have to learn about the intricacies of setting up and using them in order to write many fully functional Perl programs.

Perl also supports other communications concepts common to UNIX systems. For example, all system processes can communicate through messages and semaphores, and you can use Perl functions to create these kinds of communications. (*Messages* and *semaphores* are two different methods of process-to-process communication.)

The following functions can be found in programs that use sockets and other forms of process communications:

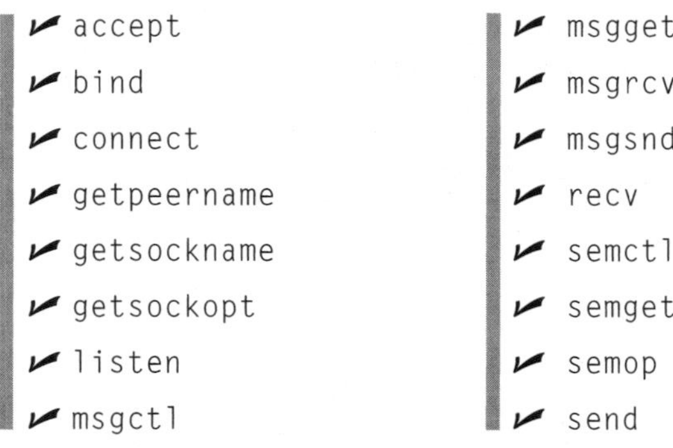

- `accept`
- `bind`
- `connect`
- `getpeername`
- `getsockname`
- `getsockopt`
- `listen`
- `msgctl`
- `msgget`
- `msgrcv`
- `msgsnd`
- `recv`
- `semctl`
- `semget`
- `semop`
- `send`

- `setsockopt`
- `shmctl`
- `shmget`
- `shmread`
- `shmwrite`
- `shutdown`
- `socket`
- `socketpair`

A Couple of Functions in a Category All Their Own

Don't you just hate it when you're organizing things into nice, neat little categories, and there are one or two things that don't seem to fit anywhere?

Two other advanced Perl functions are worth a moment of your attention, but they seem to defy any easy categorization:

- The `crypt` function is used for checking UNIX passwords; it's a one-way encryption function.
- The `syscall` function enables UNIX programmers to make operating system calls directly from Perl.

Chapter 23
Ten Great Perl Web Sites

In This Chapter

- Tapping into the latest news on Perl
- Checking out the CPAN library
- Getting information on MacPerl and PerlWin-32
- Benefiting from the development efforts of Perl experts
- Discovering software information

If you want to delve further into the intricacies of Perl than this book has taken you (and I sincerely hope that you do), the easiest and quickest way to ferret out more information is by searching around the World Wide Web for Perl resources. The Perl community has contributed thousands of hours of work to this programming language, mostly for free, and many of the fruits of their efforts are readily available on the Web. In this chapter, I tell you about ten of the best places to start your search.

The Perl Institute

The Perl Institute is a nonprofit organization, which was established to support the community of people who use Perl and the development of Perl as a viable programming language. The Perl Institute is also an organized, easy-to-reach, and knowledgeable group of people who are dedicated to keeping Perl available, usable, and free to anyone who wants to use it. The Institute acts as a coordination and communication center that connects people to information, ideas, and resources.

This great resource for finding Perl professionals, particularly trainers and programmers, can be found at

```
www.perl.org/
```

Perl Language Home Page

The Perl Language Home Page offers a wealth of information about Perl and the people supporting it. The Perl Language Home Page is fiercely (although not completely) pro-Perl and exhibits a boosterism that makes you think that it's supporting a political candidate or homecoming queen contestant. But its authors don't just talk about how wonderful Perl is, they also provide loads of worthwhile information.

The site provides the latest news about Perl, the latest versions of Perl, download software, documentation, bug reports, and links to numerous information resources. Point your browser to

```
www.perl.com/perl/
```

CPAN, the Comprehensive Perl Archive Network

CPAN is a huge network of volunteers who contribute Perl software and organize it into a readily accessible format. The Web link for CPAN doesn't actually lead to a Web page but to one of the many FTP sites that replicate CPAN. As you can see from the CD-ROM that comes with this book, an incredible amount of useful material is available from the CPAN library. (If you become a serious Perl programmer, you may even want to consider contributing to CPAN.) To find the CPAN network, head to

```
www.perl.com/CPAN/README.html
```

The Perl Journal

This site is the Web presence for the only magazine (at the time of this writing) that covers Perl exclusively. In just the past several months, the magazine has run many interesting articles that would-be Perl programmers will find fascinating. Although the actual content of the magazine isn't available online (they have to make money somehow!), the Web site has copies of the Perl programs covered in the magazine. Tables of contents for previous issues are also provided in case you want to order issues one at a time. You can find *The Perl Journal* site at

```
www.tpj.com/
```

MacPerl

MacPerl's author, Matthias Neeracher, hosts an extremely useful MacPerl resource. This page has many links to other MacPerl resources, such as sample programs, hint documents, and more. Of course, it's also a good place to get the basic MacPerl distribution (which is also on the CD-ROM that comes with this book), or to update your MacPerl.

Even if you're a Windows user, I suggest that you take a look at the MacPerl home page. The MacPerl/Mac integration is much superior to the Perl-Win32/Windows 95/98 or Perl-Win32/Windows NT integration, and this page is a good example of how Mac users try harder than their Windows-based counterparts. If you are a Perl-Win32 user and have a friend with a Mac, you may want to head to the following site and take a look at MacPerl:

```
www.iis.ee.ethz.ch/~neeri/macintosh/perl.html
```

Perl-Win32

This Web site, maintained by the people who wrote Perl for Windows 95, Windows 98, and Windows NT, is a good place to find the latest version of the Perl software for Windows and related material. The company, ActiveState, also sells Perl-related software, such as an advanced debugger and a programming environment. If you're a Perl user on Windows, it is well worth subscribing to the newsletters on this site, which you can find at

```
www.activestate.com/
```

libwww-perl

If you're creating a Web client in Perl, or just doing HTTP or FTP access, you should definitely check out libwww-perl, which is short for "Library of WWW functions, written in Perl," or something like that. (Chapter 15 contains a few examples of how to use the libwww-perl library.)

With its packages and modules that provide a simple and consistent Web interface, the library can give you precise control over how you access Web and FTP servers on the Internet. You can find libwww-perl at

```
www.ics.uci.edu/pub/websoft/libwww-perl/
```

Earl Hood's Home Page

This page is a prime example of how generous some Perl programmers are in making their work freely available to the public. The page is simple, to the point, and contains a handful of useful Perl programs, some of which are also available on CPAN and the CD-ROM that comes with this book. The programs on this site are excellent examples of how much you can accomplish with Perl if you're willing to devote some time to it.

Earl Hood has written programs that can create mailing list archives, handle HTML and SGML documents, and perform other kinds of conversions. You can find his site at

```
www.oac.uci.edu/indiv/ehood/earlsperls.html
```

Jeffrey Friedl's Home Page

Here's another example of a serious Perl hacker who gives away lots of good code. Jeffrey Friedl's page has full-featured Perl programs for tasks, such as Web access and translating Japanese characters. These programs are useful even if you don't know Perl. For example, his `search` program lets you look for particular text in an entire directory and all its subdirectories in a single command. You'll also find programs for creating transparent GIF image files, converting text files to Postscript, and more. Head to

```
enterprise.ic.gc.ca/~jfriedl/perl/
```

Perl Mongers

As Perl becomes more and more popular, Perl programmers want to get together more often to help each other out, get jobs, or to just chat. Perl Mongers is an international group whose main purpose is to help organize small groups of Perl programmers. Most Perl Monger groups are local to a particular area, but others are organized by subject interest. The main location for the Perl Mongers is

```
www.pm.org/
```

Chapter 24

Ten Cool Features Introduced with Perl 5

In This Chapter

- Finding out about the Perl 5 enhancements
- Comparing Perl 4 with Perl 5

Many people who learned to program in Perl by using Perl Version 4 may not see what all the fuss is about with Perl 5. Almost everything done in Perl 5 can be done in Perl 4, and Perl 5 doesn't do it any faster.

Some of the differences between Perl 4 and Perl 5, however, are quite significant. They allow intermediate and advanced Perl programmers to make better programs — in particular, programs that other people can use more easily. Of course, a few small changes exist mostly for convenience, but the big ones (which are listed first in this chapter) make Perl 5 a much more robust and useful language.

Multidimensional Lists

This multidimensional list feature, described in Chapter 16, enables you to create lists that consist of more than a single set of items. Multidimensional lists allow you to have lists of records for a database, for example.

Better Error Messages

The Perl 4 error messages aren't all that bad, mind you, but Perl 5 error messages are much more informative about what went wrong in your program. Of course, this makes finding the errors and fixing them all that much easier.

Objects

Perl's object-oriented features, described in Chapter 19, allow you to use parts of programs created by other people using a standardized programming interface. Creating objects is beyond the scope of this book; but using objects is a fairly simple process, and this book's companion CD-ROM provides you with access to the hundreds of Perl object modules.

Program Modules

Even without your using object-oriented programming, Perl's module approach lets you compartmentalize your programs so that variables are not seen outside of a particular module. This is useful if you are sharing code with other programmers and don't want their variables messing with yours except in a controlled fashion, such as your allowing them to change some variables in a module but not others.

Interaction with C Programs

For you more-advanced programmers, be aware that Perl 5 can be linked with programs written in C. This means that parts of Perl programs can be written in C, and parts of C programs can be written in Perl. This feature allows programmers to make the most of C while taking advantage of the best features of Perl and vice versa.

The POSIX Library

Perl 5 includes a library that allows programmers to access essentially all of the *identifiers* (or actions) in POSIX Version 1003.1. (*POSIX* is a set of standards for interoperability and, in this case, for operating systems and programming languages.) In short, corporations and government agencies who specify that all programs they use must be "POSIX compliant" can also use Perl 5 programs that include the POSIX library. It turns out that this includes a pretty large market and is a boon for Perl programmers.

Case-Changing Functions

The `lc`, `lcfirst`, `uc`, and `ucfirst` functions in Perl 5 simplify changing the case of letters in strings. You can change characters in strings from uppercase to lowercase and vice versa in Perl 4, but the case-changing functions introduced with Perl 5 are aesthetically more pleasing than the methods used in Perl 4, which means that they make more sense at a glance.

The `map` Function

The `map` function introduced in Perl 5 is a useful feature for people who frequently process lists. `map` returns a single list that is the result of repeatedly running an expression or a block on another list.

The `chomp` Function

This function may sound somewhat trivial, but I use it all the time. The `chomp` function primarily does what the `chop` function does — namely, remove the end-of-line character or characters from a string. Because some operating systems, notably MS-DOS and Windows, have two end-of-line characters instead of one, `chomp` does come in handy. The difference between `chomp` and `chop` is that `chomp` understands what kind of line-endings are used on the operating system Perl is running on and removes the correct number of characters.

More Programmers! More Free Stuff!

Although the Perl community was growing ever larger before Perl 5 was developed, the latest versions of Perl have resulted in even more people getting interested in Perl. The programming community has been enriched with much more freely accessible code, particularly through CPAN (the Comprehensive Perl Archive Network), and this is partially due to the modular and object-oriented features introduced in Perl 5.

Chapter 25

Ten Reasons Why Perl Is Better Than Java

In This Chapter

- Comparing the most overhyped language with the most useful one
- Understanding the benefits of Perl

Okay, so the title of this chapter is pretty provocative. It's just that some folks truly love Perl, and many of us are getting tired of hearing "Java, Java, Java," as if it were the only valuable programming language on earth. It's been a few years since its release, and Java still has yet to prove its worth. The wonderful Java programs that are being promised are still vaporware. Perl, on the other hand, runs on the Internet day in and day out.

By the way, don't interpret what I'm saying as, "Perl is better than Java in every way." It isn't. Java has many useful features that Perl can't match, and Java definitely excels at some tasks for which it's designed. Still, Perl can hold its own on many counts.

Java Requires Predeclaration of Variables

If you're trying to whip together a quick program, nothing gets in the way more than having to tell the programming language ahead of time the name of every variable that you're going to use and the type of variable that it is. In Java, you have to say at the beginning of a program, "I'm going to use variable *X*"; in Perl, you can just start using the variable without having to warn Perl first. Some programmers have no problems with this sort of *predeclaration,* but most folks find it tedious and the cause of many error messages when testing their programs.

Java Forces You to Use an Object Model; Perl Makes Objects Optional

Object-oriented programming, described in Chapter 19, is useful in some cases, but is overkill in others. With Java, almost every useful feature is a *class* (that is, one of a category of objects designed for a particular function). You can't even produce simple messages on screen without using object-oriented syntax. Perl is much more flexible. You can use objects if you want to or ignore them if you want to.

Strings in Java Are Much Harder to Handle Than Strings in Perl

Java has the same problems managing text that most other programming languages have: It's hampered by a limited number of functions and clunky handling of string variables. You have to create all your own string-handling features in Java; but in Perl, you don't have to. It's as if the people writing Java forgot how much people like using text. (For more information on working with text strings in Perl, see Chapter 5.)

Perl Handles Lists with Ease

The Java model says that less is more, and certainly not much in the way of list handling is built into Java. Java provides almost no help in handling lists. Perl, of course, gives you lots of different list-handling functions and operators to work with. (For information on how to use lists in Perl, see Chapters 7 and 16.)

Perl Can Do Many More System-Level Tasks

Because Java is meant to be secure against malicious or poorly-written programs that can crash your computer, it has very few built-in features for handling system-level functions, such as starting and stopping other programs, file manipulation, and so on. With Java, you have to build your own system-level library or use one of the many third-party libraries. Perl, on the other hand, has a library built in.

Perl Is Always Free

Most usable implementations of Java cost money, and sometimes a lot of money. Dozens of companies are willing to sell you Java programming environments, class libraries, debuggers, and other Java stuff. Almost everything in the Perl world, and certainly the main language system, is free to those who want it.

You Can't Write Many Useful One-Line Java Programs

If you want to do a quickie single-function program in Java, you still have to write about a dozen lines of code. Most of this is due to Java's forcing you into using object-orientated programming even when it makes little sense.

Most Sample Perl Programs Do More Than Put Animated Pictures in a Browser

As I write this, Java has been out for a few years, and most of the sample Java programs that you find are for cute little Web applets. Animated balls bouncing around are all well and good, but where's the serious Internet code, or where are the serious conversion programs that have been available to Perl programmers for so many years?

Perl Programmers Don't Tell Dozens of Dumb Oyster Jokes

This is more of a criticism of the marketing departments of Java companies and the tired headline writers of the trade press. Many industry pundits have called for a moratorium on cloying names that are related to coffee, but to no avail. Sure, caffeine is the most widely used stimulant in the world, but that's no reason to extend the joke as far as it has gone.

Perl Isn't a Name That's Associated with Violent Political Takeovers

The 1996 Nobel Peace Prize went to Carlos Felipe Ximenes Belo and Jose Ramos-Horta for their work in continuing to remind the world about the plight of East Timor, a country that was invaded by Indonesia in 1975. The government of Indonesia is headquartered on the island of Java.

Appendix A

The Great Perl Reference

Perl Operators

The following is a list of Perl's operators — those symbols that allow you to perform some sort of action on program data.

Operator	*Description*
x	Character repeat and list repeat.
.	String concatenation.
=	Assignment.
+	Add.
-	Subtract.
*	Multiply.
/	Divide.
%	Modulo divide.
-	Unary negation: negates the number it precedes.
+	Unary plus: does nothing.
*	Raise to the power.
++	Unary increment; can be used before or after a variable to increment before or after the variable is evaluated. Therefore, if `$a` is 5, `$a++` is 5 until it is evaluated, and then `$a` becomes 6; `++$a` is 6 when it is evaluated.
--	Unary decrement; can be used before or after a variable to decrement before or after the variable is evaluated. Thus, if `$a` is 5, `$a--` is 5 until it is evaluated, and then `$a` becomes 4; `--$a` is 4 when it is evaluated.
+= .= etc.	Assignment after operation. For example, `$a += 3` means "add 3 to `$a` and store that value in `$a`."
,	List separator.
..	Range.

<table>
<tr><th>Operator</th><th>Description</th></tr>
<tr><td>< > <= >= == != <=></td><td>Numeric comparisons: less than, greater than, less than or equal to, greater than or equal to, equal to, not equal to, comparison.</td></tr>
<tr><td>eq ne cmp lt gt le ge</td><td>String comparisons: less than, greater than, less than or equal to, greater than or equal to, equal to, not equal to, comparison.</td></tr>
<tr><td>not</td><td>Logical not. Can also be !.</td></tr>
<tr><td>and</td><td>Logical and. Can also be &&.</td></tr>
<tr><td>or</td><td>Logical or. Can also be ||.</td></tr>
<tr><td>xor</td><td>Logical xor.</td></tr>
<tr><td>?:</td><td>Conditional comparison: TEST ? IFTRUE : IFFALSE.</td></tr>
<tr><td>~</td><td>Bitwise logical not.</td></tr>
<tr><td>&</td><td>Bitwise logical and.</td></tr>
<tr><td>|</td><td>Bitwise logical or.</td></tr>
<tr><td>^</td><td>Bitwise logical xor.</td></tr>
<tr><td><< >></td><td>Bit shift to the left and to the right.</td></tr>
<tr><td><></td><td>I/O operator, such as <STDIN>.</td></tr>
<tr><td>=~ !~</td><td>Binds a scalar on the left to a pattern match, substitution, or translation on the right. !~ returns the inverse of the bound value.</td></tr>
<tr><td>m/PATTERN/MODIFIERS</td><td>Searches for the pattern and returns true if found. Can also be specified without the m.</td></tr>
<tr><td>s/PATTERN/REPLACEMENT/MODIFIERS</td><td>Searches for the pattern and replaces it with the specified text.</td></tr>
<tr><td>tr/FROMRANGE/TORANGE/</td><td>Returns a string with letters translated from one range to another. The tr and y operators are identical.</td></tr>
<tr><td>=></td><td>List separator; same as a comma.</td></tr>
<tr><td>' (backtick)</td><td>Runs the command between the two backticks and returns the STDOUT.</td></tr>
<tr><td>-></td><td>Dereference. Usually used with object-oriented programs as CLASS->METHOD.</td></tr>
<tr><td>\</td><td>Reference.</td></tr>
</table>

Perl's Operator Hierarchy

Although it is always safer to use parentheses to group your operations, some programmers prefer to trust Perl's rules for deciding which operators are evaluated first. The following table lists the operators in order of their precedence. Those operators with the same ranking (they're shown on the same line in the list that follows), Perl evaluates them from left to right.

For instance, the following statement

```
$a = 3 / 4 ** 2;
```

is interpreted as

```
$a = 3 / (4 ** 2);
```

because ** has higher precedence than / and is, therefore, evaluated first.

Operators are evaluated in the following order (lower numbers mean higher precedence):

1. `->`
2. `++ --`
3. `**`
4. `! ~ \ {unary +} {unary -}`
5. `=~ !~`
6. `* / % x`
7. `+ - .`
8. `<< >>`
9. `< > <= >= lt gt le ge`
10. `== != <=> eq ne cmp`
11. `&`
12. `| ^`
13. `&&`
14. `||`
15. `.`
16. `?:`

17. `= += -= *=` and other operators that end in =
18. `, =>`
19. `not`
20. `and`
21. `or xor`

Perl's Functions and Statements

The following table lists all of Perl's functions and statements in alphabetical order.

Name	Description
`abs(NUMBER)`	Takes the absolute value of the argument (that is, negative numbers are made positive).
`accept(NEWSOCKETHANDLE, GENERICSOCKETHANDLE)`	Accepts a connection on a socket.
`alarm(TIME)`	Sends the `SIGALRM` signal to the program after a specified number of seconds.
`atan2(Y, X)`	Returns the arctangent of Y/X.
`bind(SOCKET, NAME)`	Assigns a name to an existing open socket.
`binmode(FILEHANDLE)`	Tells Perl to treat the file as a binary file. It has no function under UNIX or MacOS.
`bless(REFERENCE, PACKAGE)`	Tells the item that is referred to in the reference that it is an object in the specified package. If the package is not specified, Perl uses the current package.
`caller(NUMBEROFSTACKS)`	Provides information on the stack of subroutine calls. The argument is the number of subroutine calls to unnest. With an argument, it returns a list with the package name, filename, line number, subroutine name, whether the subroutine has arguments, and whether the subroutine wants an array as its argument. Without an argument, `caller` returns just the first three list items, referring to the current subroutine.
`chdir(DIRNAME)`	Changes the working directory of a program to a specified directory or, with no argument, changes the directory to the home directory of the user. Returns true if successful, false if it isn't (for example, if the directory doesn't exist).

Name	Description
chmod(NUMMODE, LISTOFFILES)	Changes the access permissions on one or more files. The first argument must be an octal file mode, such as 0777. The function returns the number of files successfully changed.
chomp(STRINGVAR)	Removes the line ending from the end of a string variable, returning the number of characters deleted. If the last character is not a line-ending character, as defined in the special variable $/, nothing is removed. If $/ is two characters, both characters are removed. (***Note:*** This function changes the value of the variable.) You can also use the function chomp(LIST), which removes the line ending from the end of each list item.
chop(STRINGVAR)	Removes the last character from the end of the string variable, returning the character deleted. (***Note:*** This function changes the value of the variable.)
chown(USERID, GROUPID, LISTOFFILES)	Changes the user and group ownership of one or more files. The userid and groupid must be numbers, not names. The function returns the number of files successfully changed.
chr(NUMBER)	Returns the character represented by the argument.
chroot(DIRECTORY)	Changes the root directory available to a program to the specified directory. The named directory becomes the root directory to the program, and the program cannot modify or see other directories above this one in the directory hierarchy.
close(FILEHANDLE)	Closes a file that was opened with the open function.
closedir(DIRHANDLE)	Closes a directory that was opened with the opendir function.
connect(SOCKET, NETADDRESS)	Connects to another process using the specified socket.
continue { BLOCK }	Executes the block. The continue statement always follows other blocks because it is executed when other blocks exit.
cos(NUMBER)	Returns the cosine of the number, expressed in radians.

Name	*Description*
`crypt(PLAINTEXT, SALT)`	Encrypts the first argument using the salt. This function is system dependent, so you may get varying results, depending on the operating system.
`dbmclose(ARRAY)`	Breaks the binding between the array and the DBM file that was associated with the array by an earlier `dbmopen` function.
`dbmopen(ARRAY, FILENAME, MODE)`	Begins the process of associating an associative array with the named database. The mode is the octal file mode used to open the database. This function clears out any values already in the associative array.
`defined(VARIABLE)`	Returns true if the variable has been defined (that is, if it has a valid string, numeric, or reference value). This function is useful for testing undefined values returned under error conditions.
`delete($ARRAY{KEY})`	Removes a key and its value from an associative array.
`die(TEXT)`	Prints the text to the standard error output and terminates the Perl program. The program returns the value that was in the `$!` special variable.
`do { BLOCK }`	Executes the block and returns the value of the last expression in the block.
`do(FILENAME)`	Executes the statements in the file and returns the value of the last expression in the file.
`dump`	Causes a core dump, if the operating system supports it. You can also specify a label, which the program will start from if you can recreate the core from the dump.
`each(ARRAY)`	Returns a two-item list (the key and the value) for the next value in the array.
`endgrent`	Resets the cycling through the group list begun by the `getgrent` function.
`endhostent`	Resets the cycling through the host list begun by the `gethostent` function.
`endnetent`	Resets the cycling through the network list begun by the `getnetent` function.
`endprotoent`	Resets the cycling through the protocol list begun by the `getprotoent` function.

Name	Description
endpwent	Resets the cycling through the password list begun by the getpwent function.
endservent	Resets the cycling through the server list begun by the getservent function.
eof(FILEHANDLE)	Returns true if the next read on the file handle would read off the end of the file.
eval(EXPRESSION)	Causes Perl to execute the expression as though the expression were a Perl program. The expression can be one or more statements.
exec(PROGRAM)	Causes the Perl program to stop and the program named in the argument to be run. The argument can be a list, in which case each item is passed as an element of the command line to be executed.
exists($ARRAY{$KEY})	Returns true if the specified key exists in the specified array.
exit(NUMBER)	Stops the program. The argument is used as the return value for the program.
exp(NUMBER)	Returns the number *e* raised to the power of the argument.
fcntl(FILEHANDLE, FUNCTION, SCALAR)	Executes the UNIX fctl function for performing low-level file control.
File tests: -X FILENAME	Returns values based on the file. File tests include determining whether the file exists and how many bytes are in the file, and other tests.
fileno(FILEHANDLE)	Returns the numeric file descriptor of the handle given, or the undef value if the file is not open.
flock(FILEHANDLE OPERATION)	Performs low-level file locking in UNIX.
for (INITEXPR; TESTEXPR; ENDEXPR) { BLOCK }	Executes the block repeatedly. The initial expression is evaluated first, followed by the test expression. If the test expression is true, the block is executed, and the end expression is evaluated. The test expression is then evaluated, and the loop continues.
foreach VARIABLE (LIST) { BLOCK }	Executes the block repeatedly. For each item in the list, the variable is set to the item's value and the block is executed.

Name	Description
`fork`	Starts a child process and returns its process ID number.
`format NAME= FORMATLIST`	Creates a format that can be used by the `write` function. The format list consists of lines that contain picture formats, lists of arguments, or comments.
`formline(PICTURE, LIST)`	Formats a list of values according to the picture.
`getc(FILEHANDLE)`	Returns the next byte from the file, or a null string if you're at the end of the file. If called without an argument, it returns the next byte from the standard file input.
`getgrent`	Returns UNIX group information from the next line of the /etc/group file. The list returned has four items: the group name, the group password (encrypted), the group number, and a string of all the members' names.
`getgrgid(GROUPID)`	Returns information about the group, based on the group ID number. The list returned has four items: the group name, the group password (encrypted), the group number, and a string of all the members' names.
`getgrnam(GROUPNAME)`	Returns information about the group, based on the group's name. The list returned has four items: the group name, the group password (encrypted), the group number, and a string of all the members' names.
`gethostbyaddr (PACKEDADDR, ADDRTYPE)`	Returns information about the host based on its address. The address argument is packed, probably with the `pack('C4')` function, and the address type is always `2` for Internet addresses. In scalar context, `gethostbyaddr` returns the host name; in list context, it returns the host name, a string of aliases, the address type, the length of the returned list of packed addresses, and a list of packed addresses.

Name	*Description*
`gethostbyname (DOMAINNAME)`	Returns information about the host based on its domain name. In scalar context, `gethostbyname` returns the IP address, packed; in list context, it returns the host name, a string of aliases, the address type, the length of the returned list of packed addresses, and a list of packed addresses. You can unpack the IP address with the `unpack('C4')` function.
`gethostent`	Returns the next record from the /etc/ hosts file. It returns the host name, a string of aliases, the address type, the length of the returned list of packed addresses, and a list of packed addresses.
`getlogin`	Returns the current login name by querying the /etc/utmp file.
`getnetbyaddr(PACKEDADDR, ADDRTYPE)`	Returns information about the network based on its address from the /etc/ networks file. The address argument is packed, probably with the `pack('C4')` function, and the address type is always 2 for Internet addresses. In scalar context, `getnetbyaddr` returns the network name; in list context, it returns the network name, a string of aliases, the address type, and the packed address.
`getnetbyname(DOMAINNAME)`	Returns information about the network based on its name from the /etc/networks file. In scalar context, `getnetbyaddr` returns the network name; in list context, it returns the network name, a string of aliases, the address type, and the packed address.
`getnetent`	Returns information from the next line in the /etc/networks file. In scalar context, `getnetbyaddr` returns the network name; in list context, it returns the network name, a string of aliases, the address type, and the packed address.
`getpeername(SOCKET)`	Returns the socket address of the other end of a connection. The address returned is packed.
`getpgrp(PROCESSID)`	Returns the process group number for the given process number. Use an argument of `0` to indicate the current process.

Name	***Description***
`getppid`	Returns the process number of the parent process.
`getpriority(PROCESSKIND, WHO)`	Returns the priority of a process.
`getprotobyname (PROTONAME)`	Returns information about a protocol based on its name. In scalar context, the protocol number is returned. In list context, the items in the list returned are the protocol name, aliases for the name, and the protocol number.
`getprotobynumber (PROTONUMBER)`	Returns information about a protocol based on its number. In scalar context, the protocol name is returned. In list context, the items in the list returned are the protocol name, aliases for the name, and the protocol number.
`getprotoent`	Returns the next record from the /etc/protocols file. In scalar context, the protocol name is returned. In list context, the items in the list returned are the protocol name, aliases for the name, and the protocol number.
`getpwent`	Returns user information from the next line of the /etc/passwd file. The list returned has nine items: the user name, the password (encrypted), the user number, the group number, the quota field, the comment field, the gcos field, the home directory, and the default shell. In scalar context, only the user name is returned.
`getpwnam(USERNAME)`	Returns user information for the specified user name. The list returned has nine items: the user name, the password (encrypted), the user number, the group number, the quota field, the comment field, the gcos field, the home directory, and the default shell. In scalar context, only the user number is returned.
`getpwuid(USERID)`	Returns user information for the specified user number. The list returned has nine items: the user name, the password (encrypted), the user number, the group number, the quota field, the comment field, the gcos field, the home directory, and the default shell. In scalar context, only the user name is returned.

Name	Description
`getservbyname (SERVICENAME, PROTO)`	Returns information about a service based on its name. In scalar context, the port number is returned. In list context, the items in the list returned are the service name, aliases for the name, port number, and protocol name.
`getservbyport(PORT, PROTO)`	Returns information about a service based on its port number. In scalar context, the service name is returned. In list context, the items in the list returned are the service name, aliases for the name, port number, and protocol name.
`getservent`	Returns information from the next record in the /etc/services file. In scalar context, the service name is returned. In list context, the items in the list returned are the service name, aliases for the name, the port number, and protocol name.
`getsockname(SOCKET)`	Returns the socket address of the local end of a connection. The address returned is packed.
`getsockopt(SOCKET, LEVEL, OPTIONNAME)`	Returns the socket option specified.
`glob(STRING)`	Returns a list of files matching the argument; the argument may have wildcard characters.
`gmtime(TIME)`	Converts the given time into Greenwich Mean Time. In scalar context, this function returns a string that looks something like `Sat Nov 23 20:07:47 1996` (in Perl 5 and later versions only); in list context, the items are: second, minute, hour, day of month, month (January = 0, February = 1, . . .), year, weekday (Sunday = 0, Monday = 1, . . .), day of the year (January 1 = 0, January 2 = 1, . . .), and standard time (true or false). With no argument, the function assumes the current time.
`goto LABEL`	Jumps to the named label. You can use an expression instead of a label name, and Perl interprets that expression into a label name.
`grep(BLOCK, LIST)`	Evaluates the block in Boolean context on each item of the list. In scalar context, it returns the number of times that the block evaluated true; in list context, it returns the list of items matched.

Name	*Description*
`grep(REGEXP, LIST)`	Searches for the regular expression in each item of the list. In scalar context, returns the number of times that the regular expression was found; in list context, returns the list of items matched.
`hex(STRING)`	Returns the number that interprets the string as hexadecimal digits.
`if(TEST) { BLOCK1 }`	Executes the block if the test is true. The first block may be followed by `else { BLOCK2 }`. In this case, if the test is false, the second block is executed. The first block may also be followed by one or more instances of `elsif { BLOCKn }`, which acts the same as `else if`.
`import(CLASSNAME)`	This class method exports the class name to the current module.
`index(STRING, SUBSTRING, POSITION)`	Returns the position of the first occurrence of a substring in the string, or –1 if the substring isn't found. If the position is specified, Perl starts looking from that position instead of from the beginning of the string.
`int(NUMBER)`	Returns the integer portion of the number.
`ioctl(FILEHANDLE, FUNCTION, SCALAR)`	Executes UNIX's `ioctl` function for performing low-level input and output.
`join(SEPARATOR, LIST)`	Returns a string that consists of the items in the list with the separator between each item. The separator is not added to the beginning or end of the resulting string.
`keys(ARRAY)`	Normally used to return a list of all the keys in the associative array. In scalar context, it returns the number of elements in the associative array.
`kill(SIGNAL, LIST)`	Sends the signal to the list of process IDs. The signal is either the signal number or the name of the signal, for example, HUP. The function returns the number of processes signaled.
`last`	Exits the innermost loop that is executing. You can also give an argument of a label, in which case Perl exits out to the loop with that label.
`lc(STRING)`	Returns the string in all lowercase characters.

Name	Description
`lcfirst(STRING)`	Returns the string with the first character changed to lowercase.
`length(STRING)`	Returns the length of the string.
`link(OLDFILE, NEWFILE)`	Creates a new file that has a hard link to the old file. Returns true if successful.
`listen(SOCKET, MAXCONN)`	Causes the system to allow connections on the socket. The system queues up to the number of connections specified.
`local(VARIABLES)`	Makes one or more variables local to the current block, subroutine, `eval` function, or file.
`localtime(TIME)`	Converts the given time into the local time. In scalar context, this returns a string that looks something like `Sat Nov 23 20:07:47 1996` (in Perl 5 only); in list context, the items are: second, minute, hour, day of month, month (January = 0, February = 1, . . .), year, weekday (Sunday = 0, Monday = 1, . . .), day of the year (January 1 = 0, January 2 = 1, . . .), and standard time (true or false). With no argument, the function assumes the current time.
`log(NUMBER)`	Returns the natural logarithm (base *e*) of the number.
`lstat(FILE)`	Returns information about the file. The argument can be either a file handle or a string with the file's name. If the file is a symbolic link, the information is about the linked-to file, not the link itself. The following items in the list are returned: the device number of the filesystem, inode number, file permissions (number), number of hard links to the file, user number of file's owner, group number of the file's owner, device identifier for special files, size of file, last access time, last modify time, last inode change time, preferred block size, and number of blocks allocated.
`map { BLOCK } LIST`	Returns a list of the block evaluated in list context for each item in the list. During evaluation, $_ is set to the list item being evaluated.

Name	Description
`map(EXPRESSION, LIST)`	Returns a list of the expression evaluated in list context for each item in the list. During evaluation, `$_` is set to the list item being evaluated.
`mkdir(DIRNAME, PERMISSION)`	Creates a directory with the specified permissions (in octal). Returns true if successful.
`msgctl(ID, COMMAND, ARGUMENT)`	Sends a message using UNIX's `mesgctl` function.
`msgget(KEY, FLAGS)`	Returns the message ID for System V IPC messages.
`msgrcv(ID, VARIABLE, SIZE, TYPE, FLAGS)`	Receives a message with the message ID.
`msgsnd(ID, MESSAGE, FLAGS)`	Sends a message with the message ID.
`my(VARIABLES)`	Makes one or more variables local to the current block, subroutine, `eval` function, or file.
`new(CLASSNAME)`	Constructs an object from the class. You can also specify a list after the class name as arguments passed to the constructor.
`next`	Causes the innermost loop to start again from the beginning of the loop. You can also include a label with the function, in which case Perl jumps to the beginning of the loop with that label.
`no MODULE`	Removes subroutine and variable names that were imported by the `use` function after the `use` function is called on the same module name.
`oct(STRING)`	Returns the number that is the string interpreted as an octal value.
`open(FILEHANDLE, NAME)`	Opens the named file or command and associates it with the given file handle. The characters at the beginning of the name determine whether the file is opened for input, output, or appending. In the case of a command, the location of the `|` character in the command name determines whether the file handle is for reading or writing. The function returns true if the file or command is opened successfully.

Name	*Description*
`opendir(DIRHANDLE, DIRNAME)`	Opens the directory for reading and associates the directory handle with that directory.
`ord(STRING)`	Returns the ASCII value of the first character of the string.
`pack(TEMPLATE, LIST)`	Returns a string containing the items from the list put together using the template.
`package NAME`	Declares that the rest of the innermost block, subroutine, `eval` function, or file belongs to the specified package name.
`pipe(READHANDLE, WRITEHANDLE)`	Opens a pair of pipes for use by other functions.
`pop(LISTNAME)`	Shortens the list by removing the last item, and returns that item. If the list is empty, it returns the undefined value. (***Note:*** The argument must be the name of a list, not an actual list.)
`pos(VARIABLE)`	Returns the position in a variable where the last `m//g` associated with the variable left off.
`print(FILEHANDLE, LIST)`	Sends a list to the file specified by the file handle and returns true if successful. Note that the argument is a list, not a scalar; therefore, variables that are arguments to print are evaluated in list context. The `print` function is more commonly written without parentheses.
`print(LIST)`	Sends the list to the standard file output and returns true if successful. The argument is a list, not a scalar; therefore, variables that are arguments to print are evaluated in list context. The `print` function is more commonly written without parentheses.
`printf(FILEHANDLE FORMAT, LIST)`	Formats a list using the format string, sends the resulting list to the file specified by the file handle, and returns true if successful. (***Note:*** No comma appears after the file handle.)
`printf (FORMAT, LIST)`	Formats a list using the format string, sends the resulting list to the standard file output, and returns true if successful.
`push(LISTNAME, LIST)`	Adds the items of the list in the second argument to the end of the list named in the first argument.

Name	*Description*
q/STRING/	Returns a string with no interpretation of the string's contents. This function is similar to using single quotes (' '), except that you can choose the quoting character.
qq/STRING/	Quotes a string, with interpretation of the string's contents. This function is similar to using double quotes (" "), except that you can choose the quoting character.
quotemeta(STRING)	Returns the value of an argument with all of the regular expression metacharacters back-slashed as necessary.
qw/STRING/	Returns the words in a string with no interpretation. Ignores differences in white space between words.
qx/COMMAND/	Returns the output of running a command. This function is similar to using the backtick character ('), except that you can choose the quoting character.
rand(NUMBER)	Returns a random number between 0 and the specified number (including 0 but not including the specified number). If no argument is given, it returns a random number between 0 and 1. The seed used for the random number is set with the srand function.
read(FILEHANDLE, VARIABLE, LENGTH, OFFSET)	Reads the number of bytes from the file into the scalar variable. The function starts writing into the variable at the given offset, which is optional. The function returns the actual number of bytes read or 0 if you are already at the end of the file; the actual number may be less than the desired number if the function read off the end of the file.
readdir(DIRHANDLE)	Reads the next entry from a directory. In scalar context, the function returns the next filename in the directory; in list context, the function returns the rest of the filenames.
readlink(FILENAME)	Returns the name of the file pointed to by the symbolic link in the filename given in the argument. If the named file is not a symbolic link or some other error occurs, the function returns the undefined value.

Name	*Description*
`recv(SOCKET, VARIABLE, LENGTH, FLAGS)`	Receives a message on the socket and puts it in the variable.
`redo`	Restarts the innermost loop without reevaluating the conditional test for the loop. You can also give an argument of a label, which causes Perl to restart the loop with that label.
`ref(VARIABLE)`	Returns true if the variable is a reference, otherwise returns the null string. The value returned is a string indicating the type of reference.
`rename(FILENAME, NEWNAME)`	Renames a file and returns true if successful. This function does not work across file systems on UNIX.
`require(FILENAME)`	Executes the named Perl program provided that program has not already been executed.
`require(NUMBER)`	Stops the program if the Perl version number is lower than the argument.
`require(PACKAGENAME)`	Loads the package in the same way the `use` function does, except that the package is loaded while the program is running, not when it is compiled.
`reset`	Resets variables and single-match searches performed with the `??` operator.
`reset(STRING)`	Resets all variables that have a name starting with the letter in the string. If the string is more than one character, that string must be a range expressed with a hyphen, in which case all variables whose first letter starts with any letter in the given range are reset. Avoid using this function.
`return(LIST)`	Returns the specified value from a subroutine. If the subroutine is in scalar context, the first item in the list is returned; if the subroutine is in list context, the entire list is returned.
`reverse(LIST)`	Returns a list in the reverse order of the argument.
`rewinddir(DIRHANDLE)`	Sets the position of the next `readdir` function to the beginning of the directory.

Name	Description
rindex(STRING, SUBSTRING, POSITION)	Returns the position of the last occurrence of the substring in the string, or –1 if the substring isn't found. If the position is specified, Perl starts looking from that position instead of from the beginning of the string.
rmdir(DIRECTORYNAME)	Removes the directory provided the directory is empty.
scalar(EXPRESSION)	Forces an argument to be evaluated in scalar context. This function is useful if the expression may be a list and you don't want the expression to be evaluated in list context.
seek(FILEHANDLE, POSITION, RELATIVE)	Sets the position of the file pointer for the file. The value of the third argument specifies the relative position of the file pointer: 0 means it's relative to the beginning of the file; 1 means it's relative to the current position; and 2 means it's relative to the end of the file. The function returns true if successful.
seekdir(DIRHANDLE, POSITION)	Sets the position for the readdir function.
select(FILEHANDLE)	Selects the file handle to be used by the print and write functions if no file handle is specified in them. The function returns the file handle that was in use before the function was called. If you do not give an argument to the function, it simply returns the file handle being used.
select(READBITS, WRITEBITS, EXCEPTIONALBITS, TIMEOUT)	Tells you which of your file descriptors are ready to do reads or writes, or are reporting an exceptional condition.
semctl(ID, SEMNUM, COMMAND, ARGUMENT)	Controls semaphore messages on systems that support semaphores.
semget(KEY, NSEMS, FLAGS)	Returns a semaphore ID on systems that support semaphores.
semop(KEY, OPSTRING)	Performs semaphore operations on systems that support semaphores.
send(SOCKET, MESSAGE, FLAGS,TO)	Sends a message to the socket.

Name	*Description*
`setgrent`	Causes the next call to `getgrent` to start reading from the top of the /etc/groups file.
`sethostent`	Causes the next call to `gethostent` to start reading from the top of the /etc/hosts file.
`setnetent`	Causes the next call to `getnetent` to start reading from the top of the /etc/networks file.
`setpgrp(PROCESSID, PROCESSGROUP)`	Sets the process group for the process specified in the first argument.
`setpriority(PROCESSKIND, WHO, PRIORITY)`	Sets the priority for a process, a process group, or a user.
`setprotoent`	Causes the next call to `getprotoent` to start reading from the top of the /etc/protocols file.
`setpwent`	Causes the next call to `getpwent` to start reading from the top of the /etc/passwd file.
`setservent`	Causes the next call to `getservent` to start reading from the top of the /etc/services file.
`setsockopt(SOCKET, LEVEL, OPTIONNAME, OPTIONVAL)`	Sets an option on the socket.
`shift(LISTNAME)`	Shortens the list by removing the first item, and returns that item. If the list is empty, it returns the undefined value. (**Note:** The argument must be the name of a list, not an actual list.)
`shmctl(ID, COMMAND, ARGUMENT)`	Controls shared memory on systems that support shared memory.
`shmget(KEY, SIZE, FLAGS)`	Returns the shared memory ID on systems that support shared memory.
`shmread(ID, VARIABLE, POSITION, SIZE)`	Reads from shared memory on systems that support shared memory.
`shmwrite(ID, STRING, POSITION, SIZE)`	Writes to shared memory on systems that support shared memory.
`shutdown (SOCKET, HOW)`	Closes the socket.
`sin(NUMBER)`	Returns the sine of the number, expressed in radians.

Name	*Description*
`sleep(NUMBER)`	Causes the program to sleep for a specified number of seconds. If no argument is given, the program sleeps until it receives a `SIGALRM` signal from some other program. The function returns the actual number of seconds slept.
`socket(SOCKET, DOMAIN, TYPE, PROTOCOL)`	Opens a socket and returns true if successful.
`socketpair(SOCKET1, SOCKET2, DOMAIN, TYPE, PROTOCOL)`	Creates a pair of sockets and returns true if successful.
`sort { BLOCK } LIST`	Returns a list of the items in the list argument sorted using the comparison specified in the block. The block compares two variables, `$a` and $b, and the comparison determines how the sorting is done.
`sort(LIST)`	Returns a list of the items in the argument sorted in ascending string order.
`sort SUBROUTINE-NAME LIST`	Returns a list of the items in the list argument sorted using the comparison specified in the subroutine. The subroutine compares two variables, `$a` and `$b`, and the comparison determines how the sorting is done.
`splice(LISTNAME, REMOVEOFFSET, REMOVENUMBER, ADDLIST)`	Returns a list that is the named list with the specified number of items removed from the specified offset, with the list in the fourth argument added at the offset. (***Note:*** The first argument must be the name of a list, not an actual list.)
`split(/PATTERN/, STRING, LIMIT)`	Returns a list that consists of a string split at each point where the pattern matches a substring of the full string. If a limit is specified, only that limited number of items is returned, with the last item being the remainder of the string after the initial segments are split out; if no limit is specified, any number of items can be returned. In scalar context, the function returns only the number of items that would have been returned in list context. If the pattern contains parentheses, the delimiter matched in each set of parentheses is returned interspersed with the other list items.

Name	Description
`sprintf(FORMAT, LIST)`	Formats a list using the format string and returns the resulting list.
`sqrt(NUMBER)`	Returns the square root of the argument.
`srand(NUMBER)`	Sets the seed value for the `rand` function to the number specified. If you do not specify an argument, Perl uses the `time` function as the argument.
`stat(FILE)`	Returns information about a file. The argument can be either a file handle or a string with the file's name. If the file is a symbolic link, the information is about the link itself, not the linked-to file. The following items in the list are returned: the device number of the file system, inode number, file permissions (number), number of hard links to the file, user number of file's owner, group number of the file's owner, device identifier for special files, size of file, last access time, last modify time, last inode change time, preferred block size, and number of blocks allocated.
`study(SCALAR)`	Carefully examines a string in order to speed up later searches on that string.
`sub NAME { BLOCK }`	Defines a subroutine. You also include a prototype for calling the subroutine between the name and the block. If you do not specify a block, Perl notes that the name exists when it interprets your program.
`substr(STRING, OFFSET, LENGTH)`	Returns a string that is a substring of the first argument. The substring starts at the specified offset and is of the specified length, if possible. If the offset is negative, the offset is from the end of the string instead of from the beginning. If you do not specify a length, everything from the offset to the end of the string is returned. This function can also be used on the left side of an assignment, in which case the string must be a string name, and the contents of the string will change.
`symlink(OLDFILE, NEWFILE)`	Creates a new file that has a symbolic link to the old file. Returns true if successful.

Name	*Description*
`syscall(CALLNAME, LIST)`	Executes the specified system call, using the list as arguments.
`sysopen(FILEHANDLE, FILENAME, MODE)`	Opens the file using system-level calls.
`sysread(FILEHANDLE, VARIABLE, LENGTH, OFFSET)`	Reads from the file using system-level calls.
`system(COMMAND)`	Runs a command and waits for the command to finish. The function returns the exit status of the program multiplied by 256.
`syswrite(FILEHANDLE, VARIABLE, LENGTH, OFFSET)`	Writes to the file using system-level calls.
`tell(FILEHANDLE)`	Returns the file position keeper of the specified file.
`telldir(DIRHANDLE)`	Returns the directory position keeper of the specified file.
`tie(VARIABLE, NewPACKAGENAME, LIST)`	Associates a variable with a particular package so that calls to the package are reflected in the variable.
`tied(VARIABLE)`	Returns a reference to the object that is tied to the variable.
`time`	Returns the current time, which is the number of nonleap seconds from the time specified as the "beginning of time" for the operating system.
`times`	Returns a list of the amount of CPU seconds used. The items in the list include the number of seconds for user instructions for this process, system instructions for this process, user instructions for child processes, and system instructions for child processes.
`truncate(FILEHANDLE, LENGTH)`	Shortens the file to the specified length.
`uc(STRING)`	Returns the string in all uppercase characters.
`ucfirst(STRING)`	Returns the string with the first character changed to uppercase.
`umask(MODE)`	Sets the UNIX `umask` value for the current process.
`undef(VARIABLE)`	Undefines the value of the variable or sets the value of the variable to the undefined value.

Name	Description
`unless(TEST) { BLOCK1 }`	Executes a block if the test is false. The first block may be followed by `else { BLOCK2 }`. In this case, if the test is true, the second block is executed. The first block may also be followed by one or more instances of `elsif { BLOCKn }`, which acts the same as `else if`.
`unlink(FILENAMES)`	Deletes the files in the list and returns the number of files deleted.
`unpack(TEMPLATE, STRING)`	Returns a list of items that is the string examined using the template (the first argument to the function).
`unshift(LISTNAME, LIST)`	Adds the items of the list in the second argument to the beginning of the list named in the first argument.
`untie(VARIABLE)`	Unbinds a variable from a package.
`until(TEST) { BLOCK }`	If the test returns false, Perl executes the block and redoes the test in order to determine whether to execute the block again.
`use MODULE`	Imports semantics from a module into the current package. You can also specify a list of arguments for the module. Perl's pragmas are also implemented with this function.
`utime(ACCESSTIME, MODTIME, FILENAMES)`	Changes the access time and modification time on the named files. The function returns the number of files successfully changed.
`values(ARRAY)`	Returns a list of the values in the associative array.
`vec(STRING, OFFSET, NUMBITS)`	Returns the value of the element of the string that is the number of bits wide, starting at the specified offset.
`wait`	Waits for a child process to terminate.
`waitpid(PID, FLAGS)`	Waits for the specified child process to terminate and returns true when the process is dead.
`wantarray`	Returns true if the current subroutine is looking for a list value or false if it is looking for a scalar value.
`warn(LIST)`	Sends a list to the standard error output.

Name	Description
`while(TEST) { BLOCK }`	If the test returns true, Perl executes the block and redoes the test to determine whether or not to execute the block again.
`write(FILEHANDLE)`	Writes text formatted with the format function to the specified file.

Perl's Special Variables

In the following section, I describe Perl's special variables. Don't be surprised if the descriptions are somewhat puzzling at this point. Only a few of the special variables are useful for novice and intermediate Perl programmers.

General-purpose variables

Variable	Description
`$_`	The default input to many functions and operations. Most useful with the `while(<FILEHANDLE>)` function.
`$/`	The input record separator. The default depends on the operating system.
`$[`	Index of the first element in a list. The index is normally 0 (and you really shouldn't change it), but some people insist that the first item of a list should be numbered as "1."
`$|`	Forces automatic flushing to the selected file handle if this variable is set to true. If false (the default), output to the selected file handle will only be done when the operating system feels like it or when the file is closed.
`$]`	The version of Perl.
`$0`	The name of the file containing the Perl program being run.
`$^T`	Time at which this program started running.
`$.`	The input line number of the last file handle read.
`$ARGV`	Name of the current file, when using `<ARGV>`.

Variable	*Description*
`@ARGV`	Command-line arguments for the program.
`@INC`	List of directories in which Perl looks for programs named in the `do`, `require`, and `use` functions.
`%INC`	The files that have been used by `do` and `require`. Each key is the filename specified, and each value is the full path to the found file.
`%ENV`	Operating system environment variables.

Variables that relate to errors and return values

<table>
<tr><th>Variable</th><th>Description</th></tr>
<tr><td><code>$!</code></td><td>The current system error number or string.</td></tr>
<tr><td><code>$?</code></td><td>Status returned by the last <code>system</code> function, ` (backtick) command, or | (pipe). This value is actually 256 times the number returned from the process.</td></tr>
<tr><td><code>$@</code></td><td>Error message returned by the last <code>eval</code> function.</td></tr>
</table>

Special variables for regular expressions

Variable	*Description*
`$&`	The text matched by the last successful pattern match in a regular expression.
`` $` ``	The text preceding the last successful pattern match in a regular expression.
`$'`	The text following the last successful pattern match in a regular expression.
`$+`	The text that matched the last successful bracketed pattern in a regular expression.
`$digit`	The text matched by the set of parentheses in a regular expression. The digit corresponds to the number of the matched set.

Variables that relate to processes

Variable	Description
`$$`	The Perl program's process number.
`$<`	The real userid of this process.
`$>`	The effective userid of this process.
`$(`	The real groupid of this process.
`$)`	The effective groupid of this process.

Variables for formats

Variable	Description
`$%`	Current page number.
`$-`	Number of lines left on the current page.
`$=`	Page length.
`$~`	Name of the report format.
`$^`	Name of the top-of-page format.
`^L`	Text that a format puts out when doing a form feed.
`$:`	Text after which a string may be broken for format continuation fields.
`$^A`	Contents of the accumulator of format lines.

Miscellaneous variables

Variable	Description
`$,`	Output field separator, which is printed between each item in the list that is output by `print`.
`$\`	Output record separator, which is printed at the end of the list that is output by `print`.
`$"`	List separator placed between each item in a list if the list is interpreted in double-quotes, such as "`@a`".
`$;`	Separator placed between subscripts of multidimensional arrays.
`$^D`	Debugging flags.
`$^F`	Maximum system file descriptor.

Variable	Description
`$^H`	Internal compiler hints.
`$^I`	In-place edit extension.
`$^O`	Name of the operating system for which Perl was compiled.
`$^P`	Internal flag for the debugger.
`$^W`	Value of the warning switch.
`$^X`	Name that the Perl binary was compiled as.
`@F`	Holds the results of the `-a` command-line option.
`%SIG`	Signal handlers.

Perl's Predefined File Handles

File Handle	Description
`ARGV`	Iterates over the filenames in `@ARGV`.
`STDERR`	Standard error output.
`STDIN`	Standard file input.
`STDOUT`	Standard file output.
`DATA`	Anything that follows a token `__DATA__` in a program.
`_`	Cache for the `stat` and `lstat` functions and file test operators.

Appendix B
About the CD

On the CD-ROM

- Perl for UNIX, Windows (95, 98, and NT), and Macintosh
- Program listings from this book

System Requirements

Make sure that your computer meets the minimum system requirements listed below. If your computer doesn't match up to most of the following requirements, you may have problems using the contents of the CD. This list is for PCs and Macintoshes; any system running UNIX should run Perl just fine.

- A PC with a 486 or faster processor, or a Mac OS computer with a 68020 or newer processor (including PowerPC).
- Microsoft Windows 95, Windows 98, or Windows NT; or Mac OS system software 7.0 or later.
- At least 8MB of total RAM installed on your computer for Windows 95/98; 16MB of total RAM for Windows NT; 8MB of total RAM for Mac OS. For best performance, I recommend that Windows 95-equipped PCs and Mac OS computers with PowerPC processors have at least 16MB of RAM installed.
- At least 20MB of hard drive space available to install all the software from this CD for Windows, and 10MB for Mac OS.
- A CD-ROM drive — double-speed (2x) or faster is recommended.
- Windows 95 systems require DCOM for Windows 95 (this is not required for other operating systems). You can get it from the Microsoft Web site at `www.microsoft.com/com/dcom.asp`, and then load it into your system.

If you need more information on the basics, check out *PCs For Dummies,* 6th Edition, by Dan Gookin; *Macs For Dummies,* 6th Edition by David Pogue; *Windows 95 For Dummies,* 2nd Edition by Andy Rathbone; or *Windows 98 For Dummies* by Andy Rathbone (all published by IDG Books Worldwide, Inc.).

Using the CD with Microsoft Windows

To install the items from the CD to your hard drive, follow these steps.

1. **Insert the CD into your computer's CD-ROM drive.**
2. **On the Windows desktop, double-click the My Computer icon.**
3. **Double-click the icon for the D: drive.**

   Replace *D* with the proper drive letter if your CD-ROM drive uses a different letter.
4. **Double-click the icon for the Windows folder.**
5. **Double-click the file called APi502e.exe.**

   This step launches the ActivePerl installation program. Follow the steps in this program, which are described in each dialog box. (Chapter 2 has more information about some of the choices you can make.)
6. **Click Next in the first dialog box that appears.**

   The information in the dialog box warns you to not run any other program when you are installing ActivePerl. I suggest that you take this warning seriously.
7. **Agree to the license.**

   Read the license first, and then click Yes.
8. **Choose a directory in which to install Perl.**

   The suggested directory, C:\Perl, is a good choice. I assume throughout the book that you have chosen this directory, so if you choose another one, you may have to change some of the commands in other parts of the book to reflect the correct path name.
9. **Choose the components of ActivePerl that you want.**

   If you like the default choices, just leave them as they are.
10. **Verify that the additional installation options are selected in the next dialog box.**

    I suggest that you leave both of these options turned on. It's a good idea to have the Perl installer make files that have the .pl extension associated with Perl so that you can run them from Windows. It's also a good idea to have the installer place the Perl bin directory in your path so that Windows can find it when running a Perl program.
11. **Add Perl to your Start menu.**

    Use the same steps you would when installing almost any Windows software.

12. **Verify the installation settings you've chosen so far, and click Next to start copying files.**

    Perl then copies the files. This is the last prompt before the installer actually does what it is supposed to do: install.

13. **You can skip the release notes that appear.**

    Or, feel free to read them if you really want to, but there isn't much of interest in them for novice Perl users. You can always go back and read them later.

14. **Restart your computer.**

    The ActivePerl installation program requires that your computer be restarted after installation for some of the settings to take effect.

A few other things are worth noting about ActivePerl:

- A newer release of ActivePerl may be available from ActiveState. Head to `www.ActiveState.com` to update your software.
- Commercial support for ActivePerl is available through the Perl Clinic at `www.PerlClinic.com`. Peer support resources for any issues concerning ActivePerl can be found at the ActiveState Web site under "Support" at `www.activestate.com/support/`.
- The ActiveState Repository has a large collection of modules and extensions in binary packages that are easy to install and use. To view and install these packages, use the Perl Package Manager (PPM) which is included with ActivePerl.
- ActivePerl is the latest Perl binary distribution from ActiveState and replaces what was previously distributed as Perl for Win32. The latest release of ActivePerl as well as other Perl related tools are available from the ActiveState web site at `www.ActiveState.com`.
- ActiveState, ActivePerl, PerlScript, and Perl for Win32 are trademarks of ActiveState Tool Corp.

Note: ActiveState will not be providing end-user support for either customers of ActivePerl or purchasers of *Perl For Dummies, 2nd Edition.* If you do encounter any problems with this CD, please direct your inquiries to the IDG Books Worldwide Customer Service phone number: 800-762-2974 (outside the U.S.: 317-596-5430).

Using the CD with Mac OS

To install the items from the CD to your hard drive, follow these steps.

1. **Insert the CD into your computer's CD-ROM drive.**

   In a moment, an icon representing the CD you just inserted appears on your Mac desktop. Chances are, the icon looks like a CD-ROM.

2. **Double-click the CD icon on your desktop to show the CD's contents.**

   You will see the contents of this book's CD, which includes an icon with the name "MacPerl Installer."

3. **Double-click the MacPerl Installer icon.**

   This begins the installation process.

4. **Skip over the installation notes that appear.**

   Or, you can read them if you're curious. Either way, click Continue to go on from here. You'll see a dialog box asking you where you want to install MacPerl.

5. **Choose where you want to install MacPerl.**

   You can pick a folder anywhere on your hard disk from the drop-down list in the Install Location setting of the MacPerl Installer dialog box. You are also safe simply installing it in the default location, which is on the top level of your hard disk, and then moving that folder later on.

6. **Click the Install button.**

   And that's it!

What You'll Find on the CD

The CD itself is arranged by computer type. You'll find separate folders for Mac OS, UNIX, and Windows (which includes Windows 95, Windows 98, and Windows NT).

Each folder on the CD contains the example programs from this book. The program names match the file names given to the program examples in the chapters. Each folder also contains the installer for Perl.

Getting More Stuff off the Web

The Perl installations on the CD include dozens of pre-installed modules. In addition, hundreds of other modules are available for Perl. In fact, there are so many that they don't all fit on the CD! Fortunately, these modules are easy to find and download from the World Wide Web.

UNIX users will want to get their modules from the CPAN directory. CPAN is the Comprehensive Perl Archive Network, a place where you can find Perl modules for almost any task. You can find out more about CPAN at `www.perl.com/CPAN/README.html`.

Windows 95, Windows 98, and Windows NT users can find some modules at CPAN, but most of the modules at CPAN don't install easily in Perl-Win32. Instead, you can use the Perl Package Manager (PPM) that comes with ActivePerl. PPM can download the latest copies of Perl modules that have been adapted to Windows and install them on your PC. To run the PPM:

1. **Launch your Internet connection.**

   Because the PPM downloads the latest version of the module from ActiveState's Web site, you have to be connected before you use the PPM.

2. **Run the PPM by giving the following command:**

   ```
   C:\perl\5.00502\bin\perl ppm.pl
   ```

3. **When you find a module that you want to download, enter the command `install` followed by the name of the module.**

   This step both downloads the module and installs it on your computer so that you can use the module in your Perl programs.

4. **Quit from the PPM with the following command:**

   ```
   quit
   ```

In case you get stuck, you can get help on the PPM by entering the PPM `help` command.

If You Have Problems (Of the CD Kind)

I tried my best to compile Perl installations that work on most computers with minimum system requirements. Your computer may be a little bit different from most and some programs may not work properly for one reason or another.

The three most likely problems are that you don't have enough memory (RAM) for the programs you want to use, you don't have enough hard disk space (Perl installations are disk hogs), or you have other programs running that are affecting the installation or running of a program.

If you get error messages such as `Not enough memory` or `Setup cannot continue`, try one or more of the following methods and then try using the software again:

- **Turn off any anti-virus software that you have on your computer.** Installers sometimes mimic virus activity and may make your computer incorrectly believe that it is being infected by a virus.
- **Close all running programs.** The more programs you're running, the less memory is available to other programs. Installers also typically update files and programs; if you keep other programs running, installation may not work properly.
- **Have your local computer store add more RAM to your computer.** This is, admittedly, a drastic and somewhat expensive step. However, if you have a Windows 95/98 PC or a Mac OS computer with a PowerPC chip, adding more memory can really help the speed of your computer and enable more programs to run at the same time.

If you still have trouble installing the items from the CD, please call the IDG Books Worldwide Customer Service phone number: 800-762-2974 (outside the U.S.: 317-596-5430).

Index

• Symbols & Numbers •

• A •

• B •

• C •

• E •

• F •

• I •

• J •

• L •

• *M* •

• N •

• O •

• P •

• S •

• T •

• W •

• X •

• Y •

• Z •

IDG Books Worldwide, Inc., End-User License Agreement

READ THIS. You should carefully read these terms and conditions before opening the software packet(s) included with this book ("Book"). This is a license agreement ("Agreement") between you and IDG Books Worldwide, Inc. ("IDGB"). By opening the accompanying software packet(s), you acknowledge that you have read and accept the following terms and conditions. If you do not agree and do not want to be bound by such terms and conditions, promptly return the Book and the unopened software packet(s) to the place you obtained them for a full refund.

1. **License Grant.** IDGB grants to you (either an individual or entity) a nonexclusive license to use one copy of the enclosed software program(s) (collectively, the "Software") solely for your own personal or business purposes on a single computer (whether a standard computer or a workstation component of a multiuser network). The Software is in use on a computer when it is loaded into temporary memory (RAM) or installed into permanent memory (hard disk, CD-ROM, or other storage device). IDGB reserves all rights not expressly granted herein.

2. **Ownership.** IDGB is the owner of all right, title, and interest, including copyright, in and to the compilation of the Software recorded on the disk(s) or CD-ROM ("Software Media"). Copyright to the individual programs recorded on the Software Media is owned by the author or other authorized copyright owner of each program. Ownership of the Software and all proprietary rights relating thereto remain with IDGB and its licensers.

3. **Restrictions on Use and Transfer.**

   (a) You may only (i) make one copy of the Software for backup or archival purposes, or (ii) transfer the Software to a single hard disk, provided that you keep the original for backup or archival purposes. You may not (i) rent or lease the Software, (ii) copy or reproduce the Software through a LAN or other network system or through any computer subscriber system or bulletin-board system, or (iii) modify, adapt, or create derivative works based on the Software.

   (b) You may not reverse engineer, decompile, or disassemble the Software. You may transfer the Software and user documentation on a permanent basis, provided that the transferee agrees to accept the terms and conditions of this Agreement and you retain no copies. If the Software is an update or has been updated, any transfer must include the most recent update and all prior versions.

4. **Restrictions on Use of Individual Programs.** You must follow the individual requirements and restrictions detailed for each individual program in the "About the CD" appendix of this Book. These limitations are also contained in the individual license agreements recorded on the Software Media. These limitations may include a requirement that after using the program for a specified period of time, the user must pay a registration fee or discontinue use. By opening the Software packet(s), you will be agreeing to abide by the licenses and restrictions for these individual programs that are detailed in the "About the CD" appendix and on the Software Media. None of the material on this Software Media or listed in this Book may ever be redistributed, in original or modified form, for commercial purposes.

5. **Limited Warranty.**

   (a) IDGB warrants that the Software and Software Media are free from defects in materials and workmanship under normal use for a period of sixty (60) days from the date of purchase of this Book. If IDGB receives notification within the warranty period of defects in materials or workmanship, IDGB will replace the defective Software Media.

   (b) **IDGB AND THE AUTHOR OF THE BOOK DISCLAIM ALL OTHER WARRANTIES, EXPRESS OR IMPLIED, INCLUDING WITHOUT LIMITATION IMPLIED WARRANTIES OF MERCHANTABILITY AND FITNESS FOR A PARTICULAR PURPOSE, WITH RESPECT TO THE SOFTWARE, THE PROGRAMS, THE SOURCE CODE CONTAINED THEREIN, AND/OR THE TECHNIQUES DESCRIBED IN THIS BOOK. IDGB DOES NOT WARRANT THAT THE FUNCTIONS CONTAINED IN THE SOFTWARE WILL MEET YOUR REQUIREMENTS OR THAT THE OPERATION OF THE SOFTWARE WILL BE ERROR FREE.**

   (c) This limited warranty gives you specific legal rights, and you may have other rights that vary from jurisdiction to jurisdiction.

6. **Remedies.**

   (a) IDGB's entire liability and your exclusive remedy for defects in materials and workmanship shall be limited to replacement of the Software Media, which may be returned to IDGB with a copy of your receipt at the following address: Software Media Fulfillment Department, Attn.: *Perl For Dummies,* 2nd Edition, IDG Books Worldwide, Inc., 7260 Shadeland Station, Ste. 100, Indianapolis, IN 46256, or call 800-762-2974. Please allow three to four weeks for delivery. This Limited Warranty is void if failure of the Software Media has resulted from accident, abuse, or misapplication. Any replacement Software Media will be warranted for the remainder of the original warranty period or thirty (30) days, whichever is longer.

   (b) In no event shall IDGB or the author be liable for any damages whatsoever (including without limitation damages for loss of business profits, business interruption, loss of business information, or any other pecuniary loss) arising from the use of or inability to use the Book or the Software, even if IDGB has been advised of the possibility of such damages.

   (c) Because some jurisdictions do not allow the exclusion or limitation of liability for consequential or incidental damages, the above limitation or exclusion may not apply to you.

7. **U.S. Government Restricted Rights.** Use, duplication, or disclosure of the Software by the U.S. Government is subject to restrictions stated in paragraph (c)(1)(ii) of the Rights in Technical Data and Computer Software clause of DFARS 252.227-7013, and in subparagraphs (a) through (d) of the Commercial Computer–Restricted Rights clause at FAR 52.227-19, and in similar clauses in the NASA FAR supplement, when applicable.

8. **General.** This Agreement constitutes the entire understanding of the parties and revokes and supersedes all prior agreements, oral or written, between them and may not be modified or amended except in a writing signed by both parties hereto that specifically refers to this Agreement. This Agreement shall take precedence over any other documents that may be in conflict herewith. If any one or more provisions contained in this Agreement are held by any court or tribunal to be invalid, illegal, or otherwise unenforceable, each and every other provision shall remain in full force and effect.

Installation Instructions

How to use the CD using Microsoft Windows or Unix

The *Perl For Dummies,* 2nd Edition CD offers valuable information that you won't want to miss. To install the items from the CD to your hard drive, follow these steps.

1. **Insert the CD into your computer's CD-ROM drive.**

   Give your computer a moment to take a look at the CD.

2. **When the light on your CD-ROM drive goes out, double click on the My Computer icon (It's probably in the top left corner of your desktop.)**

   This action opens the My Computer window, which shows you all the drives attached to your computer, the Control Panel, and a couple other handy things.

3. **Double click on the icon for your CD-ROM drive.**

   Another window opens, showing you all the folders and files on the CD.

4. **Double click the file called License.txt.**

   This file contains the end-user license that you agree to by using the CD. When you are done reading the license, close the program, most likely NotePad, that displayed the file.

5. **Double click the file called Readme.txt.**

   This file contains instructions about installing the software from this CD. It might be helpful to leave this text file open while you are using the CD.

6. **Double click the folder, UNIX or WINDOWS, for the platform you are working with.**

7. **Find the file called perl5.005_02.tar.gz for Unix, or APi502e.exe for Windows, and double click on that file.**

   The program's installer will walk you through the process of setting up your new software. Be sure to read the About the CD appendix (much of this information also shows up in the Readme file) to learn more about installing and running Perl.

How to use the CD using the Mac OS

To install the items from the CD to your hard drive, follow these steps.

1. **Insert the CD into your computer's CD-ROM drive.**

   In a moment, an icon representing the CD you just inserted appears on your Mac desktop. Chances are, the icon looks like a CD-ROM.

2. **Double click the CD icon to show the CD's contents.**

3. **Double click the Read Me First icon.**

   This text file contains information about the CD's programs and any last-minute instructions you need to know about installing the programs on the CD that we don't cover in this appendix.

4. **Double click the MacPerl Installer icon.**

   The program's installer will walk you through the process of setting up your new software. Be sure to read the About the CD appendix (much of this information also shows up in the Read Me First file) to learn more about installing and running Perl.

After you've installed the programs that you want, you can eject the CD. Carefully place it back in the plastic jacket of the book for safekeeping.

Perl For Dummies®, 2nd Edition

Cheat Sheet

The Most Useful File Tests

Test	Description
-e	File exists
-r	File can be read
-w	File can be written to
-z	File is exactly zero bytes long
-d	Named item is a directory, not a file
-T	File is a text file (the first chunk of a file is examined, and it's a text file if fewer than 30 percent or so of the characters are nonprintable)
-B	File is a binary file (this is the exact opposite of the -T test — it's a binary file if more than 30 percent or so of the characters are nonprintable)
-s	Size of the file in bytes
-C	Creation age of file
-A	Access age of file
-M	Modification age of file

Special Characters

Character	Meaning
\n	Newline
\r	Carriage return
\t	Tab character
\f	Formfeed character
\b	Backspace character
\v	Vertical tab
\a	Bell or beep
\e	Escape character

Common List Functions

Function	`splice` Equivalent	What It Does
`push(@r, @s)`	`splice(@r, $#r+1, 0, @s)`	Adds to the right of the list
`pop(@r)`	`splice(@r, $#r, 1)`	Removes from the right of the list
`shift(@r)`	`splice(@r, 0, 1)`	Removes from the left of the list
`unshift(@r, @s)`	`splice(@r, 0, 0, @s)`	Adds to the left of the list

Perl For Dummies®, 2nd Edition

Cheat Sheet

True-False Comparison Operators

Comparison	Math	String
Equal to	==	eq
Not equal to	!=	ne
Less than	<	lt
Greater than	>	gt
Less than or equal to	<=	le
Greater than or equal to	>=	ge

Shortcuts for Character Ranges in Regular Expressions

Code	Replaces	Description
\d	[0..9]	Any digit
\w	[a-zA-Z_0-9]	Any alphanumeric character
\s	[\t\n\r\f]	A whitespace character
\D	^[0..9]	Any non-digit
\W	^[a-zA-Z_0-9]	Any non-alphanumeric character
\S	^[\t\n\r\f]	A non-whitespace character

Pattern-Matching Quantifiers in Regular Expressions

Symbol	Meaning
+	Match 1 or more times
*	Match 0 or more times
?	Match 0 or 1 time
{n}	Match exactly *n* times
{n,}	Match at least *n* times
{n,m}	Match at least *n* but not more than *m* times (these values must be less than 65,536)

Cheat Sheet $2.95 value. Item 0460-6.
For more information about IDG Books, call 1-800-762-2974.

...For Dummies: Bestselling Book Series for Beginners